PREFACE

THE TITLE of this volume—*Church, State, and Education*—was suggested to my mind by the mediaeval triad *Regnum Sacerdotium Studium*—a triad which was known to the thought of Byzantium as well as in the Latin West. Some of the contents of the volume are specifically devoted to the *Regnum* or, as we should now say, the State; others are concerned with the life and organization of the Church; the last three deal more especially with problems and issues of Education or, as the Greeks called it, *Paideia*. But there is no firm or fixed line of division between the different themes, which run naturally into one another: an essay such as that on The Unity of Mediaeval Civilization is concerned with the general nature of the community of the Middle Ages, including both Church and State as well as matters and questions of education.

The nine essays here printed appeared together for the first time (along with three others which have now been omitted because they were outmoded or because later reflection condemned them to limbo) in a volume which was published some quarter of a century ago. They are arranged not in the order of their composition, but rather in a rough chronological sequence according to the times and periods with which they are concerned. As I reflect on the different dates at which they were written, I ask myself whether they show any development—or inconsistency—of thought. I am moved, in this connection, to repeat some words which I used in the Preface to the original edition of 1930. "I am not at all sure that the essays are consistent. On the other hand I should have been surprised, and indeed alarmed, if there had been no inconsistencies. The various pieces were written during a period of remarkable change. Not to have changed with the changing times would only have argued a wooden sort of consistency."

I doubt, then, if there is any development of thought in these essays—development, that is to say, in the sense of alteration—though there may be some inconsistencies. But in the earliest essays —the second and sixth in this volume—I was perhaps more inclined to what is called 'pluralism'—an exaltation of the claim of groups *vis-à-vis* the State—than I was in later days and in my later writings. I then felt strongly the tension between the *regnum*— the 'sovereign' authority of the secular State—and the free play of the voluntary society (religious, economic, or whatever its basis might be), with its scope of liberty and ease for the unfolding of human worth and human dignity; and my sympathy then ran towards the voluntary society. Yet the essay on The Discredited State, written during that early period, in the spring of 1914, before the coming of the First World War, which brought back with a rush the claims of the State, ends with a recognition of the ultimate rights of the 'sovereign' authority of the *Regnum*—a recognition which seems to me now, as I look back on the past, to be in the nature of an unconscious prophecy of what was about to be.

I had no idea, when I wrote the last paragraph of that essay—three months before war burst suddenly on an astonished world—that the State would emerge so explosively into the foreground of men's minds, or would assert its claims so evidently and with such ready acceptance. But I already felt the tension of which I have spoken, and today, in the light of later reflection, I should say that the tension which I felt forty years ago is a tension which I have always continued to feel, simply because it is always there and always tugging at the minds of men. There is always society, voluntary society, as well as the legal and compulsive State; and sometimes the claims of the one will seem urgent and dominant, and sometimes the claims of the other will sound loudest in the ear.

At the end of one of my latest books (*Principles of Social and Political Theory*, published in 1951) I find myself still confronted by the same tension, and arguing in much the same sense as I had argued long ago in 1914. And therefore, on the whole, I see no real change in my views; I see only a different emphasis, varying from time to time, now on this and now on that side of the permanent tension between the authority of the State and the voluntary play of freely formed and freely acting groups or societies. It is impossible not to experience and confess *some* change of mind and alteration of view with the change of circumstance and the alteration of contingencies. But I do not think that this means any real or substantial change of view. The tension remains: the circumstances surrounding it change: the barometer of the reflective mind just registers the consequential change in the character and balance of the tension which must always continue to exist.

October 1956   ERNEST BARKER

CONTENTS

CHURCH, STATE, AND EDUCATION

I

THE ROMAN CONCEPTION OF EMPIRE [1]

THE Roman Empire was born in the Eastern Mediterranean ; and it was in the Eastern Mediterranean, in the city of Constantinople, that it died. We may almost say that it was Oriental in its origin : we may at any rate affirm that it was Hellenistic ; and Hellenistic means the fusion of Greek and Oriental. The process of political development which prepared its birth began in the West, in a city on the Tiber which looked across the Tyrrhenian Sea to the setting sun ; and it was the legal genius of Roman citizens—with their conceptions of *imperium* and *provincia, potestas* and *maiestas*—which gave to the Empire the framework and structure of its institutions. But the ideas on which it rested—the ideas which made it more than a structure, and gave it a root in the minds of men—were ideas which had germinated in the East. Any permanent society must rest on a body of belief and on the social will which such a body of belief creates. It was in the East that men had learned to believe in a single universal society, and in the government of that society by a king who was ' as a god among men,' and indeed was a very god ; and it was there, in the feeling of loyalty for the person of such a monarch, and even of ' adoration ' of his divinity, that a corresponding social will had found its expression. If *imperium* was a Latin word, the idea

---

[1] An Essay contributed originally to the *Legacy of Rome* (Clarendon Press, Oxford), 1923.

of an empire and the idea of an emperor were not of Latin origin. We must recognize in the Roman Empire the result of the fusion of Roman political development and Roman institutional structure with Hellenistic ideas.

But it would be a grave error to magnify the Hellenistic element in this fusion at the expense of the Roman ; and paradox would be wearing cap and bells if it proceeded to the proposition that the Roman Empire, if it was an empire, was not fundamentally Roman. If it was the Greek genius which, in its later days, rose to conceptions of the unity of humanity, it was the Roman genius which translated those conceptions, in themselves unsubstantial and unbodied, into an organized system of life. But the word 'translation' fails to do justice to Rome. It implies that the Greeks first wrote an original text, of which the Romans afterwards issued an authorized version. It would be truer to say that the Romans built first—or at any rate built independently—a *de facto* empire, on which the Greeks afterwards looked, and as they looked exclaimed, ' τοῦτ' ἐκεῖνο : this is the unity of humanity of which we have been thinking all along.' From this point of view we may almost say that Hellenistic conceptions settled upon and clustered round a Roman achievement ; adorned and even modified that achievement ; but left the solid core of achievement Roman still. It is hard to weigh men of action against men of thought : it is no less difficult to weigh a people of action against a people of thought. Perhaps it is unnecessary, as it is certainly thankless, to do either ; perhaps we may avoid contention, without shirking difficulties, if we conclude by saying that Rome built an empire in a world permeated by the preparatory thought of Greece, and that Greek thought continued to permeate, and even came to cement, the empire which Rome had built.

THERE were empires before that of Alexander. There was the Egyptian Empire, which extended to the Euphrates, of Thutmos III (*c.* 1500 B.C.) and his successors ;

there were the Semitic Empires of Sargon of Accad (*c.* 2750) and Hammurabi of Babylon (*c.* 2100), of the Assyrians of Nineveh (750–606) and the Chaldeans of Babylon (606–539) ; there was the Persian Empire (organized like the Roman in provinces, and traversed like the Roman by excellent roads) which lasted from 539 to 330 B.C. The Empire of Alexander was founded upon the ruin—and also upon the tradition—of the Persian, as the Persian had been founded upon the Chaldean and the Chaldean upon the Assyrian. Whatever the inspiration of Greek ideas under which Alexander began ; whatever his original conception of a ' crusade ' and the reduction of the ' barbarians ' under the Greeks—it is certain that he came under the sway of older traditions, and embraced a different policy. Rejecting the advice offered by Aristotle in a treatise ' On Kingship,' that ' he should distinguish between Greeks and barbarians, dealing with the former as ἡγεμών and the latter as δεσπότης,' he sought to unite East and West in a common equality. He fostered intermarriage between Greeks and Persians : he received Persians into his army ; he adopted the ceremonial of the Persian court and the Persian system of provincial government. His policy was perhaps premature ; and his successors reserved the higher offices of state for Greeks and Macedonians. But the spread of a common culture achieved what policy could not directly effect ; and in the next century Eratosthenes could declare the unity of mankind, ' refusing to agree with those who divided mankind into Greeks and barbarians, and advised Alexander to treat the former as friends and the latter as foes, and declaring that it was better to divide men simply into the good and the bad.'

This meant a great revolution in thought—a revolution which was the necessary precursor of any imperial system in the Western world. Alexander had united the known world of his time (save Italy and the confines of the West) in a single society ; and he had assumed the equality of all the members of that society. He had contradicted the two axioms hitherto current in the political thought of the

Greeks — that a multiplicity of separate self-governing and self-sufficing cities was the best constitution of politics, and that differences and inequalities between the members (enfranchised and disfranchised, citizen and alien) were inevitably implied by the very genius of the city. His conquests and his policy had implied two opposite conceptions—that of a single cosmopolis of the inhabited earth, transcending cities as it transcended tribes and nations ; and that of the equality of all men, or at any rate all free men, in the life of a common humanity. These are the two fundamental conceptions which inaugurate a new epoch—an epoch which succeeds to that of the πόλις, and precedes that of the national state ; an epoch which covers the centuries that lie between Aristotle and Alexander at one end and Luther and Henry VIII at the other, and embraces in its scope the three empires of Macedon and Rome and Charlemagne. They are again the two conceptions which we find in the teaching of St. Paul, who believed in one Church of all Christians which should cover the world, and held that in that Church there was ' neither Greek nor Jew . . . barbarian, Scythian, bond nor free.'

Implicit in the achievement of Alexander there is thus the idea of the union in a single society of the peoples both of the East and the West, who had hitherto either developed in isolation, or, if they had met, had met in conflict. He united the Eastern Mediterranean with Western Asia : it remained for Rome to add the Western Mediterranean to the amalgam which he had created. But a unity such as that which Alexander had founded needed a cohesive principle : it needed a common centre of personal attachment and loyalty ; and we must therefore proceed to examine the nature of the cohesive principle which he gave to his empire, and which Rome afterwards inherited from his successors. That principle, in a word, was the deification of the ruler. The deified king could claim the universality, and receive the universal worship, of a manifest god. On this ground Greek cities and Oriental nations could unite ; and with the throne thus elevated to an altar loyalty

could become a religion. However foreign it may seem to
the Greek idea of the state as a free association of citizens,
the conception of the deified ruler was none the less rooted in
Greek habits of thought ; and the actual deification of
Alexander may be traced among the Ionian Greeks in the
beginning of his campaign, before he touched the soil of
Egypt or of Persia. Unlike the Semites, who fixed a great
gulf between God and man, the Greeks conceived gods in
the likeness of men, and elevated men to the ranks of gods.[1]
It was their common practice to promote founders of cities
at death to the rank of hero, and to offer them ' hero-
worship ' ; and it was only an extension of this practice
when Alexander, the first leader of a united Greece and
the greatest of all the founders of Greek cities, was even in
life conceived to be not only a hero, but a god. But if
the deification of Alexander was in accordance with Greek
conceptions and practice, it was also aided by the conceptions
and practice of the East. The Egyptian kings were regarded, if not as gods in themselves, at any rate as incarna-
tions of the god Ammon or Re ; and the Persian kings
claimed ' adoration ' in virtue of the *Hvareno*, a nimbus
' conceived . . . as emanating from the sun, but also as a
token of supernatural grace.' [2] It was in the Eastern
dominions of Alexander that the worship of the deified
ruler became—what it had never been formally made by
Alexander himself—an institution of State. The kings of
Macedonia never pretended to divinity ; and indeed as they
were the kings of a single nation there was no necessity

---

[1] Goethe's poem, *Das Göttliche*, expresses the Greek conception.

Und wir verehren	Der edle Mensch
Die Unsterblichen,	Sei hülfreich und gut !
Als wären sie Menschen,	Unermüdet schaff' er
Thäten im Grossen,	Das Nützliche, Rechte ;
Was der Beste im Kleinen	Sei uns ein Vorbild
Thut oder möchte.	Jener geahneten Wesen !

[2] See H. Stuart Jones, *The Roman Empire*, p. 217. In this fascinating
matter of the deification of rulers I have followed A. Bauer, *Vom Griechen-
tum zum Christentum*, pp. 53–92, and P. Wendland, *Die hellenistisch-
römische Kultur*, vi. 4 and vii. 3. See also W. Ferguson's *Greek Imperialism* ;
and Professor Murray's *Four Stages of Greek Religion*, pp. 133–41.

that they should. It was otherwise with Egypt and Asia Minor, where there was no national feeling, and where traditions of supernatural monarchy were strong. Possibly in their lifetime, and certainly after their death, Ptolemy I and Berenice were the objects of a cult : Philadelphos and Arsinoe were worshipped as θεοὶ ἀδελφοί by 270 B.C. ; and we may still read the inscription in which Ptolemy V is celebrated as ' living for ever, beloved of Ptah, God Manifest . . . son of God and Goddess, like unto Horus, son of Isis and Osiris.' In the Seleucid kingdom the two first rulers were only canonized after death ; but Antiochus II is already θεός during his life.

It would be wrong to treat these swelling titles in any cavalier spirit. In their inception, whatever they may have become when they were staled by custom, they were more than adulation. They expressed a real gratitude of the subject for peace and good governance ; they implied a serious policy of the monarch, who knew no other way of consolidating his throne or uniting his dominions. And as they accorded with old Greek conceptions, so they also agreed with the contemporary movement of religious thought. It was the age of Euhemerism, in which gods were explained as great human ' benefactors ' and ' saviours ' who had won canonization ; and it was easy to turn a living benefactor and saviour into a present and manifest god. After all, empires have their legends. And the legend of divinity need not fear comparison with the Napoleonic legend.

GREEK philosophy was a more potent force in its decline than it was in the great days of Plato and Aristotle ; and Stoicism exerted a greater influence on the lives of men and the development of States than the Academy or the Lyceum. There is much in the philosophy of Stoicism which reflects the era of Alexander ; and it was perhaps powerful because it marched with the times. The era was one of uprooting and emigration and the mixture of peoples, in which the West moved eastwards on a steady tide, and an ebb sometimes set from the East to the West. The early Stoics came from the East, and though they might inherit Greek physics and metaphysics, they were free from the prepossessions and prejudices of Greek political thought. Zeno, the founder of the school, was a hellenized Phoenician from Cyprus : he came from that region of the Cilician gulf, fertile in its contribution to human thought, which afterwards gave to the world the hellenized Syrian, Posidonius of Apamea, and the hellenized Hebrew, Paul of Tarsus. He came to Athens at the end of the fourth century, and lived there as a resident alien. It is difficult not to believe that he was influenced in his thought by the achievement of Alexander, which must have begun its course in the days of his youth in Cyprus ; nor is it any licence of conjecture to suggest that the philosophy which he taught at Athens, at any rate on its social side, was the translation into an explicit theory of the principle implicit in that achievement.

In Stoic philosophy the whole universe is conceived as a single intelligible unity, pervaded by reason ; and the Stoic belief in a World-State is simply the political aspect of this general philosophic conception. ' The whole Universe was only one Substance, one *Physis*, in various states, and that one Substance was Reason, was God.' Reason, God, Nature (φύσις) were all synonyms—synonyms for the intelligible and homogeneous essence of the Universe. Physically, that essence was regarded as a form of matter— fire or a fiery ether—' pure and most subtil ' (as it is written in the Book of Wisdom), ' more moving than any motion,' which ' passeth and goeth through all things . . . the breath of the power of God, and a pure influence flowing from the glory of the Almighty.' In God this essential Reason was whole and pure : in man it was a fragment (ἀπό-σπασμα) ; but that fragment was ' the ruling principle ' in man, which determined the way of his life. By it, in the first place, he was knit to God and knit to his fellows ; in its virtue he was a ζῷον κοινωνικόν ; and because it was universal, the κοινωνία was universal. From it, in the second place, he derived the law of this universal κοινωνία ; for since reason was the ruling principle in each, it was the ruling principle of the society of all, and since, again, reason was the same as nature, the law of the universal society based on reason was the same as the law of nature. One universal society, one state of the whole world ; one law of nature, with which all its members must live in conformity—these are the two great tenets of Stoicism. ' He taught '—so it is recorded by Plutarch of Zeno—' that we should not live in cities and demes, each distinguished by separate rules of justice, but should regard *all* men as fellow-demesmen and fellow-citizens ; and there should be one life and order (κοσμος) as of a single flock feeding together on a common pasture (νόμος).' [1]

The teaching of Zeno had necessarily its negative aspects. He was the iconoclast of the πόλις, as he was the prophet of the World-State ; and a criticism of the institutions of the πόλις, somewhat in the vein of his predecessors the Cynics, appears more strongly in the records of his views than it does in those of his successors, who modified his asperities. We are told that he refused to admit to his ' republic ' (like Plato, he wrote a *Republic*) either temples or courts of law or currency or marriage or gymnasia or the ordinary system of education. These were perhaps the extremities of an early radicalism. More essential in his teaching was his insistence on equality. If all human beings had reason, there was a fundamental human equality ; and though one might divide the wise man from the foolish, there was no argument for distinguishing between the status of men and that of women, and little argument for distinguishing between the position of masters and that of slaves. Stoicism was thus an influence in favour of the equality of the sexes ; and if it did not make for the legal abolition of slavery, it issued in the view that slavery was an artificial institution of human law, and that in the region of the spirit all men were, or might be, equal. The graded inequality

[1] Plutarch, *de Alex. Fort.* i. 6. The word κόσμος means both ' order ' and ' world ' ; the word νόμος both ' law ' and ' pasture.'

of the city disappears before the solvent of this teaching ;
and in it we may see the emergence of a tenet, to which the
Roman lawyers gave universal currency, that ' before the
law of nature all men have an equal status ' (omnes homines
natura aequales sunt).

The vogue which Stoic philosophy came to enjoy at
Rome, from the days of the Scipios to the days of Marcus
Aurelius, is a matter known to every scholar. It imbued
the Roman lawyers with their tenets of a universal law
of nature and the equality of all men before that law. It
carried its conception of the State of the whole world
to Marcus Aurelius ; and the classical text for that conception may be found in a sentence of his Meditations :
' the poet saith, Dear city of Cecrops ; but thou—wilt
thou not say, Dear city of God ? ' The thought on which
the best of the Romans fed was a thought of the World-
State, the universal law of nature, the brotherhood and the
equality of men ; and thought of this nature inevitably
penetrated and determined the general conception which
they entertained of their empire. It is of peculiar importance, therefore, that we should understand the stage of
development which Stoicism had reached, and the form of
presentation which it had found, in the days of the establishment of the Roman Empire—the days, we may also
add, of the beginnings of the Christian Church, which also
claimed to be a universal society, and also came under the
influence of Stoicism. Here we touch the name of Posidonius of Apamea, who taught in the University of Rhodes
(Cicero, among others, was one of his pupils) in the last
century before Christ. He was not an original thinker :
he was an eclectic, who wedded Stoicism to Platonism and
(it has even been held) to the religious doctrines of the
East. It is his peculiar importance that ' the great body
of his writings expressed with unique completeness the
general mind of the Greek world at the Christian era,' [1]
and that, as such a synthesis, they formed, as it were,

[1] E. Bevan, Stoics and Sceptics, iii. See also P. Wendland, op. cit.,
pp. 60 ff. and 134 ff.

the *textus receptus* of philosophic thought on which Cicero, Virgil, and many others drew.

It has been suggested by Mr. Bevan that the formula for the activity of Posidonius may be found in a simple phrase— ' to make men at home in the Universe.' In his philosophy the universe became companionable and comfortable. Above was the fiery ether ; below the world of men. At death the fiery particle of the human soul sought to rejoin its own element, and was encouraged in its upward way by the disembodied souls who had found their goal. All was ' one great city, of which gods and men were citizens . . . a compact and knowable whole.' With the whole universe thus made a companionable society, it was natural to conceive of a human society here on earth, living in sympathy with itself as it lived in sympathy with Heaven. And if the dead thus moved upward to the ether and to God, it was also natural to think of the deification of the dead. Here Posidonius found room in his philosophy for that deification of rulers which was current in the Hellenistic East. The great dead had gone home to God and joined the Godhead ; and even the great living might be regarded as sent by ' Providence ' or ' the eternal and immortal Nature of the Universe ' to be ' saviours of the community of the human race.' [1]

The philosophy of Posidonius is really of the nature of a religion : if it is based on Stoicism, it contains elements drawn, through Plato and the Pythagoreans, from the Greek mysteries ; and it may also contain elements derived from the religions of the East. It has even been suggested that Caesar may have found in the religious system of Posidonius, with its union of philosophic speculation and popular belief, the model of a religion suited to the universal empire which he would fain have built on the lines of the absolute monarchies of the East. It is at any rate probable that Caesar knew the system of Posidonius ; and without

[1] These terms may be found in two Greek inscriptions of the time of Augustus quoted in Wendland, op. cit., pp. 409–10. The language is Stoic : the reference is to Augustus himself.

subscribing to any theory of connexion between the political ambitions of Caesar and the philosophic religion of Posidonius, we may certainly believe in a connexion between the religious development and the political evolution of the last three centuries before the Christian era. We have to remember that the ancient State was also a Church. The City had its civic religion, of which the civic magistrates were priests : ' the real religion of the fifth century,' Professor Murray writes, ' was a devotion to the City itself.' In the same way the great monarchies of the third century had their monarchical religion ; and their real religion, as we have seen, was a devotion to the deified king. With politics and religion so closely connected that they were one, it was inevitable that, just as political movements produced religious consequences, so religious movements should involve political results. Now the religious movement of the latter centuries before the birth of Christ was towards a fusion of cults and a general belief in a single God of the Universe. It would be irrelevant, and it is impossible, to describe that movement here. It is apposite, and it is necessary, to draw attention to its political consequences. A world with one religion will also tend to be a world of a single State. Granted the general conceptions of the ancient world, we may say that the growth of mono theism encouraged the growth of a universal monarchy.

MEANWHILE the political development of Rome itself was moving to meet the system of thought implicit in the Hellenistic monarchies, in the philosophy of Stoicism, and in the religious trend. The original City-State of Rome, with its municipal system of magistrates, town-council (*senatus*), and town-meeting (*comitia*), had grown to the dimensions of a State greater than even the empire of Alexander. By a process of agricultural expansion, which sowed her peasant townsmen up and down Italy, Rome had become the mistress of the peninsula at the beginning of the third century. By a process of commercial expansion, which gave her trading citizens the monopoly of

Mediterranean trade at the expense of Carthage in the West and of Corinth and other centres in the East, she had become the virtual mistress of the Mediterranean littoral in the middle of the second century. There ensued a century of troubles, from the tribunate of Tiberius Gracchus to the battle of Actium, in which the municipal constitution of Rome showed itself inadequate to solve the problems or secure the allegiance of the territories which had come under its sway. Even in Rome itself, governed under an unwritten constitution which rested on understandings, the actual supremacy acquired by an aristocratic senate in the period of expansion was challenged by a popular party in the name of the formal rights of the general body of citizens. In Italy at large the inequality between allies who were really subjects and Roman citizens who acted as sovereigns produced a second and even more menacing cleavage ; and though after the Social War a remedy was sought in the grant of Roman citizenship to the allies (88 B.C.), it is obvious that a grant of citizenship which only meant inclusion in a civic assembly that they could not attend was no real bond of union between the Italians and the city of Rome, and only proved the inability of a City-State, which, with the world in its hands, remained in the sphere of civic ideas, to form even an Italian State. But it was neither the struggles in Rome nor the cleavage in Italy which in the issue subverted the civic constitution : it was the condition and the problems of the provinces of the Mediterranean littoral. Nominally protected by regulations passed by the Senate, the provinces were actually the prey of Roman governors, who in their short term of office sought to exploit their riches, and whom the constitution provided no effective means of controlling. The result was disastrous alike to the provincials, who found that their lot was not protection but pillage, and to Rome itself, where the returned governor, with his wealth, his ambitions, and his experience of absolute power, was a menace to civic ideas. And the provinces also entailed problems of defence —problems of the frontier—which could only be solved by methods which constituted a still graver menace. Armies were necessary to face the Berber tribes in the south, the Celts and Germans in the north, the kings of Pontus and Parthia in the east. The danger was constantly recurrent : the armies accordingly became standing armies, composed of professional troops, alien in spirit from the republican constitution, and a ready instrument for monarchical ambitions. With a professional army came the professional general ; and men emerged of the type of Marius and Sulla, Pompey and Caesar — masters of legions, and masters, if they would, of Rome. The dissensions in the city between the aristocratic party of the Senate and the *populares* who appealed to the masses were the opportunity of the professional generals. They threw their swords into the scale and arbitrated ; and finally the greatest and the boldest, Julius Caesar, took the sword into his hands and ruled. He had enjoyed ten years' experience of absolute power in Gaul : he was master of the finest legions of the day ; he was allied with the popular cause ; he had a genius for men and affairs.

We may define Caesarism as a form of autocracy, backed by an army, which rests formally on some manner of plebiscite and actually — so long, at any rate, as it is successful—on a measure of popular support. So defined, Caesarism is identical with Bonapartism. But there is a fundamental difference. Bonapartism showed itself personal and transitory, an ephemeral chase of flying glory : Caesarism became a permanent institution. Modified and veiled at first by the policy of Augustus, but showing itself clearly as it grew firmer and stronger, it controlled the Mediterranean world for centuries. The reasons for its permanence were partly negative and partly positive. There was no nationalism abroad to oppose a non-national State : there were only dying City-States which had lost the instinct for autonomy, and tribal formations which had not learned to cherish political ambitions. There was no democratic spirit in the air to wither an absolute government : the temper of the times was one of acquiescence, and even of gratitude. Religion and philosophy were the occupation of stirring minds : the only opposition to the Caesars came from a group of aristocratic *frondeurs*, who accumulated memories but were barren of achievements. While there was little to oppose Caesarism, there was much to support its cause. The provinces enjoyed peace : their frontiers were defended ; their governors were supervised. Their taxes were not diminished : they were even increased in order to meet the expenses of the new system of government ; but extortion ceased, and it is significant that in the new security the rate of interest sank to one-third of what it had been under the Republic. The domestic factions of Rome died. In Italy the Romans and the Italians were equally subjects of Caesar. With the head of the army at the head of the State, the peril that the army might thrust its sword into the issues of the civil State was, if not removed, at any rate diminished. A professional soldiery might still by a *coup d'épée* depose or elect a Caesar : in the third century it dominated politics for fifty troubled years ; and the military basis of the Empire was always a weakness of the emperors. But of the first two hundred years of the Empire, at any rate, we may safely say that they were years in which the civilian power was the master of the State.

If we would understand the feelings towards the Empire which were general among its subjects in the days of its foundation, we must turn to the literature and inscriptions in which they are recorded. What Rome and the Empire owed to Augustus is testified in Virgil and Horace ; and their poetry is no adulation, but the expression of a feeling as genuine as that of Tennyson for Victoria and the Victorian Age. The language of inscriptions is even more instructive testimony, because it is more direct and more naïve. We may deduct a liberal discount on the ground of conventional flattery from some of the Greek inscriptions : they still remain significant. Augustus is 'the Saviour sent to make wars cease and to order all things ' ; ' through him have come good tidings ' (εὐαγγέλια) ; ' in him Provid-

ence has not only fulfilled, but even exceeded, the prayers
of all : sea and land are at peace : cities flourish in order,
harmony, and prosperity : there is a height and abundance
of all good things : men are filled with hopes for the future
and gladness in the present.' It is impossible to doubt,
as one reads these words, that the feeling of a new and
better order lies behind them. A century of war, of extortion, of insecurity, of misery has come to an end. A
new era is dawning. The Empire begins in hope, and con-
tinues in comfort.

> Magnus ab integro saeclorum nascitur ordo.
> iam redit et Virgo, redeunt Saturnia regna,
> iam nova progenies, caelo demittitur alto.
>
> .   .   .   .
>
> ipsae lacte domum referent distenta capellae
> ubera, nec magnos metuent armenta leones.
>
> .   .   .   .
>
> aspice venturo laetentur ut omnia saeclo !

THE Empire was the solution of a problem : it was even
more—it was a ' salvation.' Religious feelings supported its institution and continuance ; and that religious
feeling was one of adoration for a present god, sent by
Providence for the ending of war and the saving of the
community of the human race. Here we meet once more
that idea of the deified ruler, which the Hellenistic East
had known since the days of Alexander and his first
successors, and which had already been moving westwards
for many years before the reign of Augustus. Flamininus,
the victor of Cynoscephalae, was greeted by the Greeks
as deliverer and ' Saviour ' ; Chalcis decreed him divine
honours ; and like the deified rulers of the East, he struck
coins with his own image and superscription. This was
a first burst of feeling, natural in the first formal contact
of the Greeks with a grave Roman commander ; but as they
realized that the Roman State had no permanent personal
sovereign, they contented themselves for years to come with
the worship of *Roma*. *Roma* was, however, a pale goddess :
instinct, the stronger because it was now a habit, craved a

personal object of devotion ; and in the first century B.C. we find provincial governors worshipped as gods in the East. As great leaders of armies rose to new eminence in Roman politics, the monarchical instinct rose to greater heights, and found a still more swelling expression. Pompey, who had given security to the Eastern Mediterranean by his campaigns against the pirates and the King of Pontus, was not only celebrated in inscriptions as the saviour who had given peace to the world : the Athenians themselves declared him a god, and joined with the ' Pompeiasts ' of Delos (the term indicates a formal cult established in his honour) in dedicating his statue to Apollo. The type and the genius of the absolute monarchies of the East became familiar to ambitious Romans ; and when they received the shadow of divine consecration, they could not but covet the substance of absolute power which cast the shadow. The foundations of imperialism are being laid when the great leaders of the standing armies of the West begin to meet in the East the type of institution and the temper of spirit which can give a concrete body to their dreams and a definite goal to their ambitions. A Roman development meets a Greek conception. That is the genesis of the conception of the Roman Empire.

It was not Pompey, in spite of his Eastern experience and honours, who was destined to Empire : it was Julius Caesar—who, if he had studied in Rhodes and heard Posidonius, had spent his political career in the West as governor first of Spain and afterwards of the two Gauls. Caesar was a scholar and a man of genius ; and he could apprehend with a rapidity and seize with a vigour denied to Pompey the chances of a fateful hour and the opportunity for founding a ' new monarchy,' which, new as it was to the West, was an ancient pattern in the East. It was not the ' restoration ' of an archaic and half-legendary municipal monarchy which Caesar planned : it was the ' translation ' to the West of that tradition of the divine monarch of a great State which lived in the East. Like Pompey, he received divine honours in the day of his success from the Greeks

of the Eastern Mediterranean ; but it was a new and
significant thing that he received the same honours in
Rome from the Roman authorities. After the battle of
Thapsus, his statue was erected by the Senate in the temple
of Jupiter with the inscription *Semideo* ; after the battle of
Munda, a second statue was erected, in the temple of
Quirinus, with the dedication *Deo invicto*. A cult arose
in his honour, with its college of *Luperci Iuliani* and its
flamen : his image appeared on coins in token of his divinity ;
his admirers crowned his statue with the white woollen
fillet once worn by the Persian kings, and afterwards by
Alexander and his successors ; and Shakespeare has made
us all familiar with the story of Antony thrice offering
him a kingly crown—which was in effect an Eastern diadem
—on the feast of the Lupercalia.

The open and frank policy of translating to Rome an
Eastern type of monarchy failed. It was not so much a
passion for liberty, as a clinging to Roman ways and traditions in the face of a policy tending to the substitution of
Oriental forms and conceptions, that inspired the opposition
and dictated the murder of Caesar. Refusing to learn by
the lesson of his failure, Antony—the confidant of his plans
—repeated his master's attempt : taking the East for his
province, and allying himself with Cleopatra, the one living
representative of the divine monarchies of the East, he
pretended to divinity and played the part of Hellenistic
monarch. Octavian was more cautious and more ready
to profit by the teaching of experience. He disarmed the
opposition in Rome by disavowing any policy of adopting
Oriental forms, and by professing to base his power on old
Roman conceptions of consular *imperium* and tribunician
potestas. On this basis, which from one point of view we
may almost call nationalist, as from another we may call it
antiquarian, he was able to gather the Latin West to his
cause, uniting under his banner both the friends and the
foes of Caesar ; to discredit Antony as a representative of
eastern enormities ; and, defeating his rival, to unite the
East and the West under a form of government which

professed to be a partnership between the first magistrate
of Rome and its ancient Senate.

But it was an absolutism none the less ; and it was an
absolutism which from the first contained the conception
and the cult of the deified ruler. At the time of the formation of the triumvirate of Octavian, Antony, and Lepidus,
at the end of 43 B.C., a temple was consecrated, on the place
on which his dead body had been burned, ' to the genius of
divus Iulius, pater patriae, whom the Senate and people of
Rome have received into the ranks of the Gods.' This is
the worship of the dead ruler ; but, as in the Hellenistic
kingdoms, the progress to a regular worship of the living
ruler was rapid. Augustus, as the inscriptions which have
already been quoted show, was being worshipped in the
East as ' a saviour . . . through whom have come good
tidings,' by the year 9 B.C. ; and even earlier (17–12 B.C.)
he is described in another Greek inscription as ' God the
son of God, Augustus, the Benefactor.' In Egypt he enters
into the style of the Ptolemies : he is ' autocrat, Son of the
Sun, Lord of the Diadem, Caesar, living for ever, beloved of
Ptah and Isis.' [1] The language and practice of the East
were transferred, in a modified form, to the West. Provincial *concilia*, analogous to the κοινά of Asia Minor, were
associated with the imperial cult ; and in Gaul (as in Spain
and also on the Rhine) representatives chosen by the different
tribes annually elected a priest for the service of the *Ara
Romae et Augusti*. In Rome and in Italy the worship of
Augustus was nominally forbidden ; but in many of the
Italian towns we may trace a cult of the emperor, with
Augustales devoted to its service ; and in the *vici* of Rome

[1] The influence of Ptolemaic Egypt on the development of the Empire
deserves notice. It had developed a remarkable system of administration (see Bauer, op. cit., pp. 33 ff.), as well as an advanced form of divine
monarchy ; and both of these developments influenced the Roman
emperors, the more as they treated Egypt differently from all other
provinces, ruling there in their own right as successors of the Ptolemies,
and not as representatives of the city of Rome. The Egyptian system of
taxation influenced the financial policy of Augustus ; and it was when he
became successor to the Ptolemies that he necessarily became a god.

itself we find the worship of the *Lares Compitales* combined with that of the *genius* of Augustus.[1]   The house of Augustus on the Palatine Hill was united with the temple of his patron Apollo ; in his house were treasured the Sibylline oracles ; to his house was transferred the cult of Vesta.   ' The *Penates* of the *gens Iulia* were united with those of the State ; and the future and fortunes of the Roman people were now placed in the house of Augustus.'

We must not emphasize the imperial cult unduly. Augustus never allowed himself to be entitled openly a very god in Rome itself, as Caesar had done : he assumed no crown : he claimed no form of divine honour.   The poets of his age—Propertius, Virgil, Horace, and Ovid (especially Ovid)—may term him *Deus* : he acts as a plain Roman citizen.   The religion which he would foster, and in the service of which he would enlist that feeling of mingled gratitude and hope which marks his age—as of men escaped from shipwreck, eager to dedicate their dripping garment to a saving deity—is the ancient religion of his country.   He closes the temple of Janus in token of peace : he celebrates *Ludi Saeculares* to purge away the sins of the past : he dedicates an *Ara Pacis Augustae*, the crowning achievement of Augustan art.   He would associate a religious revival with the nascent empire, and consecrate his power by the association : he would cast round the new system a halo, if not of the personal worship of his own divinity (though he never frowned upon such worship), at any rate of the religious awakening which the peace of the new system had brought and the policy of the new monarch had fostered. There is policy, after all, even in the religious policy which seems least political.

The general religious reformation of the Augustan age inspired Virgil : it had little abiding result in the mass.   But the worship of the deified ruler continued and grew.   Caligula and Nero pretended to a present divinity ; but generally the emperor was elevated to the rank of *divus*, and made the object of a cult, after his death ; and during his

[1] H. Stuart Jones, op. cit., p. 28 ;   Wendland, op. cit., pp. 146–7.

life it was his *genius* which was held to be sacred. Here was found the basis of allegiance. The oath of officials and soldiers was associated with the *genius* of the present emperor and the *divi Caesares* of the past. When the new dynasty of the Flavii succeeded to the Julian dynasty in 70 A.D., it sought to prove its legitimacy by assuming a similar divinity. Magistrates of Roman towns in the provinces took an oath to the divinity of Augustus, Claudius, Vespasian, and Titus : Domitian made the residence of the Flavian family (much as Augustus had done with his house on the Palatine) into a shrine served by a college of *Flaviales* ; and, as in Egypt under the Ptolemies,[1] the women of the family received consecration along with the men. The deification of the emperor, and the allegiance which he receives in virtue of his divinity, are obviously the foundation, or at any rate the cement, of the empire. ' In this cult,' writes Wendland, ' with its peculiar mixture of patriotic and religious feeling, there was found a common expression, which served as a bond of union, for that membership of the empire which was shared by parts so different in nationality and in religion : it was the token and symbol of imperial unity.' The empire was, in effect, a politico-ecclesiastical institution. It was a Church as well as a State : if it had not been both, it would have been alien from the ideas of the ancient world. A City-State entailed a civic worship : an Empire-State entailed an empire-worship ; and an empire-worship in turn—granted the existence of a personal emperor, and granted, too, the need for a personal symbol in a State so much larger and so much less tangible than a City-State which could be personalized itself — entailed the worship of an emperor. It is not irrelevant or disproportionate to linger over this aspect of the Roman Empire. If it had not shown this aspect to its subjects, it would not have been an empire ; for it would not have been a coherent society united by a common will.

---

[1] Vespasian was first proclaimed Emperor at Alexandria, while he was in Judaea. His first act as Emperor was to occupy Egypt ; and here he wrought a supposed miracle of healing by the royal touch.

BUT the empire was not only a religion : it was also a citizenship ; and we have now to inquire into the development of a common imperial citizenship, with its corollary of a common imperial law. By the end of the Republic the municipal citizenship of Rome had already developed into a State-citizenship of Italy. Under this system, as it was inherited and developed by the early emperors, Italy was separated from and privileged above the rest of the empire ; and in other respects (no troops, for instance, were quartered in Italy, but, on the other hand, only Italians could serve in the *corps d'élite* of the praetorian cohorts) Italy enjoyed an exceptional position. But the State-citizenship of Italy was gradually widened as colonies of Roman citizens were founded in the provinces, or provincials were admitted to Roman citizenship. Here the army played a large part : military service conferred Roman citizenship ; and as troops were recruited mainly in the provinces, a broad highway was opened for the enfranchisement of provincials.[1] When the Emperor Claudius (who introduced Gaulish chieftains to the *cursus honorum* and the ranks of Senate) revived the office of censor and took a census, he found that the number of citizens had increased by more than a million since the end of the reign of Augustus. The civic body had become a new thing : if it included provincials as well as Italians, it also included freedmen as well as the freeborn. It contained different nationalities and different classes ; and its growth tended to abolish both differences.

The abolition of different nationalities meant the emergence of what we may almost call a Mediterranean nationality. We may date the emergence of this new nationality from the reign of Hadrian. He was the first emperor to diminish

---

[1] From the time of Vespasian the Italians were excused from service in the legions ; and legionaries were recruited entirely from the provinces—the eastern provinces providing troops for the East and for Africa, and the western provinces for the West. From the time of Hadrian the legions were recruited from the various areas in which they were quartered, and recruits were thus left to serve in their native country. Under this system a Briton recruited in Britain for service with one of the three British legions would receive Roman citizenship without leaving the island.

the peculiar privileges of Italy : he visited and adorned with buildings almost every province of the empire : he showed his cosmopolitan temper by recruiting special bodies of Oriental troops and by giving to a Greek the command of a frontier province ; and, as his predecessor Trajan had done on a still grander scale (especially in Dacia), he spread Roman colonies over the empire.[1] Half a century after the death of Hadrian the Emperor Septimius Severus, an African by birth, destitute of Hadrian's ideal of a new nationality, but practically impatient of any anomaly which interfered with military efficiency or ease of administration, abolished the military privileges of Italy and granted citizenship to many provincial towns, especially in his own native province. It was the culmination of the policy of Hadrian and Severus, and at the same time the result of a tendency implicit in the very conception of the empire, when in 212 A.D. Caracalla promulgated the *Constitutio Antonina*, by which all free-born members of the communities of the empire were granted Roman citizenship. With one emperor and one allegiance—an allegiance shared by all, and shared equally by all—a common citizenship naturally followed.

The edict of Caracalla not only meant the blending of nationalities in one nationality : it also meant the blending of differences of status in a common equality. The empire had been from the first a levelling force. Augustus had already followed the policy of opening a career to all talents : as he opened the Senate to knights, so he opened the ranks of the knights for the admission of members of the *plebs*. This is the natural policy of any absolute government : it would fain enrich its service by drawing freely on all classes, and it would set the dignity of its service, which it proclaims a dignity of desert, above any dignity based on descent. In its passion for equality—which was quite compatible

---

[1] Hadrian, like his cousin Trajan, was a provincial from Spain. The Julian emperors were all Roman : the Flavians were Italian, of a Sabine stock. Severus, whose family spoke Punic, and who married a Syrian wife, marks a new epoch in the principate.

with a marked preference for its own confidential servants—
imperialism came close to Stoicism, which proclaimed the
equality of citizen and alien, man and woman, bondman
and free, while it cherished a peculiar regard for the *sapiens*
who had attained to high rank in the service of Reason.
It may have been in the logic of principles other than those
of Stoicism that the Roman emperors realized the Stoic
ideal of a universal society in which all the members were
equal ; but we must remember that Stoicism influenced the
Roman lawyers' conception of a law of nature which knew
no difference of status, and that the conceptions of the
Roman lawyers influenced the policy of the Roman
emperors.

The development of a common law for the empire
accompanied, as it helped to promote, the development of a
common citizenship. From early days, far back in the
history of the Republic, the praetors had been gradually
formulating in their edict a new procedure and system of
law, which should be generally applicable to cases in which
others than Roman citizens were concerned. If we look
at the origin of this system, we shall call it the praetor's
law, or *ius praetorium* : if we look at the area of its application, we shall call it the general law, or *ius gentium*. Commercial reasons dictated the growth of the new jurisprudence :
a law was needed for commercial cases, in which foreign
traders were concerned, and which grew more and more
frequent as Rome became more and more a commercial
city. The *ius civile* of Rome, even if it had not been, as it
was, the prerogative of the Roman *civis*, was too archaic,
and too much the law of a limited agricultural community,
to suit these cases ; and the law which the praetors began
to apply, and which was thus the foundation of the *ius
gentium*, was the more modern merchant law which had
come into being, and attained a general validity, in the
Mediterranean area. Building on this foundation, and
adding to this borrowed material a native legal genius and
grasp of legal principle, the praetors formulated in their
edict a system of law which had at once the simplicity and

the absence of archaic formalism necessary for commercial cases, and the universality of application which would suit the conditions of general Mediterranean trade. This simple and universal law, thus formulated by the praetors, became connected with the conception of a law of nature. It is quite possible that the Roman lawyers realized the 'natural' character of the *ius gentium* even before they were imbued with Stoic philosophy : it is certain that, as they came to understand the Stoic conception of a universal law of nature, they came to regard the *ius gentium* as a close approximation to that conception ; and though it was never universally or completely identified with the law of nature, it was at any rate regarded as the concrete expression of such a law in actual human society—less perfect, in that it denied equality and recognized slavery ; but more serviceable, because it was actually formulated and administered in courts. As a school of jurisconsults arose at Rome, the practical application of the *ius gentium* in the praetor's court was supplemented by scientific inquiry ; and from the second century B.C. a body of trained jurists applied their skill to elucidate and develop its implications. The majesty of the *ius gentium* was recognized— and at the same time its growth was stopped—when Hadrian realized a plan which is said to have been entertained by Julius Caesar, and caused the jurist Salvius Julianus to codify the praetorian edict in a fixed and final form. By this time the work had been done : the city-law of Rome had been expanded to meet the needs of the new Mediterranean state : a *ius gentium*, regarded as valid for all free men *everywhere* (this is the meaning of *gentium*), and assuming an ideal aspect by its close connexion with the law of nature—a connexion which helped to ameliorate the lot even of the slave—was co-extensive with the whole empire. And if the expansion of this *ius gentium* was stopped by its codification, there was another source ready and able to provide a law no less universal. The emperors had the power of issuing 'rescripts' in answer to any inquiry or petition ; and these rescripts, if they dealt largely with matter of administration, were also concerned with matter of law. The Antonines used their power to advance the emancipation of slaves and to maintain the principle that all accused persons must be held to be innocent until they were proved to be guilty ; and the *constitutiones principum*—the generic name applied to imperial rescripts, edicts, and decrees—became a great agent of legal progress down to the days of Justinian. Valid for the whole empire in virtue of their origin, they continued and completed the formation of a single law for the Mediterranean world.[1]

Along with the growth of unity in citizenship and unity in law there went also a unification of government. We can hardly say that the early empire possessed a unified government. The policy of Augustus was a policy of dovetailing the new into the old and uniting the new monarchy with the ancient Republic ; and it resulted in a partnership, or ' dyarchy,' under which the prince divided authority with the Senate and People—which meant, in effect, the Senate. This dualism is most obvious in the system which gave to the prince the frontier provinces and to the Senate the rest ; but it is implicit in the whole structure. Dualism could hardly have worked under any conditions : it certainly could not work when the Senate was unable to govern, and imperfectly qualified even to oppose. The emperors, with their trained staff of officials and their supreme command of the army, were from the first the superior partners ; and a zest for efficiency as well as a love of power drove them ultimately to rule in isolation. The process of development is slow : the struggle of the emperors and the Senate is for long years the real content of the political history of the empire. It is a proof of the legal

[1] It should be remarked that, great as was the legal genius of the Romans, the development of their law owes something to Hellenistic law, which we are gradually coming to know from papyri. We cannot, indeed, speak of Graeco-Roman law as we speak of Graeco-Roman civilization. But we may safely say that the Hellenistic kingdoms, with their high civilization and intricate commerce, had developed a common jurisprudence, which affected the Roman law of mortgage and other branches of the Roman law of contract.

genius of the Romans and their instinctive respect for precedent and constitutional tradition, that even the deified Caesars, masters of all the legions, should have respected for centuries the impotent majesty of republican forms. It may be that they were not without a suspicion that even the form of constitutionalism was better than the naked fact of a military autocracy, which might reveal to the legions only too clearly the fatal secret of their power. Whatever the reason, the fact remains that the structure of Augustus, doomed from the first to failure by its inherent flaws, was none the less slow in failing utterly. It is not until three centuries have run, and we reach the days of Aurelian and Diocletian, that we can finally detect a logical and thorough-going absolutism. To this day Roman Law preserves traces of the old dualism. If it can pronounce the emperor ' a living law on earth,' and declare him ' free from all laws,' it can also proclaim that ' it is a saying worthy of the ruler's majesty that a prince should profess himself bound by the laws.' If Ulpian enunciates the absolutist dictum, that ' the will of the prince has the force of law,' he adds at once the democratic explanation, ' because the People confers upon him and into his hands all its own sovereignty and power.' We may argue with almost equal cogency that Roman Law implies absolutism, and that it implies constitutionalism.

If the transference of plenary sovereignty to the emperor is a slow process, the process may already be traced in the reign of Hadrian. As he sought to deprive Italy of its primacy, so he began to divest the Senate of its partnership. He gave an additional importance to the knights, who constituted the civil service : it was a knight who held the only considerable command which he gave to a subject ; and knights were admitted to his *consilium* along with senators. Septimius Severus, even more inimical than Hadrian to the primacy of Italy, encroached still further on the prerogatives of the Senate. In his reign senators could no longer propose decrees : when treason was in question their dignity no longer protected them from torture ; and the

Senate ceased to exercise an influence in the apportioning of provinces or the appointing of magistrates. The system of dyarchy is dying when the Senate loses even its patronage ; but the death of the system belongs to a later epoch, and it is connected with a new ascendancy of the East and a fresh movement in the sphere of religion.

FROM the first the Roman Empire had been divided into two parts—the Hellenized East and the Roman West ; the one an amalgam of Oriental nationalities and religions, united by a general diffusion of Hellenic speech and culture, which was sometimes a veneer and sometimes a deep and genuine thing ; the other a collection of Celtic cantons, Berber tribes, and Italian townsfolk, imbued with Latin speech and pervaded by Latin traditions. It is a division which history has proved to be deep : it is a division which led to the parting of the empire into Eastern and Western halves, as it led to the schism of Christianity between Eastern and Western churches. If Julius Caesar had perhaps inclined to the East, the policy of Augustus, with its strong Latin trend, had emphasized the West, and from the beginning of his principate to the accession of Vespasian we may trace, in literature as in other directions, a dominance of Latin culture.[1] From the reign of Vespasian Greek literature begins to flourish again ; after the reign of Hadrian the centre of gravity begins to shift to the East, and the process begins which Constantine sealed by the foundation of Constantinople. What is ominous for the future is that as the East becomes more preponderant in the empire, it also becomes less Hellenic. Oriental nationalities and religions, dormant under Hellenism, but influencing Hellenism even while they were dormant, quicken to a new life ; and the Roman emperors, drawn more and more eastward by the problems of Eastern turbulence and Eastern

---

[1] Latin was the official language of the Greek East, and the Greeks used the services of interpreters. Public documents (such as the famous inscription termed the *Monumentum Ancyranum*) were bilingual ; and the imperial chancery had both a Greek and a Latin department.

frontiers, fall under the fascination of Eastern institutions and cults.

Early in the third century (227 A.D.) the Sassanids established a new Persian Empire with its capital at Ctesiphon ; and under the rule of the new dynasty, Zoroastrianism—with its cult of Ahura-mazda, the ' wise lord,' the god of heaven, who fights against Ahriman and the powers of darkness—became an official religion.[1] A form or a derivative of that religion was Mithraism. In the pure Zoroastrian faith Mithra was the god of light, the messenger of Ahura-mazda, the leader of his hosts ; but as Mithraism became an independent cult he became the supreme god, the very sun, the vivifying, penetrating, conquering ruler of the universe. Greek elements entered into Mithraism : the symbol of the god slaughtering a bull, which appears in representations of Mithra, may well be such an element. As a fusion of Persian and Hellenic elements the Mithraic religion attained a great vogue, especially in the Roman army, and commanded the fervent allegiance of millions. The diffusion of Mithraism through the whole Roman Empire was prior to the third century ; but the rise of the Sassanid dynasty, the ardent champion of pure Zoroastrianism, and the dominance of the Roman army, with its cult of Mithra, in the troubled politics of that century, may both have contributed to the primary importance which sun-worship now assumes.

The deification of the emperor, in the form inherited by the Romans from the Hellenistic monarchies, had by the third century become a lifeless and exhausted thing. It had no longer the glamour of a new thing from the East ; and the feeling of hope and gratitude, which had inspired the worship of Augustus in the early days of the empire, was irretrievably gone. The period of the fifty tyrants (235–70 A.D.) had seen the name of emperor cheapened : it had combined civil war with foreign invasion, and exceeded the horrors of the period of slaughter which preceded

[1] The compilation of the Zend-avesta belongs to the period of the Sassanid dynasty.

the principate of Augustus. Some new system of government was once more needed, as it had been needed at the
end of the first century B.C. : some new consecration, which
would take the place of the cult of the *divi Caesares* as a
bond of union and basis of allegiance, must support that
system and gain it a general acceptance. Aurelian began
and Diocletian completed the introduction of a new system
of Oriental absolutism ; and Aurelian made an Oriental
cult the religion of the empire, and bade his subjects regard
him as the earthly vicar and emanation of the Unconquered
Sun.

The cult of the Sun introduced by Aurelian was not in
itself Mithraism, though it had its connexions with the
worship of Mithra, and was calculated to attract the ready
allegiance of all his worshippers. It was a Syrian form of
religion, which he had come to adopt in his Eastern campaigns : it was a nature-cult, directed indeed to the worship
of the brightest of the heavenly bodies, but not different
in kind—except in its monotheism—from the worship of
the planets and other forms of ' astral religion ' which were
current in the East. What it was in itself is perhaps no
great matter, and at any rate does not greatly concern us
here. The fact and the consequences of the adoption of
an Oriental cult are of profound importance. That adoption meant a revolution in the position of the emperor ;
and it meant a revolution in the conception of the
empire.

The revolution in the position of the emperor consisted
in the change to an Oriental despotism. The old worship
of the emperor as a god in himself may appear to us servile ;
but it had been compatible with the spirit of liberty and
the forms of constitutionalism. After all, the conception
of the deified ruler was fundamentally Hellenic, and not
Oriental ; and that conception could exist by the side of
Hellenic and Roman ideas of the self-respect of the subject
and the freedom of the commonwealth. When Aurelian
claimed a new worship, not as a god in himself but as the
incarnation or emanation of a god, he may seem to have

claimed less, but he was really exacting more. He was moving in the sphere of Oriental ideas : he was asking for a blind prostration before a radiant divinity. He asserted a divine right, which could not be shared in any partnership : the Senate now lost even the formal privileges which it hitherto retained.[1] The purple, Aurelian told his troops, was the gift of God, who alone could limit His gift :

> The breath of worldly men cannot depose
> The deputy elected of the Lord.

But the emperor was more than a ' deputy ' : he was the image and epiphany of *Sol Invictus*. His was the nimbus emanating from the sun, which conferred a supernatural grace ; and if he left to the sun the title of ' Lord of the Roman Empire,' he might yet claim to be himself both ' Lord and God ' (*dominus et deus*). He wore the diadem and the great jewel-embroidered robe copied from the Sassanids : he adopted the throne and footstool, before which all subjects must prostrate themselves in adoration. All this means a new and eastern empire ; and all this passes into the system of Diocletian, which shows in the clear light of midday the results of the tendencies which dawn in the reign of Aurelian.

It was the work of Diocletian to exhibit with an exact logic the administrative consequences of the revolution in the position of the emperor which marked the end of the third and the beginning of the fourth century. He has been compared with Jeremy Bentham ; and he was certainly no less impatient of survivals and anomalies, and no less anxious to make a clean sweep and establish a new system. He made no particular profession of divinity, if he maintained the solemn state of robe and diadem and adoration ; but he pruned with a radical utilitarianism all the dead branches of the Roman past. The last trace of dyarchy disappeared, when the Senate became the municipal council of the city of Rome and its suburbs,

[1] Its members were excluded from military commands : it lost the old right of issuing bronze coins : the formula *Senatus Consulto* disappeared.

and a new division and regrouping obliterated any distinction between imperial and senatorial provinces. The empire became an intricate bureaucratic state, organized on a new basis of division, under which the military arm was independent of civil control, and one set of civil officials was jealously pitted against another. At the centre of the great cobweb, its 'universal spider,' the emperor held the threads and spun the filaments in a lonely absolutism. Italy ceased to enjoy any primacy, and was taxed like any other area : Rome ceased to be a capital, and the centre was shifted eastwards to Nicomedia. Losing its roots in the past, the empire became a new autocracy : severing its connexion with Rome and Italy, it found a fresh basis in the East, where it might at once feel more at home in sentiment and sit closer to its work in the details of administration.

In the conception of Diocletian the empire was still a unity : in the actual process of history the deserted West tended more and more to become a unit on its own account. Diocletian implicitly recognized, as he definitely hastened, this tendency, when he divided the empire, for convenience of administration, into an eastern and a western half by a line drawn through Illyria. The old Graeco-Roman civilization, pivoted on the middle Mediterranean, and organized on the basis of a single political community, had shown signs of fissure for the last two hundred years. After the reign of Diocletian it cracked and split. The East fell away into Byzantinism : the West broke away into Latin Christianity. This meant a double change. The world became two instead of one (though men still clung for centuries to the conception of the one universal society) ; and in one of the two halves the Church became the basis of life in place of the State. It is the latter change which demands our attention ; for it is here that we may see a fundamental revolution in the very conception of the empire—a revolution already implied in the reign of Aurelian, but first explicit in the policy of Constantine.

WHEN Aurelian made the worship of the Sun into the religion of the empire, and himself into the earthly emanation of the Sun, he was unconsciously acknowledging a great transference in the balance of human interest. The world in which the Unconquered Sun is proclaimed ' the Lord of the Roman Empire '—in which a temple is dedicated to his majesty upon his ' birthday ' [1]—is not the world of Pericles or Alexander, of Cicero, or even of Hadrian. For many centuries — for the thousand years, we may say, from 700 B.C. to 300 A.D.—the basis of political life had been found in the political interest, and men had thought and acted as ζῷα πολιτικά. The State was the unit of life : religion was an attribute or dependency of the State. The State might be a small city—an Athens, worshipping Athene as the incarnation of itself : it might be a ' great society '— an empire, worshipping a deified emperor as the incarnate ' genius ' of its imperialism : the dominant motive in either was political, secular — a motive of this world and the life of this world. This is the essence of Graeco-Roman civilization. By the third century A.D. there comes a transfer of interest. Human life seems to swing round on a pivot : the religious motive—long growing in strength ; long spreading westward from its home in the East—acquires the dominance. For many centuries to come — for the next thousand years, we may almost say, down to 1300 A.D., when the great Church of the Middle Ages began to totter in the pontificate of Boniface VIII — the basis of human organization is the religious motive, and human society is ecclesiastical in its primary inspiration. There are still states : there is indeed still an empire. But it is the Church which counts ; and kings who are kings by the grace of God are in the last resort kings by the grace of the Church. We cannot indeed assert the proposition of the whole Mediterranean world ; but we may assert it at any rate of the West. And here we touch a paradox. The East,

---

[1] The birthday of the Sun was fixed on December 25, at the time of the winter solstice. Constantius vindicated the day for Christianity, and made it Christmas Day—the birthday of our Lord.

which gave religion and the Church to the West, fell under
the control of the State. The West, which gave politics
and the State to the East, came under the sovereignty
of the Church. We may almost say that there was an
interchange of gifts and of rôles. The western State moved
into the East, to Constantinople, and subjugating the Church
produced Byzantinism. The Church which arose in the
East moved into the West, to Rome, and enthroning the
Papacy produced Latin Christianity.

A religion which was an attribute or dependency of the
State, and in the last resort a worship of the State, could
never satisfy the religious instinct. The achievements of
an Alexander, or the pacific triumphs of an Augustus, might
create a gratitude and an adoration for the head of a State,
which might last beyond the lifetime of their creator.
But the State has its defeats as well as its victories ; and
the abiding religious instinct, with its own aspirations towards a society and its own hope of controlling human life
by its principles, stood ready to take advantage of its
defeats. The religious appeal became ever stronger in the
ancient world, as the process of syncretism developed and
monotheism moved to victory. Christianity grew to an
irresistible volume. The worship of Mithra and of Isis,
the worship of the Unconquered Sun and of the great
mother Cybele—with their intimate societies, their arresting
rites, their consolation and their passion—all drew their
votaries and kindled a deep devotion. By the time of
Diocletian the State had lost its appeal and become a
structure based upon fear. It was a cobweb of suspicion :
its activity was an activity of extraction of taxes, relentless,
remorseless, to support an army and a mass of officials :
it tied the artisan to his guild, the serf to his plot, the
councillor to his town, in order that each, duly penned in his
place, might do his State-service and pay his State-dues.
There was no spontaneous social cohesion to constitute
a political community : there was no voluntary social
will to support a government. In this conjuncture the
religious motive entered into the foreground of life, and

swung forward to its triumph. The State, if it was to survive at all, could only survive by making the Church its ally, or, to speak more exactly, by becoming the ally of the Church. Thus the Roman Empire was driven in its last days by the mere instinct of self-preservation to adopt a religious creed as the basis—the only basis—on which it could still remain in existence. It sought to survive as an empire by becoming also, and indeed primarily, a Church. In the new religious temper of the times this was the only solution.

But why was the Christian Church in the issue the chosen ally of the pagan State ? The State had persecuted the Church : the Church had regarded the State as anti-Christ : on what ground could they unite ? We may meet these questions by the answer that, whatever the previous relations of the Christian Church and the Roman Empire, the peculiar conditions of the fourth century, as they have just been delineated, were such as to make an entirely new relation possible. The conflict between the two had depended on conditions which had ceased to exist. In the days in which the empire had found its basis in the worship of a deified emperor, the government had persecuted Christians because they had refused to participate in that worship; and in the Book of Revelation the Church had shown itself stung by such persecution to a passion of rebellion against the city of ' Babylon ' and the worship of the ' dragon.' But Christianity, if it protested against the persecuting State, was not in its essence opposed to the State in any of its forms or activities. St. Paul recognizes that the powers that be are ordained of God ; and prayers for the emperor and those in authority were customary among the early Christian communities. Christianity could recognize the State : what it could not recognize was the doctrine that religion was an attribute or dependency of the State ; and as long as that doctrine lasted, in the form of emperor-worship and the enforcement of emperor-worship as an essential article of citizenship, there could be no alliance between Christianity and the empire. By the end of the third century emperor-worship was passing : the empire was feeling its way towards a new form in which political unity would no longer involve a form of political religion, but community of religion would create, or at any rate sustain, political unity. If the empire was to be united on this basis, Christianity, with its aspiration towards the Gentiles and its vision of an oecumenical Church, was ready to constitute the basis. It offered itself as a world-religion to hold together on the ground of religious unity an empire which was doomed to dissolution if it sought to remain on the ground of political unity. The emperors accepted the offer. They became the powers ordained of God for the guidance of things temporal in a new empire now conceived as a Christian society. They did not realize, nor did the Church itself realize, that as the Christian society elaborated its own principle of life, a new ecclesiastical emperor would arise in the Pope, and a new struggle of Church and State would ensue, in which secular emperors and kings would seek to vindicate an independent political sphere against the claims of a theocracy. These results lay in the future. What happened in the reign of Constantine and his successors was that the autocratic emperors, remaining autocrats, agreed that the essential unity of the empire should henceforward be found in a common allegiance to the Christian creed. A bureaucratic machine controlled by an Orientalized emperor was united with a religious community based on the love of God and the brethren.

It was in 312 A.D. that Constantine, about to join battle with the legions of Maxentius, fighting under the banner of the Unconquered Sun, adopted a Christian symbol as his badge and marched to victory at the battle of the Mulvian bridge. He would oppose to the Unconquered Sun, deepseated in the allegiance of Roman legionaries, the unconquerable Christ whose votaries no persecutions could daunt, and whose coming triumph he already recognized. His victory over the army of Maxentius was the victory of Christianity (as it were in the ordeal of battle) over Sunworship and Mithraism and all the pagan cults. But it

did not result in the immediate establishment of Christianity
as the religion of the State. Constantine was content to
recognize Christianity as one of the public worships of the
empire. For the next seventy years the old pagan rites
were officially performed in Rome ; and the emperor, even
while he was a Christian, and presided in Christian synods,
was also the *Pontifex maximus*. But with the emperors
confessing the Christian faith, and, still more, with the
pressing need for a unification of the empire on a common
religious basis, the establishment of Christianity as the one
acknowledged religion of the empire was inevitable. The
Emperor Gratian (375–83 A.D.) refused to wear the robes of
the *Pontifex maximus*, and abolished the official recognition
of pagan rites. The Emperor Theodosius I (379–95 A.D.),
the last creative emperor, first as the colleague and then
as the successor of Gratian, completed the work. He sum-
moned in 381 A.D. the synod of Constantinople, which ended
the Arian heresy in the empire and defined the Christian
creed ; and he prohibited pagan profession as he proscribed
heretical opinion. Behind the figures of both emperors
stands Ambrose, Bishop of Milan, who inspired the weak
Gratian as he curbed the stormy Theodosius. When in
390 A.D. Theodosius, solemnly rebuked and excluded for
months from the Church on the ground of a massacre committed by his troops at Thessalonica, divested himself at
last of the purple in Ambrose's cathedral at Milan, and after
public penance was restored to the Christian communion,
he showed not only that the empire had become a Christian
society, but also that in that society (at any rate in the
West) the officers of the Church might become the censors
of the acts of the State.

HISTORIANS have proclaimed the fall of the empire, or
at any rate of the ' Western Empire,' in the year 476
A.D. ; and we may thus be led to conclude that the empire
collapsed when it became a Christian society. Here we must
make a distinction. In one sense the empire did not and
could not fall, because it was one with Christian society,

and Christian society still stood, and grew even firmer and stronger, as it absorbed into its life the barbarian invaders from the north. It may be urged, indeed, that what remained was a Christian Church, and not a Roman Empire ; that the old universal State had gone, if a new universal Church had come ; that in place of the old universal Graeco-Roman State there were now barbaric *regna*, hardly worthy to be called states, and only loosely united by a common profession of Christianity. Such a contention rests on a false antithesis—the antithesis between Church and State, conceived as separate societies. The Christian Church had fused with the Roman State in a single society, a Christian commonwealth, which was an empire as well as a Church and a Church as well as an empire. The continuity of the Christian Church involved the continuity of the empire, because the Church and the empire were not two societies, but two aspects of a single society. It may be urged again that, if this be so, the empire only survived as an ' aspect ' —that is to say, as a mental conception—and that in the tangible world of institutions and administration it had no body and no existence. We may well admit that there is a large measure of truth in such a contention—though we may also urge that a conception which influenced the political development of Western Europe for many centuries was more than a ghost—and we must accordingly turn to consider the sense in which the empire, after all, ' fell ' in 476 A.D.

In the first place, the empire fell asunder into the two divisions of East and West. The cleavage was indeed far from being absolute, and the idea and even the form of unity long survived. So long as men cherished the idea of a single Christian society, they could hardly admit to themselves the existence of two separate societies and two separate empires. The Church of the East, though it diverged more and more from the West, especially in the days of the iconoclastic controversy (*c.* 700 A.D.), was not repudiated by the West as schismatic until the eleventh century ; and the Byzantine emperors were recognized as emperors even in the West until the coronation of Charlemagne, alike by barbarian kings and by the Bishop of Rome. None the less the East had finally diverged from the West ; and we may, if we will, date that divergence in 476 A.D. It is a matter of choice. We may equally well date it earlier, from Diocletian's administrative division of the empire, or from Constantine's foundation of Constantinople, or from the dynastic division of Theodosius I ; or later, from the coronation of Charlemagne or the final schism of the Churches. What matters is the fact that the East had steadily withdrawn itself into its own life from the second century of the Christian era, and that it gradually built a polity of its own fundamentally different from that of the West—a polity in which there was no Papacy, but the emperor was himself the head of the Church, and the Church was a department of the administration of the State. This is Byzantinism ; and the essential conceptions of Byzantinism were inherited on the one hand by the Russian Tsars,[1] successors of the Caesars by marriage and governors of their Church through the Holy Synod, and on the other by the Turkish Sultan, at once Keisar-i-Rum in virtue of Constantinople and Commander of the Faithful in virtue of succession to the Prophet. Augustus had strange successors. But Augustus was of the West ; and Aurelian, son of a Pannonian peasant, and Diocletian, son of an Illyrian freedman, both of the East and both absolute rulers, might have recognized a closer kinship with an Ivan or a Selim.

In the second place, the empire in the West after 476 A.D. was in abeyance for some hundreds of years, so far as a visible emperor, or a capital, or a system of administration

[1] Ivan III, who married Sophia Palaeologus, used the title of Tsar (in old Slavonic *tsésar*) on documents and on coins : he termed himself *samodérzhets*, or autocrat of the Russias, in translation of the Byzantine αὐτοκράτωρ : he adopted the Byzantine crest of the double-headed eagle. Ivan IV was the first Russian sovereign to have himself crowned Tsar (1547 A.D.). It was Peter the Great who finally subdued the Russian Church to the State, and abolishing the patriarchate instituted a layman as procurator-general of the Holy Synod to govern the Church.

was concerned. There was no emperor to be seen, whether at Rome or Milan or Ravenna, and there was no imperial system of administration.[1] The splendour of the emperor at Constantinople might cast a shadow westwards, and men might feel, as long as they saw the shadow, that there was somewhere a substance of empire ; but the substance was not in the West. If empire means an emperor, a capital, an administration, then Count Marcellinus was right when he wrote of the year 476 A.D., *Hesperium gentis Romanae imperium . . . cum hoc Augustulo periit*. But if empire means a society and a community, then we can only say that the empire survived in the West ; and the whole of mediaeval history would be unintelligible if we did not realize that it survived. It survived as a *respublica Christiana*, a Christian commonwealth recognizing the formal suzerainty of the Byzantine successors of Constantine, but gradually developing a spiritual ruler of its own in the Bishop of Rome.

IN the *De Civitate Dei* St. Augustine faced the question whether the empire collapsed when it became a Christian society. He wrote before 476 A.D., but he wrote under the impression of the sack of Rome by Alaric ; and he sought to meet the pagan argument that the adoption of Christianity was the ruin of Rome. Rome, he replies, had known vicissitudes and misery even under paganism. But this is only a negative answer ; and Augustine quickly rises to the height of the true Christian argument. The love and enjoyment of God, which Christianity alone can give, are the true happiness of humanity ; and they stand triumphant above all the chances and calamities of temporal events. Along this line Augustine moves to the theme of the Two Cities, which had already been handled by Marcus Aurelius— the City of Rome and the City of God ; he sets one form of social life against another, and pits the heavenly against

[1] Justinian reconquered Italy, and it was under Byzantine government until 568 A.D. Even after that date there was a Byzantine exarch at Ravenna until 752 A.D. But that was all.

the earthly. He is far from identifying the heavenly city with the community gathered in the Roman Empire ; and we may even doubt whether he identified the *Civitas Dei* with the visible and organized Christian Church. Scholars are divided on the issue : some have held that his city of God was ' a real institution with a definite organization ' ; others have thought that it was an unseen society, not built with hands, a spiritual society of the predestined faithful, distinct from the visible communion of baptized Christians. But we are probably justified in believing that even in the thought of St. Augustine himself, and certainly in the interpretation of later generations, the mantle of the city of God descended upon the visible Church. ' The conception of the Church as a social entity wielding governing powers,' wrote Dr. Figgis, ' owes much to St. Augustine. He did much to strengthen the Church as an imperial force.' [1]

The Church which could thus be conceived as a social entity and an imperial force gradually acquired an imperial organization. The genius and the structure of the old imperial system passed into the organization of the Church. Residence in Rome, with the emperor far removed in distant Constantinople, contributed to establish the Bishop of Rome as the successor of the Caesars in the West ; and the habit of looking to Rome for political guidance was continued in the tendency, which we may trace in the Church as early as the second century, to turn to Rome, as the guardian of the pure apostolic tradition, for guidance in all religious controversies. Hobbes wrote of the Papacy as ' the ghost of the deceased Roman Empire, sitting crowned on the grave thereof.' The author of the forged Donation of Constantine (perhaps compiled in Italy, in the latter part of the eighth century) expressed the same idea when he made Constantine give to Sylvester I his palace, diadem, and robes, ' with the city of Rome and all provinces, places, and cities of Italy or the western regions.' We must not exaggerate the inheritance, or conclude that the position of the Papacy was simply and solely the con-

[1] *The Political Aspects of St. Augustine's City of God*, pp. 71-2.

tinuance in the religious sphere of the power previously wielded by the emperor in the political. A sacramental and sacerdotal Church, such as the Latin Church of the West, demanded in its own inner logic, and apart from any inheritance, a central fountain, abounding in a *plenitudo potestatis*, from which there might emanate to the bishops, and through the bishops to their clergy, the dignity of their office, the sacramental power, and the substance of the tradition they were set to teach. But if papalism, with its sovereignty and its infallibility, was inherent in the essence of such a Church, we may still believe that tradition and environment fostered the growth of what was innate.

A city of God conceived as a visible Church, and organized as a spiritual empire, may seem to leave little room for any *terrena civitas*. But it was many centuries before the claim of ecclesiastical dominance, if it was already implicit in the Church at the end of the fourth and in the fifth century, was finally asserted. Ambrose of Milan subdued Theodosius to penitence in 390 A.D. : it was not until 1077 A.D. that Henry IV knelt in penitence before Gregory VII at Canossa. In a world of barbaric German chieftains the times were not ripe for the sway of the Church ; and during the long interval a theory of what we may call parallelism was held. There was indeed one society, men thought, and one only ; but there were two governments, each with separate powers. This is the theory expressed by Gelasius I (and scholars have accordingly termed it Gelasian) in a letter to Anastasius, the eastern emperor : ' there are two things by which this world is principally ruled—the sacred authority of the Popes and the royal power.' The one is set over things spiritual and the other over things temporal ; but the burden of the Popes is the heavier, as they must answer even for kings at the divine judgment. Two parallel sovereigns of one society, the Pope at Rome and the Emperor at Constantinople— this is the theory which is held in the West till the coronation of Charlemagne in 800 A.D. By that event a change was made, not in the relations of the two powers, but in the residence of the temporal power. There was a ' translation of the empire from the Greeks to the Germans ' (not, we may note, a division, but a transference of a single and undivided empire) ; and henceforth, till the pontificate of Gregory VII, the Pope at Rome and the Emperor at Aix-la-Chapelle are parallel rulers of the society of the western world. The East is recalcitrant. The empire has been ' translated ' ; but an East Roman Empire persists in remaining among the Greeks.

In the pontificate of Gregory VII we reach the days of ecclesiastical dominance. The system of parallelism—we may almost call it a new dyarchy, of a very different type from that devised by Augustus—is abandoned : the Church Universal, through its universal bishop, seeks to control the whole of human life : universal in extension, it would also be universal in its intensity of action. Society was recovering from the time of barbaric dispersion : trade was bringing the whole of Western Europe together : the Crusades and the spread of international orders were beginning to cement the unity. Gregorianism succeeds to Gelasianism ; and Gregorianism means a gallant attempt of the Church, through its Papacy, to bring a united Christian commonwealth, in its every reach, under the control of Christian principle. In politics and in social life, in economics and in the studies of universities, the Church would be dominant : it would control kings in their government ; by its canon law of marriage and of wills, as by its penitentiary system, it would guide the social life of the family and the individual ; it would regulate prices and prohibit usury ; it would build a great body of scholastic knowledge to satisfy every student. Gregorianism as an ideal (it could never be realized) means one universal society, which is a Church, based utterly on the law of Christ and controlled ultimately by Christ's vicar. Here the new development of the human spirit, the new trend to the religious life, which first found recognition at the end of the third and the beginning of the fourth century, attains its zenith. The combination of a religious society with an autocratic political society which we find under Constantine ; the modified form of

that combination preached by Gelasius, in which the
religious society acquires a religious as well as a political
government—both disappear. The religious society attempts its logical complement in a theocracy.

But the political instinct of humanity is not readily
quenched. The Holy Roman Empire, against which
Gregorianism was pitted, was not, it is true, a strong embodiment of that instinct. A Charlemagne might have the
force of a Frankish Empire at his back : the German emperors from Otto I onwards (962 A.D.) were only kings of
Germany and Italy ; and while Germany was divided by
tribalism and distracted by feudalism, Italy was the home
of practically independent cities. Even Charlemagne,
though his coins bear the inscription *Renovatio Romani
Imperii*, had no tradition ; and his successors were equally
destitute of any connexion with antiquity. With no root
in their own realms, and no tradition for their support, the
German emperors of the Middle Ages were not adequate to
the struggle with the Church ; and though they might seek
to vindicate an independent political sphere, they were
worsted in argument and defeated in policy by the papalist
forces. It was when a lay sentiment, fostered by the
lawyers, arose in France, and associated itself with national
feeling, that the Church found a stubborn enemy, and Boniface VIII at last met with defeat (1303 A.D.). A lay society,
founded on a national basis, vanquished the conception of a
universal empire in the form which that conception had
more and more assumed during the thousand years since
the death of Aurelian—the form of an ecclesiastical society.
And the Reformation, in which the lay State, alike in
England and in Germany, asserted the priority of the
political motive and the supremacy of its king over all
persons and in all causes as well ecclesiastical as temporal,
marks the final defeat and disappearance of the conception
of the Roman Empire.

THE UNITY OF MEDIAEVAL CIVILIZATION [1]

Ergo humanum genus bene se habet et optime, quando secundum quod potest Deo adsimilatur. Sed genus humanum maxime Deo adsimilatur quando maxime est unum ; vera enim ratio unius in solo illo est. Propter quod scriptum est : ' Audi, Israel, Dominus Deus tuus unus est.'—DANTE, *De Monarchia*, I. viii.

I

HE who shuts his eyes to-day to make a mental picture of the world sees a globe in which the mass of Asia, the bulk of Africa, and the length of America vastly outweigh in the balance the straggling and sea-sown continent of Europe. He sees all manner of races, white and yellow, brown and black, toiling, like infinitesimal specks, in every manner of way over many thousands of miles ; and he knows that an infinite variety of creeds and civilizations, of practices and beliefs—some immemorially old, some crudely new ; some starkly savage, and some softly humane—diversify the hearts of two thousand million living beings. But if we would enter the Middle Ages, in that height and glory of their achievement which extended from the middle of the eleventh to the end of the thirteenth century, we must contract our view abruptly. The known world of the twelfth century is a very much smaller world than ours, and it is a world of a vastly greater unity. It is a Mediterranean world ; and ' Rome, the head of the world, rules the reins of the round globe.' From Rome the view may travel to the Sahara in the south ; in the east to the Euphrates, the Dniester, and the Vistula ; in the north to the Sound and the Cattegat (though some, indeed, may have

[1] A Paper read before a ' Unity ' Summer School at Birmingham in 1915.

heard of Iceland), and in the west to the farther shores of Ireland and of Spain. Outside these bounds there is something, at any rate to the east, but it is something shadowy and wavering, full of myth and fable. Inside these bounds there is the clear light of a Christian Church, and the definite outline of a single society, of which all are baptized members, and by which all are knit together in a single fellowship.

Economically the world was as different from our own as it was geographically. Money, if not unknown, was for the most part unused. It had drifted eastwards, in the latter days of the Roman Empire, to purchase silks and spices ; and it had never returned. From the days of Diocletian, society had been thrown back on an economy in kind. Taxes took the form either of payments of personal service or of quotas of produce : rents were paid either in labour or in food. The presence of money means a richly articulated society, infinitely differentiated by division of labour, and infinitely connected by a consequent nexus of exchange. The society of the Middle Ages was not richly articulated. There were merchants and artisans in the towns ; but the great bulk of the population lived in country villages, and gained subsistence directly from the soil. Each village was practically self-sufficing ; at the most it imported commodities like iron and salt ; for the rest, it drew on itself and its own resources. This produced at once a great uniformity and a great isolation. There was a great uniformity, because most men lived the same, grey, quiet life of agriculture. The peasantry of Europe, in these days when most men were peasants, lived in the same way, under the same custom of the manor, from Berwick to Carcassonne, and from Carcassonne to Magdeburg. But there was also a great isolation. Men were tied to their manors ; and the men of King's Ripton could even talk of the ' nation ' of their village. If they were not tied by conditions of status and the legal rights of their lord, they were still tied, none the less, by the want of any alternative life. There were towns indeed ; but towns were themselves very largely agricultural—the homes of *summa rusticitas*—

and what industry and commerce they practised was the perquisite and prerogative of local guilds. Custom was king of all things, and custom had assorted men in compartments in which they generally stayed. The kaleidoscopic coming and going of a society based on monetary exchanges—its speedy riches and speedy bankruptcies, its embarrassment of alternative careers all open to talents—these were unthought and undreamed of. The same uniformity and the same isolation marked also, if in a less degree, the knightly class which followed the profession of arms. A common feudal system, if we can call that a system which was essentially unsystematic, reigned over the whole of Western Europe, and, when Western Europe went crusading into Syria, established itself in Syria. Historians have tried to establish distinctions between the feudalism of one country and that of another—between the feudalism of England, for instance, and that of France. It is generally held nowadays that they have failed to establish the distinction. A fief in England was uniform with a fief in France, as a manor in one country was uniform with manors in other countries, and a town in one country with towns in others. ' One cannot establish a line of demarcation between German and French towns,' says a famous Belgian historian, ' just as one cannot distinguish between French and German feudalism.' [1] The historian of the economic and institutional life of the Middle Ages will err unless he proceeds on the assumption of its general uniformity. But the uniformity of the fief, like that of the manor and the town, was compatible with much isolation. Each fief was a centre of local life and a home of local custom. The members of the feudal class lived, for the most part, local and isolated lives. Fighting, indeed, would bring them together ; but when the ' season ' was over, and the forty days of service were done, life ran back to its old ruts in the manor-hall, and if some of the summer was spent in company, much of the winter was spent in isolation. On a society of this

[1] Pirenne, *Revue Historique*, liii. p. 82.

order—stable, customary, uniform, with its thousands of isolated centres —the Church descended with a quickening inspiration and a permeating unity. Most of us find a large play for our minds to-day in the competition of economics or the struggles of politics. The life of the mind was opened to the Middle Ages by the hands of the Church. We may almost say that there was an exact antithesis between those days and these latter days, if it were not that exact antitheses never occur outside the world of logic. But it is as nearly true as are most antitheses that while our modern world is curiously knit together by the economic bonds of international finance, and yet sadly divided (and never more sadly than to-day) [1] by the clash of different national cultures and different creeds, the mediaeval world, sundered as it was economically into separate manors and separate towns, each leading a self-sufficing life on its own account, was yet linked together by unity of culture and unity of faith. It had a single mind, and many pockets. We have a single pocket, and many minds. That is why the wits of many nowadays will persist in going wool-gathering into the Middle Ages, to find a comfort which they cannot draw from the golden age of international finance.

But retrogression was never yet the way of progress. It is probable, for instance, that the sanitation of the Middle Ages was very inadequate, and their meals sadly indigestible ; and it would be useless to provoke a revolt of the nose and the stomach in order to satisfy a craving of the mind. An uncritical mediaevalism is the child of ignorance of the Middle Ages. Sick of vaunting national cultures, we may recur to an age in which they had not yet been born—the age of a single and international culture ; but we must remember, all the same, that the strength of the Middle Ages was rooted in weakness. They were on a low stage of economic development ; and it was pre-cisely because they were on a low stage of economic develop-

---

[1] This Paper belongs to the days of the war. I have thought it best to leave the marks of its origin.

ment that they found it so easy to believe in the unity
of civilization. Unity of a sort is easy when there are
few factors to be united ; it is more difficult, and it is
a higher thing, when it is a synthesis of many different
elements. The Middle Ages had not attained a national
economy : their economy was at the best municipal, and
for the most part only parochial. A national economy
has a higher economic value than a municipal or parochial
economy, because it means the production of a greater
number of utilities at a less cost, and a richer and fuller
life of the mind, with more varied activities and more
intricate connexions. A national economy could only
develop along with—perhaps we may say it could only
develop through—a national system of politics ; and the
national State, which is with us to-day, and with some of
whose works we are discontented, was a necessary condition
of economic progress. With the coming of the national
State the facile internationalism of the Middle Ages had
to disappear ; and as economics and politics ran into
national channels, the life of the spirit, hitherto an international life, suffered the same change, and national religions, if such a thing be not a contradiction in terms,
were duly born. But a national economy, a national
State, a national Church were all things unknown to the
Middle Ages. Its economy was a village economy : its
mental culture was an international culture bestowed
by a universal Church (a village culture there could not be,
and with a universal Church the only possible culture was
necessarily international) ; while, as for its politics, they
were something betwixt and between—sometimes parochial,
when a local feudal lord drew to himself sovereignty ;
sometimes national, when a strong king arose in Israel ;
and sometimes, under a Charlemagne, almost international.

A consideration of the linguistic factor may help to
throw light on the point in question. Here again we may
trace the same isolation and the same uniformity which
we have also seen in the world of economics. There was
an infinity of dialects, but a paucity of languages, in the

Middle Ages. One is told that to-day there are dialects in the Bight of Heligoland and among the Faroes which are peculiar to a single family. Something of the same sort must have existed in the Middle Ages. Just as there were local customs of the manor, the town, and the fief, there must have been local dialects of villages and even of hamlets. But here again isolation was compatible with uniformity. There were perhaps only two languages of any general vogue in the central epoch of the Middle Ages, and they were confined by no national frontiers. First there was Latin, the language of the Church, and since learning belonged to the Church, the language of learning. Scholars used the same language in Oxford and Prague, in Paris and Bologna ; and within the confines of Latin Christianity scholarship was an undivided unity. Besides Latin the only other language of any general vogue in the middle of the Middle Ages was vulgar Latin, or Romance. To Dante, writing at the close of the thirteenth century, Romance was still one *idioma*—even if it were *trifarium*, according as its ' yes ' was *oïl*, or *oc*, or *si*.[1] Of the three branches of this *idioma*, that of *oïl*, or Northern France, was easily predominant. The Norman conquest of England carried it to London : the Norman conquest of Sicily carried it to Palermo : the Crusades carried it to Jerusalem. With it you might have travelled most of the mediaeval world from end to end. It was the language of courts ; it was the language of chansons ; it was the language of all lay culture. It was the language of England, France, and Italy ; and St. Francis himself had delighted in his youth in the literature which it enshrined.

The linguistic basis of mediaeval civilization was thus Latin, either in its classical or in its vulgar form. There were of course other languages, and some of these had no small vogue. Just before the period of which we are treating—the period which extends from 1050 to 1300— Norse had a very wide scope. It might have been heard not only in Scandinavia and the Northern Isles, but in a

[1] *De Vulgari Eloquio*, i. viii.

great part of the British Islands, in Normandy, in Russia
—along the river-road that ran to Constantinople—and
in Constantinople itself. But the fact remains that the
linguistic basis of mediaeval thought and literature was
a Latin basis. The Romance University of Paris was the
capital of learning : the Romance tongue of Northern
France was the tongue of society. And as the linguistic
basis of mediaeval civilization was Romance, so, too, was
mediaeval civilization itself. The genius of Latin Christianity was the source of its inspiration : the spirit of the
Romance peoples was the breath of its being. The souvenir
of the old Roman Empire provided the scheme of its political
ideas ; and the Holy Roman Empire, if a religious consecration had given it a new sanctity, was Roman still. Yet
the irruption of the Teutons into the Empire had left its
mark ; and the emperor of the Middle Ages was always
of Teutonic stock. It was perhaps at this point that the
unity of the mediaeval scheme betrayed a fatal flaw. It
would be futile to urge that the dualism which showed itself
in the struggles of papacy and empire had primarily, or even
to any considerable extent, a racial basis. Those struggles
are struggles of principles rather than of races ; they are
contentions between a secular and a clerical view of life,
rather than between the genius of Rome and the genius of
Germany. Hildebrand stood for a free Church—a Church
free from secular power because it was controlled by the
papacy. Henry IV stood for the right of the secular power
to use the clergy for purposes of secular government, and
to control the episcopacy as one of the organs of secular
administration. But the fact remains that a scheme which
rested on a Teutonic emperor and a Roman pontiff was
already a thing internally discordant, before these other
and deeper dissensions appeared to increase the discord.

Such were the bases on which the unity of mediaeval
civilization had to depend. There was a contracted world,
which men could regard as a unity, with a single centre of
coherence. There was a low stage of economic development, which on the one hand meant a general uniformity

of life, in fief and manor and town, and on the other hand meant a local isolation, that needed, and in the unity of the Church found, some method of unification. With many varieties of dialect, there was yet a general identity of language, which made possible the development, and fostered the dissemination, of a single and identical culture. Nationalism, whether as an economic development, or as a way of life and a mode of the human spirit, was as yet practically unknown. Races might disagree ; classes might quarrel ; kings might fight ; there was hardly ever a national conflict in the proper sense of the word. The mediaeval lines of division, it is often said, were horizontal rather than vertical. There were different estates rather than different states. The feudal class was homogeneous throughout Western Europe ; the clerical class was a single corporation through all the extent of Latin Christianity ; and the peasantry and the townsfolk of England were very little different from the peasantry and the townsfolk of France. We have to think of a general European system of estates rather than of any balance of rival powers.

II

THE unity which rested on these bases begins to appear, as a reality and not only an idea, about the middle of the eleventh century, and it lasts till the end of the thirteenth. It was a unity, as we have seen, essentially ecclesiastical. It was the product of the Church : we may almost say that it was the Church. Before 1050 the Catholic Church, however universal in theory, had hardly been universal in fact. The period of the Frankish, the Saxon, and the early Salian emperors had been a period of what German writers call the *Landeskirche*. The power of the Bishop of Rome had not yet been fully established ; and the great churches of Reims and Mainz and Milan were practically independent centres. Independent of the papacy, they were not independent of the lay rulers within whose dominions they lay. On the contrary, their members were deeply engaged in lay activities ; they were landlords, feudatories, and officials in their various countries. In the face of these facts, the Gregorian movement of the eleventh century pursues two closely interconnected objects. It aims at asserting the universal primacy of the papacy ; it aims at vindicating the freedom of the clergy from all secular power. The one aim is a means to the other : the pope cannot be universal primate, unless the clergy he controls are free from secular control ; and the clergy cannot be free from secular control, unless the universal primacy of the papacy effects their liberation. Gregorianism wins a great if not a thorough triumph. It establishes the theory, and in a very large measure the practice, of ecclesiastical unity. The days of the *Landeskirche* are numbered : the days of the Church Universal under the universal primacy of Rome are begun. But when the universality of the Church has once been established in point of extension, it begins to be also asserted in point of intensity. Once it is ubiquitous, the papacy seeks to be omnicompetent. Depository of the truth, and only depositary of the truth, by divine revelation, the Church, under the guidance of the papacy, seeks to realize the truth in every reach of life, and to control, in the light of Christian principle, every play of human activity. Learning and education, trade and commerce, war and peace, are all to be drawn into her orbit. By the application of Christian principle a great synthesis of human life is to be achieved, and the *lex Christi* is to be made a *lex animata in terris*.

This was the greatest ambition that has ever been cherished. It meant nothing less than the establishment of a *civitas Dei* on earth. And this kingdom of God was to be very different from that of which St. Augustine had written. His city of God was neither the actual Church nor the actual State, nor a fusion of both. It was a spiritual society of the predestined faithful, and, as such, thoroughly distinct from the State and secular society. The city of God which the great mediaeval popes were seeking to establish was a city of this world, if not of this world only. It was a fusion of the actual Church, reformed by papal direction and governed by papal control, with actual lay society, similarly reformed and similarly governed. Logically this meant a theocracy, and the bull of Boniface VIII, by which he claimed that every human creature was subject to the Roman pontiff, was its necessary outcome. But theocracy was only a means, and a means that was never greatly emphasized in the best days of the papacy. It was the end that mattered ; and the end was the moulding of human life into conformity with divine truth. The end may appear fantastic, unless one remembers the plenitude of means which stood at the command of the mediaeval Church. The seven sacraments had become the core of her organization. Central among the seven stood the sacrament of the Mass, in which bread and wine were transubstantiated into the divine body and blood of our Lord. By that sacrament man could touch God ; and by its mediation the believer met the supreme object of his belief. Only the priest could celebrate the great mystery ; and only those who were fit could be admitted by him to participation. The sacrament of penance, which became the antechamber, as it were, to the Mass, enabled the priest to determine the terms of admission. Outside the sacraments stood the Church courts, exercising a large measure of ethical and religious discipline over all Christians ; and in reserve, most terrible of all weapons, were the powers of excommunication and interdict, which could shut men and cities from the rites of the Church and the presence of the Lord. Who shall say, remembering these things, that the aims of the mediaeval Church were visionary or impracticable ?

For a time, and in some measure, they were actually accomplished. Let us look at each estate in turn, and measure the accomplishment—speaking first of the knightly world, and the Church's control of war and peace ; then of the world of the commons, and the Church's control of trade and commerce ; and last of the clerical world, and the Church's control of learning and education.

THE control of war and peace was a steady aim of the Church from the beginning of the eleventh century. The evil of feudalism was its propensity to private war. To cure that evil the Church invented the Truce of God. The Truce was a diocesan matter. The 'form' of Truce was enacted in a diocesan assembly, and the people of the diocese formed a *communitas pacis* for its enforcement. There was no attempt to put an absolute stop to private war; the Truce was only directed to a limitation of the times and seasons in which feuds could be waged, and a definition of the persons who were to be exempted from their menace. But from seeking to limit the fighting instinct of a feudal society, the Church soon rose to the idea of enlisting that instinct under her own banner and directing it to her own ends. So arose chivalry, which, like most of the institutions of the Middle Ages, was the invention of the Church. Chivalry was the consecration of the fighting instinct to the defence of the widow, the fatherless, and the oppressed; and by the beginning of the eleventh century liturgies already contain the form of religious service by which neophytes were initiated into knighthood. This early and religious form of chivalry (there was a later and lay form, invented by troubadour and trouvère, which was chiefly concerned with the rules for the loves of knights and ladies) culminated in the Crusades. In the Crusades we touch perhaps the most typical expression of the mediaeval spirit. Here we may see the clergy moulding into conformity with Christian principle the apparently unpromising and intractable stuff of feudal pugnacity: here we may see the papacy asserting its primacy of a united Europe by gathering Christian men together for the common purpose of carrying the flag of their faith to the grave of their Redeemer. Here the permeating influence of Christian revelation may be seen attempting to permeate even foreign policy (for what are the Crusades but the foreign policy of a Christian commonwealth controlled and directed by the papacy ?) ; and here again even the instinct for colonial expansion, so often the root of desperate wars, was brought into line with the unity of all nations in Christ, and made to serve the cause of Him ' in whom alone is to be found the true nature of the One.'

There is another aspect of the clerical control of peace and war in the interest of Christian unity which must not be forgotten. The papacy sought to become an international tribunal. The need for such a tribunal was as much a mediaeval as it is a modern commonplace. Dante, who sought to vindicate for the emperor, rather than for the pope, the position and power of an international judge, has started the argument in famous words. ' Between any two princes, of whom the one is in no way subject to the other, disputes may arise, either by their own fault, or by that of their subjects. Judgment must therefore be given between them. And since neither can have cognizance of the other, because neither is subject to the other, there must be a third of ampler jurisdiction, to control both by the ambit of his power.'[1] Such ampler jurisdiction, which might indeed be claimed for the emperor, but which he had never the power to exercise, was both claimed and exercised by the papacy. The papacy, which sought to enforce the Christian canon of conduct in every reach of life and every sphere of activity, would never admit that disputes between sovereign princes lay outside the rule of that canon. Innocent III, in a letter to the French bishops defending his claim to arbitrate between France and England, stands very far from any such admission. ' It belongs to our office,' he argues, ' to correct all Christian men for every mortal sin, and if they despise correction, to coerce them by ecclesiastical censure. And if any shall say, that kings must be treated in one way, and other men in another, we appeal in answer to the law of God, wherein it is written, " Ye shall judge the great as the small, and there shall be no acceptance of persons among you." But if it is ours to proceed against criminal sin, we are especially bound so to do when we find a sin against peace.'[2] Here,

[1] *De Monarchia*, I. x.
[2] Cf. Carlyle, *Mediaeval Political Theory in the West*, ii. 219–22.

in these words of Innocent, the clerical claim to control of peace and war touches its highest point. In the name of a Christian principle, permeating all things, and reducing all things to unity, the dread arbitrament of war is itself to be submitted to a higher and finer arbitration. The claim was too high to be sustained or translated into effect. It is not too high to be admired.

Nor was it altogether remote from the actual life of the day. Even to the laity of the Middle Ages, war was not a mere conflict of powers, in which the strongest power must necessarily prevail. It was a conflict of rights before a watching God of battles, in which the greatest right could be trusted to emerge victorious. War between States was analogous to the ordeal of battle between individuals : it was a legal way of testing rights. Now ordeal by battle was a mode of procedure in courts of law, and a mode of procedure whose conduct and control belonged to the clergy. If, therefore, war between States is analogous to ordeal, it follows, first, that it is a legal procedure which needs a high court for its interpretation (and what court could be more competent than the papal curia ?), and, next, that it is a matter which in its nature touches the clergy. Such ideas were a natural basis for the Church's attempt to control the issues of war and peace ; and if we remember these ideas, we shall acquit the Church of any impracticable quixotism.

THE attempt to control trade and commerce was no less lofty and no less arduous. It is perhaps still easier to stop war than to stop competition ; and yet the Church made the attempt. The Christian law of love was set against the economic law of demand and supply. It was canonical doctrine that the buyer should take no more, and the seller offer no less, than the just price of a commodity—a price which would in practice depend on the cost of production. The rule for prices was also the rule for wages : the just wage was the natural complement of the just price. The prohibition of usury and of the taking of interest was another factor in the same circle of ideas. If prices and wages are both to be returns for work done, and returns of an exact equivalence, then, on the assumptions which the canonists made—that the usurer does no work, and that his loan is unproductive of any new value —it necessarily follows that no return is due, or can be justly paid, for the use of borrowed money. Work is the one title of all acquisition, and all acquisition should be in exact proportion to the amount of work done. This is the basic principle, and it is the principle of the Divine Law : *In sudore frontis tuae comedes panem tuum.* Once more, therefore, and once more in an unpromising and intractable material, we find the Church seeking to enforce the unity of the Christian principle and to reduce the Many to the One. In the same way, and from the same motive, that private war was to be banished from the feudal class in the country, competition—the private war of commerce— was to be eliminated from the trading classes in the towns. Nor was the attack on competition, any more than the attack on war, so much of a forlorn hope as it may seem to a modern age. Even to-day, custom is still a force which checks the operation of competition, and custom covered a far greater area in the Middle Ages than it does to-day. The rent of land, whether paid in labour or in kind, was a customary rent ; and in every mediaeval community the landed class was the majority. It was an easy transition from fixed and customary rents to the fixing of just prices for commodities and services. Lay sentiment supported clerical principle. Guilds compelled their members to sell commodities at a level price, and in a spirit of collectivism endeavoured to prevent the making of corners and the practice of undercutting. Governments refused to recognize the ' laws ' of demand and supply, and sought, by Statutes of Labourers, to force masters to give, and workmen to receive, no more and no less than a ' just ' and proper wage.

It was not only by the regulation of trade and commerce that the Church sought to penetrate the life of the towns.

The friars made their homes in the towns in the thirteenth
century ; and the activity of the friars—Franciscan and
Dominican, Austin and Carmelite—enabled the Church to
exercise an influence on municipal life no less far-reaching
than that which she sought to exert on the feudal classes.
Towns became trustees of property for the use of the
mendicant orders ; and the orders of Tertiaries, which
flourished among them, enabled the townsfolk to attach
themselves to religious societies without quitting the
pursuits of lay life. A mediaeval town—with its trade and
commerce regulated, however imperfectly, by Christian
principle ; with its town council acting as trustee for religious orders ; and with its members attached as Tertiaries
to those orders—might be regarded as something of a type
of Christian society ; and St. Thomas, partly under the
influence of these conditions, if partly also under the influence of the Aristotelian philosophy of the πόλις, is led
to find in the life of the town the closest approach to the
ethics of Christianity.

THE control of learning and education by the Church is
the most peculiar and essential aspect of her activity.
The control of war and peace was a matter of guiding the
estate of the baronage ; the control of trade and commerce
was a way of directing the estate of the commons ; but
the control of learning and education was nothing more
nor less than the Church's guidance of herself and her
direction of her own estate. *Studium* may be distinguished
from *sacerdotium* by mediaeval writers ; but the students
of a mediaeval university are all ' clergy,' and the curricula
of mediaeval universities are essentially clerical. All
knowledge, it is true, falls within their scope ; but every
branch of knowledge, from dialectic to astronomy, is studied
from the same angle, and for the same object—*ad maiorem
Dei gloriam*. Here, as elsewhere, the penetrating and
assimilative genius of the Church moulded and informed a
matter which was not, in its nature, easily receptive of a
clerical impression. The whole accumulated store of the

lay learning of the ages—geometry, astronomy, and natural science ; grammar and rhetoric ; logic and metaphysics— this was the matter to be moulded and the stuff to be per- meated ; and on this stuff St. Thomas wrought the greatest miracle of genuine alchemy which is anywhere to be found in the annals of learning.

The learning which the Church had to transform was essentially the learning of the Hellenic world. Created by the centuries of nimble and inventive thought which lie between the time of Thales and that of Hipparchus, this learning had been systematized into a *corpus scientiae* during that age of Greek scholasticism which generally goes by the name of Hellenistic. In its systematized Hellenistic form, it had been received by the Roman world, and had become the culture of the Roman Empire. By writers ranging from Ptolemy to Boethius the body of all known knowledge had been arranged in a digest or series of pandects ; and along with the legal codification of Justinian it had been handed to the Christian Church as the heritage of the ancient world. The attitude of the Church to that heritage was for long unfixed and uncertain. The logic, and still more the metaphysics, of Aristotle were not the most comfortable of neighbours to the new body of Christian revelation committed to the Church's keeping. In the hands of Berengar of Tours the methods of Greek logic proved a corrosive to the received doctrine of the Mass. In the hands of Abelard, in the *Sic et Non*, they served to suggest the need of criticism of the text of Christian tradition. If unity was to be preserved, a bridge must be built between the secular science of the Greeks and the religious faith of the Church. In the thirteenth century that bridge was built. Aristotle was reconciled with St. Augustine ; the *Organon*, the *Ethics*, and the *Politics* were incorporated in the body of Christian culture ; and the mediaeval instinct for unification celebrated its greatest and perhaps its most arduous triumph.

The thirteenth century thus witnessed a unity of civilization alike as a structure of life and as a content of the human mind. On the one hand, there rose a single governing scheme of society, which culminated in the universal primacy of Rome and the Roman pontiff. On the other hand, set in this scheme, and contained in this structure, there was a single stuff of thought, directed to the manifestation of the eternal glory of God. The framework we may chiefly ascribe to Gregory VII ; the content to St. Thomas Aquinas. But the whole resultant unity is less the product of great personalities than of a common instinct and a common conviction. Men saw the world *sub specie unitatis* ; and its kaleidoscopic variety was insensibly focused into a single scheme under the stress of their vision. The heavens showed forth the glory of God, and the firmament declared His handiwork. Zoology became, like everything else, a willing servant of Christianity ; and *bestiaria moralizata* were written to show how all the beasts were made for an ensample, and served for a type, of the one and only truth. All things, indeed, were types and allegories to this way of thinking ; and just as every text in the Bible was an allegory to mediaeval interpretation, so all things in the world of creation, animate and inanimate, the jewel with its ' virtue ' as well as the beast with its ' moral,' became allegories and parables of heavenly meanings. Thus the world of perception became unreal, that it might be transmuted into the real world of faith ; and symbolism like that of Hugh of St. Victor dominated men's thought, making all things (like the Mass itself, if in a less degree) into *signa rei sacrae*.

The unity of knowledge was thus purchased at a price. Things must cease to be studied in themselves, and must be allegorized into types, in order that they might be reduced to a unity. Perhaps the purchase of unity on terms such as these is a bad bargain ; and it is at any rate obvious that in such an atmosphere scientific thought will not flourish, or man learn to adjust himself readily to the laws of his environment. From the standpoint of natural science we may readily condemn the Middle ages and all their works ; and we may prefer a single *Opus* of

Roger Bacon to the whole of the *Summa* of St. Thomas. But it is necessary to judge an age which was destitute of natural science by some other criterion than that of science ; nor must we hasten to say that the Middle Ages found the Universal so easily, because they ignored the Particular so absolutely. The truth is, that though mediaeval thinkers knew far more of the writings of Aristotle than they did of those of Plato, they were none the less far better Platonists than they were Aristotelians. If they had been better Aristotelians, they would have been better biologists ; but as they were good Platonists, they had a conception of the purpose and system of human life in society, which perhaps excuses all, and more than all, the defects of their biology. Any survey, however brief, of the political theory of the Middle Ages will show at once its Platonic character and its incessant impulse towards the achievement of unity.

III

TO mediaeval thought, as to Plato, the unity of society is an organic unity, in the sense that each member of society is an organ of the whole to which he belongs, and discharges a function at once peculiar to himself and necessary to the full life of the whole. Monasticism, so often misrepresented, attains its true meaning in the light of this conception. The monk is a necessary organ of Christian society, discharging his function of prayer and devotion for the benefit not of himself solely, or primarily, but rather of every member of that society. He prays for the sins of the whole world, and by his prayer he contributes to the realization of the end of the world, which is the attainment of salvation. In the same way the conception of a treasury of merits, afterwards perverted in the system of indulgences, belongs to an organic theory and practice of society. The merits which Christ and the saints have accumulated are a fund for the use of the whole of Christian society, a fund on which any member can draw for his own salvation, just because each is fitly joined and knit together with all the rest in a single body for the attainment of a single purpose. But we need not take isolated instances of the Platonism of mediaeval thought. The whole basic conception of a system of estates, which recurs everywhere in mediaeval life, is a Platonic conception. The estates of clergy, baronage, and commons are the Platonic classes of guardians, auxiliaries, and farmers. The Platonic creed of τὸ αὑτοῦ πράττειν (' Do thine own duty ') is the Christian creed of ' doing my duty in that state of life to which it shall please God to call me.' The Middle Ages are full of a spontaneous Platonism, and inspired by an *anima naturaliter Platonica*. The control which the mediaeval clergy exercised over Christian society in the light of divine revelation repeats the control which the guardians of Plato were to exercise over civic society in the light of the Idea of the Good. The communism of the mediaeval monastery is reminiscent of the communism of the Platonic barracks. And if there are differences between the society imagined by Plato and the society envisaged by the mediaeval Church, these differences only show that the mediaeval Church was trying to raise Platonism to a higher power, and to do so in the light of conceptions which were themselves Greek, though they belonged to a Greece posterior to the days of Plato. These conceptions—which were cherished by Stoic thinkers ; which penetrated into Roman Law ; and which from Roman Law flowed into the teaching and theory of the early fathers of the Church—are mainly two. One is the conception of human equality ; the other, and correlative, conception is that of a single society of all the human race. The equality of men, and the universality of the city of God in which they are all contained, are conceptions which were no less present to Marcus Aurelius than they were to St. Augustine. They are conceptions which made the instinctive Platonism of the mediaeval Church even more soaring than that of Plato. While the Republic of Plato had halted at the stage of a civic society, the *respublica Christiana* of the Middle Ages rose to the height of a single *humana civilitas*. While Plato had divided the men of his Republic into classes of gold and silver and bronze, and had reserved the ecstasy of the aspect of the divine Idea for a single class, the mediaeval Church opened the mystery of the Mass and the glory of the fruition of God to all believers, and, if she believed in three estates, nevertheless gathered the three in one around the common altar of the Redeemer. Serfdom might still remain, and find tolerance, in the economic working of society ; but in the Church herself, assembled together for the intimate purposes of her own life, there was ' neither bond nor free.'

The prevalence of Realism, which marks mediaeval metaphysics down to the end of the thirteenth century, is another Platonic inheritance, and another impulse to unity. The Universal *is*, and is a veritable thing, in which the Particular shares, and acquires its substance by its degree of sharing. The One transcends the Many ; the unity of mankind is greater than the differences between men ; and the university of mortal men, as Ockham writes, is one community. If there be thus one community, and one only, some negative results follow, which have their importance. In the first place, we can hardly say that the Middle Ages have any conception of the State. The notion of the State involves plurality ; but plurality is *ex hypothesi* not to be found. The notion of the State further involves sovereignty, in the sense of final and complete control of its members by each of a number of societies. But this, again, is *ex hypothesi* not to be found. There is one final control, and one only, in the mediaeval system—the control of Christian principle, exerted in the last resort, and exerted everywhere, without respect of persons, by the ruling vicar of Christ. But if plurality and sovereignty thus disappear from our political philosophy, we need a new orientation of all our theory. We must forget to speak of nations. We must forget, as probably many to-day would be very glad to forget, the claims of national cultures, each pretending to be a complete satisfaction and fulfilment of the national mind ; and we must remember, with Dante, that culture (which he called ' civility ') is the common possession of

Christian humanity. We must even forget, to some extent, the existence of different national laws. It is true that mediaeval theory admitted the fact of customary law, which varied from place to place. But this customary law was hardly national : it varied not only from country to country, but also from fief to fief, and even from manor to manor. It was too multiform to be national, and too infinitely various to square with political boundaries. Nor was customary law, in mediaeval theory, anything of the nature of an ultimate command. Transcending all customs, and supreme over all enactments, rose the sovereign majesty of natural law, which is one and indivisible, and runs through all creation. ' All custom,' writes Gratian, the great canonist, ' and all written law, that are adverse to natural law, are to be counted null and void.' Here, in this conception of a natural law upholding all creation, we may find once more a Stoic legacy to the Christian Church. ' We ought not to live in separate cities and demes, each distinguished by separate systems of justice '—so Zeno the Stoic had taught—' but there should be one way and order of life, like that of a single flock feeding on a common pasture.' Zeno, like St. Paul, came from Cilicia.[1] Like St. Paul, he taught the doctrine of the one society, in which there was neither Jew nor Gentile, neither Greek nor barbarian. We shall not do wrong to recognize in his teaching, and in that of his school, one of the greatest influences, outside the supreme and controlling influence of the Christian principle itself, which made for the dominance of the idea of unity in mediaeval thought.

Before we proceed to draw another negative conclusion from the principle of the one community, we must enter a brief caveat in regard to the conclusion which has just been drawn. We cannot altogether take away the State from the Middle Ages by a stroke of the pen and the sweep of a paradox. There were states in mediaeval Europe, and there were kings who claimed and exercised *imperium*.

[1] See above, p. 8, and cf. E. R. Bevan, *Stoics and Sceptics*.

These things caused the theorists, and particularly the Roman lawyers, no little trouble. It was difficult to reconcile the unity of the *imperium* with the multiplicity of kings. Some had recourse to the theory of delegation, and this seems to be the theory of the *De Monarchia of* Dante. But there was one thinker, almost a contemporary of Dante, who said a wise thing, prophetic of the future. *Rex in regno suo*, wrote Bartolus of Sassoferrato, *est Imperator regni sui.*[1] In that sentence we may hear the cracking of the Middle Ages. When kings become ' entire emperors of their realms ' (the phrase was used in England by Richard II, and the imperial style was affected by Henry VIII), unity soon prepares to fly out of the window. But she never entirely took flight until the Reformation shattered the fabric of the Church, and made kings into popes as well as emperors in their dominions.

We may now turn to draw another conclusion from the mediaeval principle of unity. To-day the world recognizes, and has recognized for over three centuries, not only a distinction between States, but also a distinction between two societies in each State—the secular and the religious. These two societies may have different laws (for instance, in the matter of marriage), and conflicts of duties and of jurisdictions may easily arise in consequence. The State may permit what the Church forbids ; and in that case the citizen who is also a churchman must necessarily revolt against one or other of the societies to which he belongs. The conflict between the two societies and the different obligations which they impose was a conflict unknown to the Middle Ages. Kings might indeed be excommunicated, and in that event their subjects would be compelled to decide whether they should disobey excommunicated king or excommunicating pope. But that was only a conflict between two different allegiances to two different authorities ; it was not a conflict between two different memberships of two different societies. The conflict

[1] The dictum is not original in Bartolus (cf. C. N. S. Woolf's book on Bartolus, p. 380). But it attained vogue through his writings.

between the two societies—Church and State—was one which could hardly arise in the Middle Ages, because there was only a single society, an undivided Christian commonwealth, which was at one and the same time both Church and State. Because there was only one society, baptism counted as admission both to churchmanship and to citizenship, which were one thing, and one only, in the Christian commonwealth ; and for the same reason excommunication, which shut the offender from all religious life, excluded him equally and by the same act from every civil right. The excommunicated person could not enter either the Church or the law court ; could not receive either the eucharist or a legacy ; could not own either a cure of souls or an acre of soil. Civil right and religious status implied one another ; and not only was *extra ecclesiam nulla salus* a true saying, but *extra ecclesiam nullum ius* would also be very near the truth. Here again is a reason for saying that the State as such can hardly be traced in the Middle Ages. The State is an organization of secular life. Even if it goes beyond its elementary purpose of security for person and property, and devotes itself to spiritual purposes, it is concerned with the development of the spirit in its mortal existence, and confined to the expansion of the mind in the bounds of a mortal society. The Middle Ages thought more of salvation than of security, and more of the eternal society of all the faithful, united together in Christ their Head, than of any passing society of this world only. They could recognize kings, who bore the sword for the sake of security, and did justice in virtue of their anointing. But kings were not, to their thinking, the heads of secular societies. They were agents of the one divine commonwealth—defenders of the Faith, who wielded the secular sword for the furtherance of the purposes of God. Thus there was one society, if there were two orders of ministering agents ; and thus, though *regnum* and *sacerdotium* might be distinguished, the State and the Church could not be divided. Stephen of Tournai, a canonist of the twelfth century, recognizes the two powers ;

but he only knows one society, under one king. That society is the Church : the king is Christ.

Under conditions such as these—with the plurality of States unrecognized by theory, even if it existed in practice, and with distinction between State and Church unknown and unenforced—we may truly say with a German writer, whose name I should like to mention *honoris causa*, Professor Tröltsch, that ' there was no feeling for the State ; no common and uniform dependence on a central power ; no omnipotent sovereignty ; no equal pressure of a public civil law ; no abstract basis of association in formal and legal rules—or at any rate, so far as anything of the sort was present, it was a matter only for the Church, and in no wise for the State.' [1] So far as social life was consciously articulated in a scheme, the achievement was that of the clergy, and the scheme was that of the Church. The interdependencies and associations of lay life—kingdoms and fiefs and manors—were only personal groupings, based on personal sentiments of loyalty and unconscious elements of custom. A mixture of uniformity and isolation, as we have seen, was the characteristic of these groupings : they were at once very like one another, throughout the extent of Western Europe, and (except for their connexion in a common membership of the Church Universal) very much separated from one another. But with one at any rate of these groupings—the kingdom, which in its day was to become the modern State—the future lay ; and we shall perhaps end our inquiry most fitly by a brief review of the lines of its future development.

IV

THE development of the kingdom into the State was largely the work of the lawyers. The law is a tenacious profession, and in England at any rate its members have exercised a large influence on politics from the twelfth to the twentieth century—from the days of Glanville, the

[1] *Die Soziallehren der christlichen Kirchen*, p. 242.

justiciar of Henry II, to the days of Mr. Asquith, the prime minister of George V. It is perhaps in England that we may first see the germs of the modern State emerging to light under the fostering care of the royal judges. Henry II is something of a sovereign : his judges formulate a series of commands, largely in the shape of writs, which became the common law of the land ; and in the Constitutions of Clarendon we may already see the distinction between Church and State beginning to be attempted. With a sovereign, a law, and a secular policy all present, we may begin to suspect the presence of a State. In France also a similar development, if somewhat later than the English, occurs at a comparatively early date. By the end of the thirteenth century the legists of Philippe le Bel have created something of *étatisme* in their master's dominions. The king's court begins to rule the land ; and proud of its young strength it enters the lists against Boniface VIII, the great prophet of the Church Universal, who proclaimed that every human creature was subject to the Roman pontiff. The collapse of Boniface at Anagni in 1303 is the traditional date of the final defeat of the mediaeval papacy. Everywhere, indeed, the tide seemed on the turn at the close of the thirteenth century. The Crusades ended with the fall of Acre in 1291. The suppression of the great international order of the Templars twenty years later marked a new leap of the encroaching waves. The new era of the modern national State might seem already to have begun.

But tides move slowly and by gradual inches. It needed two centuries more before the conditions in which the modern State could flourish had been fully and finally established. Economic conditions had to change—a process always gradual and slow ; and a national economy based on money had to replace the old local economy based on kind. Languages had to be formed, and local dialects had to be transformed into national and literary forms, before national States could find the means of utterance. The revival of learning had to challenge the old clerical structure of knowledge, and to set free the progress of secular science, before the minds of men could be readily receptive of new forms of social structure and new modes of human activity. But by 1500 the work of preparation had been largely accomplished. The progress of discovery had enlarged the world immeasurably. The addition of America to the map had spiritual effects which it is difficult to estimate in any proper terms. If the old world of the Mediterranean regions could be thought into a unity, it was more difficult to reduce to the One the new world which swam into men's ken. Still more burdened with fate for the future generations was the vast volume of commerce, necessarily conducted on a national basis, which the age of discoveries went to swell. Meanwhile, men had begun to think and to write in national languages. Already by the reign of Richard II the dialect of the East Midlands, which was spoken in the capital and the universities, had become a literary language in which Chaucer and Wyclif had spoken to all the nation. Still earlier had come the development of Italian, and a little more than a century after the days of Wyclif Luther was to give to Germany a common speech and a common Bible. It was little wonder that in such times tne old unity of the Christian commonwealth of the Middle Ages shivered into fragments, or that, side by side with a national language, there developed—at any rate in England and in Germany —a national Church. The unity of a common Roman Church and a common Romance culture was gone. *Cuius regio eius religio.* To each region its religion ; and to each nation, we may add, its national culture. The Renaissance may have begun as a cosmopolitan movement, and have found in Erasmus a cosmopolitan representative. It ended in national literatures ; and a hundred years after Erasmus, Shakespeare was writing in England, Ariosto in Italy, and Lope de Vega in Spain.

In the sixteenth century the State was active and doing after its kind. It was engaged in war. France was fighting Spain : England was seeking to maintain the balance :

Turkey was engaged in the struggle. It is a world with which we are familiar—a world of national languages, national religions, national cultures, national wars, with the national State behind all, upholding and sustaining every form of national activity. But unity was not entirely dead. Science might still transcend the bounds of nations, and a Grotius or Descartes, a Spinoza or a Leibniz, fill the European stage. Religion, which divided, might also unite ; and a common Calvinism might bind together the Magyars of Hungary and the French of Geneva, the Dutchman and the Scot. Leyden in the seventeenth century could still serve as a meeting ground of the nations ; it could play the part of an international university, and provide a common centre of medical science and classical culture. But the old unity of the Middle Ages was gone—gone past recall. Between those days and the new days lay a gulf across which no voice or language could carry. Much was lost that could never be recovered ; and if new gold was added to the currency of the spirit, new alloys were wrought into its substance. It would be a hard thing to find an agreed standard of measurement, which should cast the balance of our gain and loss, or determine whether the new world was a better thing than the old. One will cry that the old world was the home of clericalism and obscurantism ; and another will say in his bitterness that the new world is the abode of two other evil spirits—nationalism and commercialism. One thing is perhaps certain. We cannot, as far as human sight can discern, ever hope to reconstruct unity on the old basis of the Christian commonwealth of the Middle Ages. Yet need is upon us still—need urgent and importunate—to find some unity of the spirit in which we can all dwell together in peace. Some have hoped for unity in the sphere of economics, and have thought that international industry and commerce would build the foundations of an international polity. Their hopes have had to sleep, and years of war have shown that ' a synchronized bank-rate and reacting bourses ' imply no further unity. Some again may hope for unity in the field of science, and may trust that the collaboration of the nations in the building of the common house of knowledge will lead to co-operation in the building of a greater mansion for the common society of civilized mankind. But nationalism can pervert even knowledge to its own ends, turning anthropology to politics, and chemistry to war. There remains a last hope—the hope of a common ethical unity, which, as moral convictions slowly settle into law, may gradually grow concrete in a common public law of the world. Even this hope can only be modest, but it is perhaps the wisest and the surest of all our hopes. *Idem scire* is a good thing ; but men of all nations may know the same thing, and yet remain strangers one to another. *Idem velle idem nolle in re publica, ea demum firma amicitia est.* The nations will at last attain firm friendship one with another in the day when a common moral will controls the scope of public things. And when they have attained this friendship, then—on a far higher level of economic development and with an improvement by each nation of its talent which is almost entirely new— they will have found again, if in a different medium, something of the unity of mediaeval civilization.

III

A HUGUENOT THEORY OF POLITICS:
THE *VINDICIAE CONTRA TYRANNOS* [1]

IN 1559 France was plunged into the melting-pot, and she remained there for the next forty years, until 1598, when a new Bourbon France emerged with the ending of the war against Spain and the issue of the Edict of Nantes. Two things had happened in 1559. In the first place, there had come to an end a long series of foreign wars, almost continuous since the French invasion of Italy in 1494. That raised a serious question of unemployment. What was to be done with a nobility which for over sixty years had found both distraction and occupation in war, and now had idle hands and empty pockets ? Here was a chance for Satan to find some mischief. In the second place, there had died the last strong king of the House of Valois, Henry II, leaving behind him a widow (who was a Florentine of the house of the Medici) and a young family of four sons and three daughters. That raised a serious problem of government. It is written in the Book of Ecclesiastes, ' Woe to thee, O land, when thy king is a child.' I have more than once thought, in my reading of history, that the words might be added, ' And woe to thee even more when thy regent is a woman, and woe above all when she is a foreigner.' Here indeed was a chance for Satan, when an Italian queen dowager, brooding with fierce eyes over a young family, confronted an unemployed nobility—and, in addition, as if that were not enough, a body of ambitious Princes of the Blood who were only agreed in a common desire to relieve her of her tutelary care.

[1] Based upon a Paper read to the Huguenot Society of London in January 1930.

Could France, under these conditions, remain a unitary State, controlled by a single and effective sovereignty ? The prospect seemed dubious. Apart from the immediate questions of aristocratic unemployment and royal government, there was a more permanent and general problem. France was still a congeries of annexed provinces, united only in the person and office of the monarchy which had made the annexations. The 'spirit of the province' was still strong in Dauphiné, Brittany, Gascony, Provence. Provinces had their own 'liberties,' their own provincial assemblies of Estates, their own provincial bodies of law. Nor was this all. Within the province itself there was the fief and the municipality. Besides the localism of the province there was also that of the feudatory, anxious to be Seigneur over his fief ; there was also that of the city, resolute to be master within its walls. Add feudalism and municipalism to provincialism, and the result is a triad of localisms, accumulating an almost intolerable load of stresses and strains upon the arch of the monarchy. Could it carry the load ? Or would France disintegrate under the pressure into a loose federation on the model of contemporary Germany ? Looking back over the centuries, we can easily give an answer in the first sense. We can see that there was in France an indomitable instinct of political unity—whether inherited from the centralization of ancient Rome, or rooted still deeper in a common passion for French soil and a common feeling of French blood and culture— which would successfully thwart every tendency towards disintegration. But to those living at the time an answer was far less easy ; and the odds might well seem to be in favour of a collapse. The practical example of Germany, which was now a loose confederation, offered a standing invitation to the separatist instincts of provinces, princes and towns. Nor was the theory of unitary monarchy as yet established in European thought. Machiavelli, indeed, had preached the Prince one and irresistible, the State one and indivisible ; but the name of the great Florentine was not a name by which men could conjure, least of all in

France, in the days of the Florentine woman Catherine de Medici. The French jurist Bodin was to establish a theory of sovereignty in his *Six Books of the Republic* : but that massive work did not appear until 1576, and years had to pass before its teaching could sink deeply into men's minds. Meanwhile the theory of politics was still largely in the hands of civilians trained in the Roman law ; and among them the great name was still that of Bartolus, a jurist who had taught and written in Perugia in the first half of the fourteenth century. Now Bartolus was an apostle of federalism rather than of unity—of liberty rather than of sovereignty. Living among Italian City States, he had sought to defend in theory the independence which they had attained in practice, and he had evolved the doctrine of the *civitas sibi princeps* — the city which is Prince for itself. That is a theory which looks towards federalism. Living, again, at a time when tyrants were arising in the city-states, he had sought to find a juristic basis for the right of civic self-government ; and his treatise *De Tyrannia* was a mediaeval counterpart (still known and cherished in the latter half of the sixteenth century) to Mill's Essays on *Liberty* and *Representative Government*. If political theory affects political practice (and that is perhaps a large assumption), we may say that the political theory current in 1559 boded ill for the unity of France.

IN this conjuncture of the stars of France there swung into the sky the meteor of religion, the army of French Calvinism, the ranks of the Huguenots. It was one of the noblest movements of thought in a country ever fertile and ever generous in such movements ; and even to think of it now, after all these years, still stirs the blood. They who were ' of the religion ' were gallant men : they fought a good fight : they endured tribulations : they are counted among the salt of the earth. But what did they mean for France ; and what was their contribution to the problem of French unity—or French disintegration ? That is the question we have to face. What is the answer which we must give ?

If the Huguenots could have brought the monarchy over to their side ; if Charles IX, the second of the sons of Henry II, who reigned from 1560 to 1574, had joined their cause ; and if, through that junction, their cause had become successful—then, and on that large assumption, we may say that the Huguenots would have been a force making for the unity of France, on a constitutional and Protestant basis. In that case France would have undergone, somewhere about 1572, a revolution comparable to our own Whig Revolution of 1688—our own Revolution of which, I should like to say in passing, I believe that the Huguenots, even in their failure, and perhaps because of their failure, and owing to the Whig doctrines of resistance produced by their failure, may be accounted the spiritual ancestors. We may even imagine, on this basis of hypothesis, a Huguenot France which pushed unity to excess, insisting in its hour of triumph upon unity of religion no less rigorously than the Puritans of Massachusetts, in the days of their triumph, insisted upon a similar unity between 1630 and 1690. In any case I should contend that Huguenotism was not, in its essence, inimical to the unity of France—in its essence, I repeat ; in its pure logic ; in the form which it would have taken if only it could have worked out freely its immanent potentiality. *Per accidens*, it is true, it did become inimical : time and contingency made it a minority ; and, as a minority, it was forced to struggle against a scheme of compulsory unity. But its original and native instinct was towards the monarchy, the unity of France, the great-ness of France. It was the policy of Coligny, one of the greatest of the Huguenots, to capture the mind of Charles IX : to turn France towards hostilities against Philip of Spain in the Netherlands : to bring a united France to aid the cause of liberty and religion on her northern frontier, and to cement her unity by common effort in a common cause. The policy failed ; and the day of its failure was St. Bartholomew's Day, August 24, 1572. Massacre was the answer to Coligny ; and all hope of the Huguenots guiding France died with the massacre. Perhaps there never had been any hope : perhaps there never could have been any hope. For the massacre was no mere move on the part of the queen-mother, resolved, at any price, to prevent her son from escaping from her tutelage and falling into the arms of Coligny. It was a popular massacre : we may even say that it was a national massacre. It was popular, because the people at large threw themselves into it heart and soul. After all, the Huguenots were an *élite*— an aristocratic *élite* : a civic *élite*—and the people had no liking for the *élite*. Again, it was national, as well as popular : it raged all over France : it made Lyons a shambles as well as Paris. Thirty thousand were killed. It is, says a German scholar, ' as if we might detect in this terror the will to unity of the French people, which can suffer no foreign bodies, no disunion.' [1] One remembers a similar terror and a similar will to unity in 1793.

After that ' day ' in 1572 the Huguenots were a minority, and, for the moment, a scattered minority. Mornay—whose wife's memoirs of his life, published in the Broadway Series of Translations under the title of *A Huguenot Family in the Sixteenth Century*, are a precious mine—fled overseas to England. Others escaped to Geneva, where the Frenchman Beza was now the head of Calvin's Church : others found a refuge in Germany and the Netherlands. What remained to this scattered minority ? What remains to a minority always, and that is—thought, and the appeal to thought. The Huguenots sat down by their waters of Babylon, and they thought—thought and wrote. They recited their history : they published their philosophy ; and by that history and philosophy they appealed to Caesar—to the conscience of Christian Europe. There is a series of writings in the seven years that followed St. Bartholomew's Day, 1572–9, which should never be forgotten by any who confess the cause of liberty, civil and religious. The great Beza himself published anonymously, about 1574, a treatise *De jure magistratuum*. Not only had he to publish it

[1] Elkan, *Die Publizistik der Bartholomäusnacht*, p. 16.

anonymously : he had even to suggest on the title-page that it was only an amplified edition of a previous work, by ' those of Magdeburg,' of the year 1550 ; and even so he was driven from pillar to post to find a printer. Hotman, professor of law in the University of Geneva founded by Calvin, published at Geneva in 1573 his *Franco-Gallia*, which sought to vindicate the ancient constitutional liberties of France. It was a work destined to a large vogue : it crossed the seas to England : it became one of the inspirations of English Whigs who also sought to vindicate the ancient constitutional liberties of *their* country. Three other works also deserve mention, both in themselves and because they are all linked together by a curious tie. One is a treatise of the year 1573, *de furoribus Gallicis*, an account of the massacre, said to be written by one Ricaud, a preacher of Lyons, who entitles himself on his title-page by the name of Ernestus Varamundus Frisius. A second is two dialogues, in which Hotman may have had a hand, published together in 1574 under the title of the *Réveille Matin* (a trumpet to call ' the French and their neighbours ' to arms against the murderers of the Huguenots), and professing to be written by one Eusebius Philadelphus Cosmopolita. A third is the *Vindiciae Contra Tyrannos* of the year 1579, whose anonymous author entitled himself Stephanus Junius Brutus Celta, and which contains a philosophy of liberty in Church and State. The curious tie that unites all three is that they are all stated on their title-pages to have been printed at Edinburgh.[1] None of them were, but the actual press had to be hidden ; Edinburgh was a far cry and a safe attribution ; moreover it was a home of Calvinism and the residence of George Buchanan, a Scottish scholar well known to many friends in France, who wrote a radical treatise *de Jure Regni apud Scotos*, which actually *was* printed at Edinburgh in 1579.

[1] On the title-page of the *Réveille Matin* the name of the printer is given. It is *Jaques James*. The words ' avec permission ' are added by way of an additional witticism.

OF all these writings I can deal here only with one—the *Vindiciae contra Tyrannos*. It is the most famous ; it had the deepest influence, especially in England ; I am inclined to think it the most profound ; and in any case it suffices abundantly to show the temper and the philosophy of the Huguenots after the massacre, in the middle of those forty years during which, as I have said, France was plunged into the melting-pot. But there is a preliminary question, which I confess is a matter of caviare, but about which I feel bound to say one word. It is the question of the authorship of the *Vindiciae*. For the last forty years, since a German scholar called Lossen wrote a paper on the subject in 1887, it has been customary to say that Mornay, the Huguenot I have already mentioned, who afterwards served Henry of Navarre and wrote a number of theological treatises, was the man who called himself Stephanus Junius Brutus. The more I have looked into the matter, the less I believe that he was. It is true that his wife records that in 1574 he wrote upon ' the lawful power of a prince over his people ' (a phrase which corresponds to part of the sub-title of the *Vindiciae* [1]), and that what he wrote was ' afterwards printed and published, but without its being widely known that he was the author.' Mornay may well have written on so obvious a topic ; but this does not prove that he wrote the 240 Latin pages of the *Vindiciae*, packed with legal learning and backed by an armoury of references, which appeared in 1579. I do not see how he could possibly have done so, even on the mere ground of time, during that brief breathing-space among forays and excursions which he spent at Jametz in the early half of 1574 (and to which his wife

---

[1] The full sub-title runs ' Concerning the lawful power of a prince over his people and of a people over its prince.' There is certainly a parallel between Madame Mornay's phrase and the first part of the sub-title. But the phrase was a commonplace. The full title of Beza's *De jure Magistratuum* is ' concerning the right of magistrates over subjects and the duty of subjects towards magistrates.' Again, the *Dialogue d'Archon et de Politie*, published in 1576, has the sub-title ' Concerning the authority of princes and the liberty of peoples.' Madame de Mornay's phrase might apply to either of these as well as to the *Vindiciae*.

refers his essay on the lawful power of a prince); and I become the more sceptical when I reflect that he was falling in love about this time. In any case, I cannot but feel that Mornay's legal scholarship was not equal to the task : that his real interest was in theology rather than in political philosophy : that his recorded views on politics do not square with those of the *Vindiciae* [1] : that he was too young a man in 1574 (for he was then only in his twenty-fifth year) to have written a treatise such as the *Vindiciae* ; and that it is difficult to see why a work composed in 1574 should never have seen the light until 1579. I put Mornay therefore on one side, for these and for many other reasons which I must forbear to mention ; and I turn to another possible author, for whom the *Vindiciae* was vindicated by the great Bayle about 1690, and to whom it was steadily ascribed by scholars for nearly two hundred years. This is Hubert Languet, a Burgundian, born in 1519 (and therefore thirty years older than Mornay), who lived for much of his life in Germany. He was a lawyer so distinguished as twice to have been offered chairs of law in German Universities ; he was a scholar who had lived for years with Melanchthon ; he was a traveller and a diplomat who knew the cities and the minds of men from Lapland and Stockholm to Vienna and Padua ; and he was a man of affairs, who spent the last four years of his life, from 1577 to 1581, in the service and friendship of William of Orange. His life, his attainments, his opinions, all square with the *Vindiciae*. He knew law ; and it is full of legal knowledge. He knew the history and conditions of most European countries ; and it is full of references to their history and conditions. Nor is this all. The *Vindiciae* has close analogies with the *Apology* for his actions published on behalf of William of Orange in 1580. Good testimony ascribes the composition of that *Apology* to Languet ; [2]

---

[1] His wife records that in 1576 he was ' exposing the worthlessness of all Estates, whether provincial or general.' The argument of the *Vindiciae* is directed to establishing the value of both.

[2] The author of the *Vita Huberti Langueti* (Philibert de Marre, who, by

and this suggests that he also composed the *Vindiciae*, which it resembles. Again, the *Vindiciae* is quoted repeatedly in the annotations to the *Acta* of a congress held at Cologne for the purpose of mediating between the Netherlands and Philip of Spain, at the end of 1579. Languet was present as an envoy at that congress ; and his book may well have glided into the notes appended to the record of its acts. The more I think about the matter, the more I am inclined to say ' aut Languet aut diabolus.' But I confess that I may be mistaken, and the real author may be neither. I will only add that Languet died in 1581, two years after the publication of the *Vindicae*. If he wrote it, he carried the secret with him to the grave. Mornay lived for over forty years after the publication of the *Vindiciae*. If he wrote it, he kept the secret for a long time. . . .[1] And he was not a secretive man.

I turn to the substance of the *Vindiciae*. I will ask you to imagine a man sitting down, some three hundred and fifty years ago, to write on the vital problems of contemporary politics. The year is somewhere about 1579 ; the place is possibly Antwerp. In France, since the Treaty of Bergerac

the way, attributes the *Vindiciae* to Languet) states that he had heard from Languet's heirs that, a few days before his death, he sent to each of them a copy of the *Apology, quasi a se exaratus*. I noted lately, in reading Irving's *Memoirs of Buchanan*, that in 1581 Languet wrote to Buchanan (now well known abroad for his *de jure Regni*), reminding him that they had met in Paris about twenty years ago, and enclosing a copy of the *Apology*. It seems unlikely that Languet should have written to recall his existence after so many years, and to enclose a pamphlet, unless the pamphlet he enclosed was of his own composition. That is the way of authors.

[1] There is a story, coming from the middle of the seventeenth century, that a certain Daillé, who lived with Mornay for seven years, was regularly sent by him, when visitors came to inspect his library, to remove a copy of the *Vindiciae* from a cupboard in which he kept together copies of his own writings. This seems to suggest that Mornay *had* written the *Vindiciae*, and was troubled by the secret. But all that the story proves, if it be true, is that Mornay had some sort of a connexion with the *Vindiciae*, which led him to keep a copy of it among his own writings. He was a friend of Languet. He may have written some of the Latin verses attached to the *Vindiciae*. He may, again, have been responsible for the French translation of the *Vindiciae*, which appeared in 1581. See p. 108, below *infra*.

in 1577, which was tolerably favourable to the Huguenots, there is now comparative peace ; and that peace is destined to continue, except for a short war in 1580, until 1585. In the Netherlands, on the other hand, everything is marching to a crisis. The man who sits down to write is a Frenchman, and France is his exemplar (*in quo, tanquam caeterorum exemplari, diutius haereo*) ; but he has surveyed the world, and he has a full mind. You must imagine that he knows the Bible thoroughly, but that, with a lawyer's training, he throws a legal colour over its records and texts. In law he is thoroughly steeped : he knows the *Digest* of Justinian : he knows the writings of the great Bartolus and his theories of the *civitas sibi princeps* and the nature of tyranny. He is a classical scholar to his finger-tips : he quotes Greek — and rare Greek at that, such as only an accomplished scholar would know — with facility : he knows the *Politics* of Aristotle, the *Cyropaedia* of Xenophon, the *Republic* of Plato : he knows his Latin authors, and not least Seneca's letters and Cicero's *de Officiis*. He had obviously read, though he never quotes, the passage of Calvin's *Institutes* which deals with the State : he has read and he quotes St. Augustine ' On the City of God ' ; he has also read, and he also quotes, the *Summa* of St. Thomas Aquinas. He knows a good deal about German history, a good deal about French, and something about English, Scottish, and Scandinavian history : he is tolerably versed in Polish affairs : he can quote the *Sachsenspiegel* of Germany, the *Liber Feudorum* of Lombardy, and what he calls the ' Spanish Code.' He has probably read Beza's *De jure magistraruum* : he has almost certainly read Hotman's *Franco-Gallia* ; perhaps he knows something about Bodin's *Six Books on the Republic* : he may also have read the work of Salamonius, *De Principatu*, just republished in France in 1578, and he may have digested its theory of a social contract. Anyhow, he has material enough : he has passion : he has a clear incisive style, sometimes rising to eloquence, sometimes adorned with picturesque images ; [1] and he has a singular

[1] On the style of the *Vindiciae*, see Note A, at the end of this Essay.

gift of logic, which makes him resolved, ' in the manner of a geometer ' (as it is written in the Preface) to discover the axioms and to deduce the propositions of politics.   He writes his work, in its four parts : he entitles himself Stephanus, in memory, perhaps, of the first martyr ; Junius Brutus, in memory of the protagonist of Roman liberty ; and Celta, to show that he is French : he adorns his work, or gets it adorned by another (the style is certainly different), with a preface professing to be written by a Gascon : he adorns it further with a prefatory poem masquerading as the work of a Belgian, and with a final poem disguised as the composition of a Spaniard from Tarragona.   He has, you will see, wrapped up political science in a mystery.   I doubt if we shall ever penetrate some of the mystery, or know who wrote the preface or the poems ; and I doubt if we shall ever be quite sure who wrote the main work itself. . . . But Mornay was a young friend of Languet.   He was living in Antwerp about the same time.   He liked to write Latin verses—and possibly prefaces.   That is all I can say.

THE serious matter, however, is not who said what, but what was actually said.   We must abjure the scholar's temptation to play with riddles of authorship, and we must face the scholar's real task, which is that of recovering and understanding an author's thought.   The author of the *Vindiciae* had two problems to face.   One was the problem of the duty of the individual when confronted with a State which commands him to do or believe what he cannot do or believe.   It is the problem of Antigone face to face with Creon : it is the problem of the conscientious objector face to face with the law of conscription : it is the problem of English Nonconformity, the Antigone of our national history, confronted by penal statutes.   Here the author of the *Vindiciae* had before him the doctrine of the *Institutes* of Calvin, in the twentieth chapter of Book IV ; and that was a doctrine of non-resistance.   The powers that be are ordained of God ; and the duty of obedience to those powers is a divine imperative.   Whatever they command we are bound to obey ; and if they command evil, our only remedy is patience and prayer. The author of the *Vindiciae* follows the master. Private persons cannot resist the public authority. They have no commission from God. To plead the right of private conscience in this matter is dangerous. ' If any man arrogate that authority to himself, as though he were one breathed upon by the Holy Spirit, let him beware that he be not puffed up by arrogance, that he be not a god to himself, that he be not himself assuming for himself these great spiritual motions, that he be not conceiving vanity and bringing forth a lie.' [1] What then remains ? Two choices. First, to do as our Lord said : ' When they persecute you in this city, flee ye into another.' Next, and if it be not given to flee elsewhere, ' to renounce life rather than God, and to be crucified rather than crucify Christ afresh.' [2] Exile or death— that is the choice for the private person when he stands face to face with the will of an ungodly State. It was the choice which thousands of Huguenots made. We know from the records of history how they accepted the saying of Jesus, and fled into another city, accepting dispersion among the nations, and fructifying the cities among which they were dispersed. The cities of London and Canterbury : the cities of Switzerland, Germany, and the Netherlands— all these received them. Across the Atlantic, in the far country of South Carolina, after the revocation of the Edict of Nantes, the city of Charleston—at that time one of the greatest of American cities—also received them. ' Commerce is of noble origin in South Carolina,' wrote its first historian. Is it fanciful to ascribe to this Huguenot recep-

[1] *Vindiciae*, pp. 68-9 (edition 1579).

[2] Ibid., p. 67. Here the author is discussing the rights of private resistance on religious grounds. But he is equally opposed to private resistance on political grounds ; and in the face of political oppression he bids the people beware that ' in seeking to cross the sea dry-shod under the guidance of some impostor, it fall not headlong into the abyss ; in seeking a *vindex* for tyranny, it follow not one who may transfer tyranny to himself, after the tyrant has been expelled : in seeking to serve the commonwealth, it aid not the private greed of a person ' (p. 214).

tion the fact, remarked by the latest historian of the United States, that ' in 1920 Charleston had only 68,000 inhabitants, but more distinction and flavour than any one of the hundred American cities that exceeded it in size ' ? [1]

But there was another problem, and for our purposes a profounder problem, which the author of the *Vindiciae* had to face. Private resistance may be impossible. But what is to be said of public resistance ? Let us suppose that the king has become a tyrant, and a persecutor of ' the religion.' Is there no resource ? If individuals are powerless, what is to be said of the people as a body, a corporation, *non ut singuli, sed ut universi* ? What is to be said of parliaments, or meetings of the three Estates, which represent the people as an epitome ? What is to be said of the public authorities, central and local, which are connected with the people, represent the people, and may act on the people's behalf ? Here the author of the *Vindiciae* had another passage in the *Institutes*, from a later section of the same chapter of the same book, to give him guidance. ' If there be magistrates constituted for the defence of the people, to bridle the excessive cupidity and licence of kings, such as the Ephors in Sparta,[2] the tribunes at Rome . . . and to-day, it may be, in each kingdom the Three Estates assembled ; they have not only the right, but the duty, to oppose and resist the intemperance of kings, according to the obligation of their office ; and they may even be accused as guilty of perjury by reason of any deception, whereby treacherously they betray the liberty of the people, of which they ought to recognize themselves as ordained trustees (*tutores*) by the will of God.' I am inclined to think that Book IV, chapter xx, section 31 of the *Institutes* is one of the seed-beds of modern liberty. It passed into the Huguenot

[1] S. E. Morison, *Oxford History of the United States*, i. p. 35.

[2] This would seem to be the origin of what we may call ' the doctrine of the Ephorate.' It is adopted not only in the *Vindiciae*, but also in other Huguenot writings and in the *Politica* of Althusius (c. xviii. §§ 48 sqq.). The author of the *Vindiciae* takes as one of the two mottoes of his book a passage from Justin, *de Lycurgo Legislatore*, which naturally carries our thoughts to Sparta and its legislator and Ephors.

writings of the years 1572–9, and particularly into the argument of the *Vindiciae*. Through them it passed into the Dutch Declaration of Independence, or Act of Abjuration, of 1581, which breathes ideas I cannot but believe to have been inspired by Huguenots then living and working in the Netherlands. Through them, again, it passed, by ways I shall endeavour to trace, into the English Revolution and Bill of Rights of the year 1689 ; and it continued thereafter to be a source—little known and yet active—of the principles of the great Whig party.

The passage which I have quoted from Calvin underwent a great development in the hands of the writer of the *Vindiciae*. Briefly, I should summarize that development by saying that he made explicit, singularly explicit, the notion of the sovereignty of the people implied by Calvin ; that he connected with that notion, as corollaries, the three ideas of contract, trusteeship, and resistance, which were all to acquire a universal vogue ; and that he also connected with it, as a peculiar corollary, an idea of federalism, which, it is true, appeared, and was even extended, in the thought of Althusius and in connexion with the federation of the United Provinces of the Dutch, but which never attained the general vogue of the other three ideas.

THE people and its sovereignty are facts which appear to be simply assumed. We are not told, so far as I can see, how a *populus* comes into existence, or how it acquires sovereignty, or indeed what it is.[1] The author seems to

---

[1] The author explains, in an interesting passage which has some affinities with Locke's second *Treatise*, why the people turns itself into a State by creating a government and instituting a king (pp. 107–9). What he does not explain is the origin of the people and the reason for its sovereignty. He simply assumes, as the basis of his argument, (1) that the people exists *per se*, whereas the king can only exist *per populum*, and that it is therefore prior to the king (p. 82) ; (2) that the people, being as it is prior, and instituting as it does the government, is also *potior* (p. 85) ; and (3) that the people, existing *a se*, and possessing priority and superiority, has imprescriptible rights, inherent in its nature as an immortal corporation or *Universitas* (p. 104). 'As the Rhine, the Seine, and the Tiber are the same as they were a thousand years ago, so the German, the Gallic,

assume the given fact of the existence of what he calls the *populus* ; and he seems to assume that by what we should call natural law ' the people ' has sovereignty. In this sense he is one of the founders of that school of natural law which extends through Grotius, and Puffendorf, and Locke, in the seventeenth century, to the American Declaration of Independence in 1776, with its reference to ' the laws of Nature and of Nature's God,' and to Tom Paine's *Rights of Man* in 1791. But we must add that the writer of the *Vindiciae* also feels that the divine law of the Scriptures, no less than natural law, will justify the sovereignty of the people ; and he quotes the Old Testament again and again to prove the rights of the people of God in ancient Israel. This addition may lead us to another reflection. The *populus* of the author of the *Vindiciae* is really two things, though the author never makes the distinction clear. In the first place, it is a people of God : it is the people *sub specie religionis* : it was what we may call a Church— an *ecclesia*. This is a difficult saying when we reflect that the Huguenots, for whom the author is speaking, were by no means co-extensive with the people of France, and indeed, on the contrary, were only a small minority of that people. None the less, it is a saying which is implied in the argument of the *Vindiciae* ; and it must even be considered as an integral part of the argument. But in the second place, the people is also what we may call a natural people, with the rights of natural law ; or again we may say that it is a political people, with the political right of sovereignty ; or again, and more simply, we may say that it is a State. Populus and Respublica are thus one : l'Etat, c'est le peuple. We may add that if populus is thus respublica as well as ecclesia, if the people is the State as well as the Church, it also follows that State and Church are one. L'Eglise, c'est l'Etat : l'Etat, c'est l'Eglise.[1]

or the Roman people is the same ; nor can their rights be changed one jot or tittle either, by the flow of their waters, or by the alteration of their individual members.'

[1] The co-extension (identification is perhaps too strong a word) of

WE may now turn to the notion of Contract. This is the specific contribution of the author of the *Vindiciae*. True, the idea of a political contract had appeared in the Middle Ages : it is as old as St. Thomas, and even older : true, again, it had been used in recent times by Salamonius. It none the less remains also true that the idea of the ' original contract,' which served such solemn uses in our own Revolution Settlement, starts on its modern history with the publication of the *Vindiciae* in 1579. The author is very clear about contract, and indeed about *two* contracts which correspond to the two senses in which we may under-stand the ' people.' In the first place, the people as the people of God makes a covenant with God, that ' it will be and will remain the people of God.' This comes straight from the Old Testament and its covenant. Indeed, what is Vetus Testamentum but παλαιὰ διαθήκη, and what is διαθήκη but covenant or contract ? We cannot speak of the Old Testament without speaking also of covenant—the covenant of El, who is God, with Isra-el, ' the warriors of

people and Church is an assumption common to Lutherans, Calvinists, and Anglicans in the sixteenth century. It is only in the theory of the seventeenth century (among the Jesuits and in Calvinist writers such as Voetius) that we find the idea of the Church as a society separate from and not necessarily co-extensive with the people. There is a phrase in the schedule to the Church of Scotland Act of 1921 which recalls the ideas of the sixteenth century—a phrase in which the Church of Scotland is de-scribed as ' a national church representative of the Christian faith of the Scottish people.' In this phrase the Church of Scotland and the Scottish people seem to be co-extensive and even identical. Gierke, in the fourth volume of his *Genossenschaftsrecht* (especially pp. 363–71), throws light on the whole matter.

It must be added that in his fourth ' question,' when he is discussing the problem ' whether neighbouring princes may aid the subjects of a prince afflicted by reason of the pure religion,' the author of the *Vindiciae* alters his ground. He has to argue that such princes are bound to protect the one pure religion wherever it be, and that the pure religion is a single Church, irrespective of boundaries and peoples, which must be protected in all places and among all peoples. Here, therefore, he distinguishes Ecclesia, *quae una omnium est, quae una universaque singulis commissa est* and Respublica, *quae alia aliorum esse potest, alia aliis . . . commendata est* (p. 229). Here the identity of Populus with Ecclesia and Respublica, and therefore of Respublica with Ecclesia, disappears.

God.' The author of the *Vindiciae* adds a refinement to this covenant, which he gathers from the Scriptures. When kings arose in Israel, the covenant or contract altered its character : it ceased to be simply an agreement between God and the people : it became an agreement between God on the one side, and the people *and* the king on the other. People and king are thus *copromissores* ; and it follows, on the logic of *copromissio*, that if the king violates his promise and obligation by departing from God, the people are bound, for the sake of keeping their promise and obligation, to resist or constrain or even depose the king. What was true for Israel of old is true for all peoples to-day ; for the polity of Israel was an ideal polity, proceeding ' not from Plato and Aristotle,' but from God. Here is a first ground laid for resistance ; but it is not the only ground. There is a second contract to be considered. The people, besides making a covenant with God, in its religious capacity, also makes a covenant with the king in its natural or political capacity—a covenant ' to obey the king truly while he rules truly.' This is a covenant also expressed in the Scriptures, where we are told that the kings of Israel made covenants with Israel : it is a covenant which is moreover implied in the coronation ceremony of contemporary kingdoms, where the king promises to rule truly, and the people promises to obey truly in return ; it is a covenant to which the example of Aragon explicitly testifies.[1] It follows on this covenant, once more, that if the king violates his obligation by infringing its terms, the people may resist or constrain or even depose the king. There is, however, a difficulty in this second or political contract, which escapes the author of the *Vindiciae*, but is inherent in all theories of a contract between king and people. Parties to a contract are separate and independent parties. If you make

[1] The author of the *Vindiciae* (quoting, I think, from the *Franco-Gallia*, where the original Spanish is cited) twice refers to the proud claim of the Aragonese nobles : ' We, who have as much worth as you, and more power than you, elect you king, *on such and such conditions*.' Bodin (pp. 131–2 of the Frankfort edition of 1594) refers to the Aragonese custom, but refuses to admit its application.

king and people contractors, you make king and people separate and independent parties. The people ceases to be identical with the State, and the State is split into a duality of king and people. Unity is lost ; and as long as you talk in terms of a contract of king and people it will never be recovered. It is a better thing to talk of a contract, not between king and people, but between the members of the people, one with another, for the purpose of forming a body politic. On that basis you may say that the body politic so formed proceeds to delegate powers to a king, who is thus a delegate or trustee, but not a contractor. On the same basis you may further say that the body politic also, and *pari passu*, delegates powers to other public authorities as well as the king, and that these bodies stand by the side of the king in the same capacity of delegates or trustees. I believe that this is what Locke said, or tried to say, in 1689 ; and I am sure that it is what Burke was saying in 1770, in the *Thoughts on the Causes of the Present Discontents*. Both Locke and Burke believed in a contract of the sort which constitutes the people a body politic, and both of them regarded political power as a delegation or trust proceeding from that body politic. The author of the *Vindiciae* follows a different and less consistent theory. *His* people is an unexplained body politic. *His* king is a separate contractor with that unexplained body politic. And yet his king, and other public magistrates also, are somehow, at the same time, no more than trustees or delegates.

WE are thus brought to another idea which appears in the *Vindiciae* ; and that is the idea of trusteeship. I cannot see that it goes logically with the idea of contract between king and people. I cannot see that the king can be at one and the same time a separate and independent contractor and a delegate or trustee. But that is what he is, according to the theory of the *Vindiciae*. Along with the argument about contract, there is also an argument that the king is a *tutor*, which is the word that Calvin had used and which in Roman law approximates, I suppose, to our English word trustee. Having used this word, the author dilates, with a good deal of lore drawn from Roman law, on the origin and duties of the *tutor*—on his origin, in the choice and designation of the people ; [1] on his duties, in virtue of his mandate or trust. He goes further. He argues that the king is not the only authority in the State vested with this capacity. Calvin's hint about ephors in ancient times and the three Estates in modern kingdoms receives a large development. There are two sorts of public authorities, according to the author of the *Vindiciae*, which must be considered as parallel with the king. In the first place there are the *officiarii regni*, as distinct from the *officiarii regis*. These are the great public officers, such as the Constable : they draw their authority from the people, like the king himself, and not (like the king's private officers) from the king : they are ' assessors and consorts ' of the king : collectively they are even greater than the king ; and if they are true to the tutorial authority vested in them by the people, they will, as is their bounden duty, restrain a king who infringes the terms of his trusteeship. All this may well remind us of the position assumed by the great Whig magnates after the Revolution of 1688. In the second place, there are the delegates of the orders, the representatives of the three Estates, or, as we should say, the Parliament of the realm The Estates General of France, intermitted for many years before 1559, had been resumed during the troubles which followed ; and the author of the *Vindiciae* is clear that the Estates are a

[1] Strictly speaking, kingship proceeds both from God and the people. As St. Thomas had taught, and Burke long afterwards repeats, God gives the *principium* of political authority, but the people determines the *modus* (or form of government), and attributes the *exercitium* (or actual exercise of authority) to a definite person or body of persons. In the same sense the author of the *Vindiciae*, who had read and twice quotes the *Summa* of St. Thomas, holds that kings rule *a Deo quidem, sed per populum et propter populum* (p. 79). In the same sense Burke writes, ' although government certainly is an institution of divine authority, yet its forms, and the persons who administer it, all originate from the people ' (*Thoughts on the Causes of the Present Discontents*).

representation of the people, an epitome of the people, vested by it with authority to give consent on all great issues, to rebuke the king, and even to change the succession to the Crown. This emphasis on the Estates has equally its affinities with the Whig Parliamentarianism of our eighteenth century.

WE may now turn to the third of the ideas which we ascribed to the author of the *Vindiciae*—the idea of resistance. It follows from what has been said about contract that the people may resist the king on the ground of breach of contract. It follows on what has been said about the trusteeship of *officiarii*, and the representative position of the Estates, that both of these *can* resist, and both indeed *must* resist, if the king violates his trusteeship and delegation, since otherwise they will be failing in their own trusteeship and representation. The right of public resistance runs through the whole argument—resistance of the people of God, for breach of the first contract ; resistance of the political people, for breach of the second ; resistance of officers of State and the three Estates, on grounds of public trusteeship and representation. By resistance kings must be kept within the divine law of the word of God ; and by it they must be kept within the law of the land—a law not of their making, even if they have concurred in its making, a law according to which they have sworn at their coronation to rule, a law of which they are only the servants.[1] Such resistance may go to the length of deposition ; and shall we not say, considering this zeal of popular liberty and popular vigilance, that kings have become a little thing, and no more than dust in the balance ? If kingship was necessary to maintain the unity of France, the author of the *Vindiciae* leaves very little kingship to

[1] The idea of the sovereignty of law over the ruler is strongly enforced by the author of the *Vindiciae*. One of his two mottoes is the famous passage from the Codex Theodosianus, *Digna vox est majestate regnantis legibus alligatum se principem profiteri*. See Note B at the end of this essay.

maintain that unity. Yet we must beware of exaggerating the amount of popular liberty which he vindicates. We have to look carefully into the meaning of the word ' people ' in the *Vindiciae*. The author is not, after all, a democrat. He is really, we soon discover, an aristocrat. This becomes plain in an early part of his argument. Can the people, he imagines some doubter asking, really resist—the people in the sense of the universal multitude, that beast of innumerable heads ? He replies, ' When we speak of the *universus populus*, we mean those who have authority from the people—the magistrates . . . chosen by the people . . . consorts, as it were, of sovereignty and ephors (or over-seers) over monarchs. We mean also assemblies, which are nothing else but epitomes of the people. . . . In a word, whatever we have said to be conceded or committed to the whole people, belongs to its *officiarii* ; whatever to Israel, belongs to the Princes and Elders of Israel.' [1] This argument, in its aristocratic implication, consorts with the genius of Calvinism. Calvinism was not democratic, but aristocratic : it was government not by the congregation, but by the presbyter and elders of the congregation. It consorts again with the Whiggism of the eighteenth century, which was aristocratic liberalism. That is the worst of the conception of trusteeship in its application to politics. The political trustee is apt to regard himself as acting from above, on behalf of beneficiaries who are always below and always in a minority. The *curator* or *tutor*, to use the language of the *Vindiciae*, has a perpetual tutelage of his *pupilli*.[2]

THERE remains to be mentioned, in conclusion, the fourth and last idea of the author of the *Vindiciae*—the idea of federalism. Federalism, again, is perhaps an idea

---

[1] *Vindiciae*, pp. 46–8.

[2] Bodin, on the other hand, regards the conception of *curator* or *tutor* as derogating from the sovereignty of the true king. In a passage which seems like a rebuke to the argument of the *Vindiciae*, he contends that any one using *aliena potestas* either by way of *curatio* or by mere right of magistracy, whether for a time or in perpetuity, has no sovereignty (p. 119).

natural to Calvinism, which unites congregations in presbyteries, presbyteries in synods, and synods in a general
assembly.   But it was an idea which meant life and death
to the Calvinists of France.   It was all very well to talk of
the *universus populus*, but the Huguenots were not the
universal people of France.   They might indeed form the
populus of a seignory under a Huguenot noble : they might
again form the *populus* of an *urbs* or *civitas* which had embraced the religion of Calvinism.   Even so, they were only
a *populus* within the *populus* : they were what we may call
a *sub-populus*.   Some way must be found of vindicating
the position of such a *sub-populus*.   The author of the
Vindiciae attempts a way, perhaps remembering Bartolus'
doctrine of the Italian *civitas sibi princeps*.   He would make
French cities, at any rate those of ' the religion,' as independent of the French monarchy as Bartolus had made
the Italian cities independent of the Empire : and he would
thus turn France into a sort of Germany.   This was the
danger of Huguenotism—the danger which made the
political unitarianism of France turn upon it under
Richelieu, and, more drastically still, under Louis XIV.
The argument of the *Vindiciae* is significant on this point.
Not only has the *universus populus* made a double compact: the *populus* of a city—for a city is a people, and not a
place or ' a heap of stones ' [1]—has also made *its* double
compact.   *It* must keep its heavenly compact with God,
and may resist the king in the strength thereof ; and *it*
may insist that the king shall keep his earthly pact with
it, and observe the municipal conventions to which he has
sworn.   This postulates a multitude of pacts, or at any
rate two sorts of pacts, each of them double—the double
central pact of the *universus populus*, and the double
local pacts of the provinces and cities, pacts as many in
number as there are provinces and cities concerned.   And it
is to be noticed that both sorts seem to be of equal validity
with one another.   In the light of such arguments the
question may be raised whether we are justified in applying

[1] *Vindiciae*, p. 58.

even the term 'federalist' to the theory of the *Vindiciae*.
Is not the term pitched too high ? Are we not confronted
by something lower than federalism—something of the
nature of a loose confederation—something like what
Germany was already becoming, and was formally recognized as being by the Treaty of Westphalia in 1648 ?
Or shall we rather compare the theory of the *Vindiciae*
with the federal form which the Seven United Provinces
were soon afterwards to assume ? If we do so, we shall be
led to notice a matter of some importance ; and that is the
similarity between the federal theory of the State in the
Vindiciae and the similar theory of the State in the work of
Althusius, *Politica methodice digesta* (published in 1603)—
a work which seems to owe much of its inspiration to a study
of Dutch conditions. The *Vindiciae* (we may then say),
if it looks back to Bartolus and his theory of the *Civitas
sibi princeps*, looks also forward to Althusius, and anticipates
his theory of the State as an association composed of provinces and cities, each of which may retain its own 'majesty,'
or (as we should say) its sovereignty, and so be a ' prince for
itself.'

IF time and space had sufficed, some words might have
been said at this point in regard to the influence of the
general theory of the *Vindiciae* upon the course of the
Dutch war of independence. I can only say, without proof
of my guesses, that I would venture three conjectures in
this connexion. First, I am inclined to believe, as I have
already had occasion to observe, that the famous *Apology*
of the Prince of Orange, issued in 1580 in answer to the
ban pronounced by Philip II of Spain, was largely drafted
by Languet, who, as I have attempted to argue, was probably
the author of the *Vindiciae*. Secondly, I am inclined to
think that the Dutch Act of Abjuration of 1581—an Act
as solemn as the Declaration of Independence of 1776—
owed something to the same inspiration. Thirdly, I suspect
that the instructions given by the Dutch ' States ' to the
envoys who were to justify the Abjuration before the Diet

of the Empire (of which they were still nominally a part), in 1582, were also indebted to that inspiration. Contract was the basis of these instructions—contract and again contract. 'The contracts which the king has broken,' the envoys said, 'are no pedantic fantasies.' I would add that the contracts of which the author of the *Vindiciae* spoke were also more than pedantic fantasies. They helped, I think, to make history—both in the age in which they were first put forward, and in succeeding ages.

The *Vindiciae* was a popular book. There were six Latin editions between 1579 and 1599, and six more before the Peace of Westphalia in 1648—some printed in one place and some in another, from which we may guess the general vogue of the work. It was often printed along with the *Prince* of Machiavelli, by way (I suppose) of a corrective.[1] The first French translation was printed at Geneva, as early as 1581; and there was another published in 1615. English translations also began to appear. The first of which I know was a translation only of a small part—the part which deals with the question whether neighbouring princes may aid the subjects of another prince suffering from persecution or tyranny ; but this was exactly the part which had a lively interest for the England of Elizabeth, confronted as it was with that very question in France and in Holland. The translation appeared in London in 1588, under the title of *A Short Apology for Christian*

---

[1] Generally the *Vindiciae* appeared as a sequel to the *Prince*. In one instance, however, the *Prince* (in Latin) appears as a sequel to the *Vindiciae* (E. Armstrong, *Eng. Hist. Rev.*, iv. p. 17). The Huguenots naturally professed to be anti-Machiavellian, in order to throw odium on Machiavelli's countrywoman, Catharine de Medici. In the preface to the *Vindiciae* much is made of the fact that the book is diametrically opposed to the evil arts, the wicked counsels, and the false and pestiferous doctrine of the *Prince*. The prefatory poem also begins with a denunciation of that *contemptor superûm* who is *nomine notus Maculosi Velleris*— a curious pun. Actually I have only noted one explicit reference to Machiavelli (p. 176) ; and against that I would set the fact that there is also a reference (not indeed *nominatim*) to Ariosto and Tasso (pp. 196–7). The *Vindiciae* is not written to controvert the *Prince*, and its argument would have been just the same if the *Prince* had never been written.

Soldiers. More important is the translation of the whole of the *Vindiciae* which appeared in London in 1648, and was reprinted again in London in 1689. It is a striking fact that this translation should first have appeared in the year before the execution of Charles I, and that it should have been reprinted in the year of the deposition of James II.

The history of the book in England, whether in the original or in translations, is curious. In the early part of the seventeenth century the book was ascribed in England to the Jesuits. This may seem paradoxical ; but the reason is simple. The book was anti-monarchical : the Jesuits in England were anti-monarchical ; therefore the book was written by a Jesuit. James I spoke of its author as ' an anonymous writer, perhaps an emissary of Roman Church, anxious by its means to cause a dislike for the Reformed Religion among princes.' A common report assigned the authorship to the Jesuit Parsons. The Puritans of England must have known better. They must have guessed that the book came from the ranks of the reformed religion for which they fought ; and it must have been from some Puritan source that the translation of 1648 was derived.

That translation was made by a certain William Walker. Thomas Hollis, a famous antiquarian and Radical of the eighteenth century, to whom I shall recur, possessed a copy of the original Latin edition of 1579, on a blank page of which was written the motto, ' Will and Walke aright,' with the name of William Walker underneath ; and Hollis believed that it was from this copy that Walker had made his translation. There is a story about this William Walker that he came from Darnal, near Sheffield, and that he was the man who cut off the head of Charles I. The story appears in a note, written by some owner, in a copy of Walker's translation of the *Vindiciae* now in the British Museum ; and there was a discussion of the story in the *Gentleman's Magazine* for November 1767. I should be inclined to guess that an ingenious guesser jumped to the conclusion that the translator of the *Vindiciae contra Tyrannos* must himself have committed tyrannicide. A truer light is thrown on Walker, and the circumstances of his translating the *Vindiciae*, in an account which is given in Blackburne's *Memorials of Thomas Hollis*. In 1649, we are told, the Presbyterian ministers had to defend themselves against an imputation of anti-monarchical principles, which their adversary, a Catholic priest, declared them to have drawn from Beza, the author of the *Vindiciae*. (Beza, along with Hotman and George Buchanan, was one of its many supposed authors : and as late as 1660 an edition appeared at Amsterdam with the imprint, *Stephano Junio Bruto sive ut putatur Theodoro Beza auctore.*) The ministers replied that the *Vindiciae* was written by Parsons the Jesuit. They added (somewhat inconsistently, one cannot but feel) that a member of Parliament now sitting in the House had caused the *Vindiciae* to be translated into English by the same Walker who had written the *Monthly Mercuries*. Walker, it would appear, was a journalist rather than a tyrannicide ; and it was an English journalist, acting on the suggestion of an English M.P., who gave to his countrymen a full-dress presentation of a current and standard defence of religious and civil liberty.

The *Vindiciae* was obviously a live book in England in the first half of the seventeenth century. It continued to live in the latter half. In 1683, during the period of Tory reaction at the end of the reign of Charles II, the University of Oxford passed in its Convocation ' a judgment and decree against certain pernicious books and damnable doctrines, destructive to the sacred persons of princes, their State and Government, and of all human society.' Damning *imprimis* the doctrine that ' all civil authority is derived from the people,' the University consigned to the flames, in the Bodleian quadrangle, the *Vindiciae contra Tyrannos*, along with George Buchanan's *De jure regni apud Scotos* and Milton's *Defensio pro populo Anglicano*. The decree was passed, and the bonfire lit, on the day on which Russel was executed. A graduate of Christ Church wrote a copy of Latin hexameters in celebration of the *flammae ultrices*, and the decree was presented to Charles II. It is perhaps worth mentioning that in 1710 the decree, by order of the House of Lords, was publicly burned along with Sacheverel's sermon.

Between the burning of books by the Oxford decree and the burning of the Oxford decree by order of the House of Lords, there had intervened the Revolution of 1688.[1] That Revolution was in itself a solemn enactment of the principles for which the author of the *Vindiciae* had contended—principles which had now entered into English thought, and were backed by the memory of the Long Parliament and the policy of the Whig party. These principles found a new formulation in 1690 in Locke's *Two Treatises of Government*, which henceforth became the Bible of the Whigs. The similarity of the principles of Locke to those of the author of the *Vindiciae* is obvious. The basis of natural law ; the assumption of the ultimate sovereignty of the people ; the theory of contract (if in a different form) ; the doctrine of the people's right to institute, to oppose, and even to depose, kings ; above all, the idea of political trusteeship (which is fundamentally important in Locke's *Treatises*, as it also bulks largely in the *Vindiciae*)—all these are common to Locke with his forerunner. It does not follow that Locke borrowed directly from the *Vindiciae*. The essence of its argument—an argument which also appears, if less fully and trenchantly stated, in the works of other Huguenot and Calvinist writers after 1572—had been wrought into the general substance of what we may call progressive political thought ; and Locke would readily find what was now universally current. But there can be no doubt that Locke knew the *Vindiciae*. It is true that he does not expressly refer to the book. He was a shrewd man, and in his shrewd way he preferred to cite conservative writers in order to justify

[1] It is only fair to Oxford to say that its heart had been changed, by events at Magdalen College and elsewhere, as early as 1688. While the Prince of Orange was still in the far West, after his landing at Torbay, some of the Heads of the Colleges sent the Warden of All Souls to meet him, ' assuring him that they would declare for him, and inviting him to come thither ' (Burnet). It is only fair to Oxford also to say that Cambridge had burned the *Vindiciae* as early as about 1620.

liberal opinions. He cites, for example, the judicious
Hooker throughout his second *Treatise* ; and he cites in one
passage the royal Solomon, James I. But there is also
another book which Locke cites, and with which, indeed,
he deals at some length towards the end of the second
Treatise. It is not the *Vindiciae* ; it is an attempt at a re-
futation of the *Vindiciae*. It is Barclay's *De regno et
regali potestate, adversus Buchananum, Brutum, Boucherium
et reliquos monarchomachos*. Barclay was a Scotsman from
Aberdeen, who became a Professor of Civil Law at Angers,
and published his book in 1600. When he wrote *adversus
Brutum*, he was controverting the author of the *Vindiciae*,
who was generally styled by his pseudonym. If Locke
knew Barclay, as he certainly did, he must also have known
the *Vindiciae*, even if he only knew it through Barclay.
But a reprint of the English translation appeared, as we
have seen, in the year before that in which Locke published his *Two Treatises* ; and he may well have read the
translation, if not the original. In any case there is, in more
than one respect, a curious parallel between Locke and the
author of the *Vindiciae*. Whether Languet or Mornay wrote
the *Vindiciae*, it was composed by a person living in Holland
(for both of them were there in the year before its publication,
and in the year of its publication), and it was composed under
the influence of Huguenot feeling. When Locke began his
Two Treatises, he too was living in Holland ; and while he was
writing them, the feeling caused by the Revocation of the
Edict of Nantes was dominant in his circle. ' It may be said,'
writes one of the most recent students of Locke,' that it was
in Holland, and in consequence of the intellectual fermenta-
tion caused by the Revocation of the Edict of Nantes, that
his political doctrines arrived at maturity.'[1]

HERE the wheel has come full circle, and here the argument might fitly conclude. But a word of sum-
mary may perhaps be added. The political thought of the

[1] Ch. Bastide, *John Locke*, pp. 96–7. On parallels between Locke
and the author of the *Vindiciae*, see Note C at the end of this Essay.

Huguenots, as it is expressed in the *Vindiciae*, found no home and no welcome in France. A chance, indeed, seemed to offer itself during the years of the Fronde (1648–1653) ; but the Fronde was a short-lived movement, which, if it began with the cause of liberty, ended in the cause of class privilege. In 1789, again, it might seem at first sight as if the Huguenot principles had at long last entered into their own ; but it is only a matter of seeming. If the French Revolution adopted the principle of the sovereignty of the people, it made popular sovereignty as powerful and as unitary as ever monarchical sovereignty had been during the last two centuries ; and it left little room for rights of resistance or federal principles. But the principles which were alien to the political unitarianism of France found a more congenial home in Holland, with its mixed system of popular rights and federal institutions ; and while the Huguenots themselves found sympathy and an eventual refuge in the United Provinces, the theory of the *Vindiciae* was developed in that of Althusius—a German, indeed, but a German who lived and worked in Friesland, on the very borders of Holland, and who drew on federal Holland as well as on the federal Germany of his day for the material of his speculation. In England, too, with the rise of the Free Churches, the consolidation of local self-government, and the growth of parliamentarianism, the Huguenot theory found a second congenial home. The federal element of the theory might not appeal to England, but the doctrines of the sovereignty of the people, of the contract, of resistance, of trusteeship, were all readily welcome ; and even the narrow Huguenot conception of the people, under which it was identified with the *officiarii* and the three Estates, found its parallel in the Whig identification of the English people with the magnates and the Commons.

In the English home which it had found at the end of the seventeenth century we may say ' Good-bye ' to the Huguenot theory of politics. Perhaps it had now served its turn and done its work. But it survived, at any rate for a few, well into the eighteenth century. Robert Molesworth (afterwards Viscount Molesworth), a supporter of the Orange cause in Ireland, who went on a mission to the Danish Court which ended in trouble and a lively *Account of Denmark*, published in 1694, was a Whig Member of Parliament, first in Dublin and afterwards at Westminster, with a taste for letters and political theory. He published, in 1711, a translation of Hotman's *Franco-Gallia* (welcome to the Whigs as a vindication of ancient constitutional liberties, even *in terra aliena*), and he adorned his translation with a long and lively preface. The memory of Molesworth's translation survived until the beginning of the Radical movement in 1770, and it was republished for the London Association in 1775.[1] Even more curious is the story of Thomas Hollis and his passion for the *Vindiciae*. Hollis (1720–1774) described himself in one of the many copies of the work which he collected as *T. H. Anglus, Hospitii Lincolniensis, Regalis et Antiquoru msocietatum socialis, libertatis patriae praestantisque ejus constitutionis anno 1688 recuperatae amator studiosissimus*. He was a ‘ republican ’ Whig, who presented to Sidney Sussex College, Cambridge, its portrait of Oliver Cromwell (he was a ready giver, and presented books to Harvard and other Universities), and who wrote at the end of Molesworth's preface to his translation of the *Franco-Gallia* the two simple words, ‘ My Faith.’ A wealthy man, he had a habit of reprinting works of political theory devoted to the cause of liberty, and of adorning his reprints with emblems of liberty. He republished Locke's *Letters on Toleration* and his *Two Treatises of Government* ; Sidney on *Government* : Neville's *Plato Redivivus* ; and other works. We learn from Blackburne's *Memorials* that the *Vindiciae* was ‘ a favourite book with Mr. Hollis.’ ‘ Many have been the editions of the *Vindiciae* : Mr. Hollis picked up as many of them as he could meet with ’—among the rest (as I have already mentioned) the copy used by Walker, and an edition printed at Paris, in 1631, under the altered

[1] It was reprinted under the title of *The True Principles of the Whigs*.

title of *Vindiciae Religionis*. He acquired an original painting of Languet (whom he firmly believed to be the author, though some of the grounds he alleged were highly dubious) ; and 'intending to procure a new edition of the *Vindiciae*, he caused an elegant engraving of Languet's head to be taken ' (it is figured in the *Memorials*), with a design of prefixing it to the new edition. The edition never appeared. New stars dawned in the firmament ; and when the *Contrat Social* of Rousseau began to shine in 1762, there was no more place, except in the scholar's library, that refuge of extinct stars, for the *Vindiciae contra Tyrannos* of Stephanus Junius Brutus.

NOTE A

The Style of the 'Vindiciae'

One mark of the style of the *Vindiciae* is a sort of epigrammatic *brusquerie*, combined with a perpetual cultivation of antithesis. This gives a forced lucidity and a hard precision to the argument. It suggests to the mind of the reader the habit of the University lecturer, or, again, that of the ' painful preacher.' It suggests, too, the influence of the sharp formulation of Calvinistic theology. To one who has found himself yielding to the temptation of the double or triple antithesis, and has trembled to think that he might be twisting the truth to suit the needs of antithetical necessity, the author of the *Vindiciae*—certainly a fellow-sinner— is at once a comfort and a warning. He even uses the resources of the Latin language to make what may be called punning antitheses. A good instance of his method comes on p. 76 : *Ostendimus antea Deum Reges instituere, Regna Regibus dare, Reges eligere : dicimus jam Populum Reges constituere, Regna tradere, electionem suo suffragio comprobare.*

But the style remains generally trenchant, and sometimes eloquent. ' You talk to me ' (he imagines an objector saying) 'about your patricians and *optimates* and *officiarii regni*. I, on the other hand, can see nothing in them but ghosts and old trappings like those of tragedies. I can see scarcely a single trace anywhere of your antique liberty and authority ' (p. 103).

Such objections stir him to a stinging reply. ' Let not Electors, Palatines, Patricians, and other *optimates* think that they are only created and instituted in order that once, may be, in their lives, at a royal coronation, they may show themselves on view in the trappings of an antique fashion, to play a sort of romantic drama—to take the part, just for the day, of a Roland, an Oliver, a Rinaldo, or some other hero, as if they were on the stage ; to represent, in a sort of a mummery, the Round Table of Arthur ; and then, when the audience has gone home, and the Music has pronounced the epilogue, to think they have admirably played their part. Such things are *not* done in play : they are *not* done perfunctorily : they are *not* the games of boys ' (p. 197). He returns to the theme later, when he imagines *optimatium unus aliquis*, who, instead of facing tyranny like a man, is content simply to admonish the tyrant's aiders and abettors. It is folly as well as cowardice. ' Not only is such admonishment dangerous, and counted as a capital offence, in a state of tyranny ; the man would be acting like one who despised all other assistance, threw his arms away, and quoted the laws and delivered a sermon on justice to a band of brigands in the middle of a wood. That, if you will, is to carry reasonableness to the point of madness. But what is to be done ? Is he to be deaf to the groans of the people, and dumb at the approach of brigands : is he just to gape and fold his arms ? No : if the law assigns the penalties of treason to the soldier who pretends sickness for fear of the enemy, what penalty can be enough for the man who, in malice or cowardice, betrays the people he has undertaken to protect ? ' (p. 206).

I will only add—turning from the style to the scholarship of the author of the *Vindiciae*—that his knowledge of Greek, as I have said in the text of the essay, is more than respectable. He quotes, for example (p. 43), a fragment of a Greek comic writer which proves that he must have read the edition of Stobaeus (who gives the fragment) printed at Venice in 1535. He cites, again, in another passage (p. 171), the so-called Pythagorean writings ; and he quotes, and quotes correctly (probably from Pollux), the oath of the Athenian Ephebi (p. 185).

NOTE B

The Sovereignty of Law in the 'Vindiciae'

Two of the most recent works on Political Theory are Professor M'Iver's *The Modern State* (1926), and Professor Krabbe's *Die Moderne Staatsidee* (1919). It is curious to notice how political theory is still wrestling with the same problems, and wrestling with them almost in the same terms, as it was in 1579, when the *Vindiciae* was published. This is not to say that there is nothing new under the sun. Still less is it to say that the thinkers of to-day are simply the pupils and *glossatores* of the thinkers of an earlier age. It is only to say that the problems remain constant, and that, while each age must wrestle with them in reference to its own conditions, and must keep itself fresh by rethinking solutions afresh in reference to those conditions, there will none the less be repetitions of ancient truths, and sometimes there may even be striking, if undesigned, repetitions of the very forms in which those truths have been couched before.

Professor M'Iver, starting from the theory of ' community ' as the fundamental fact, argues that the State must be regarded as an ' association ' which acts as an ' organ of community.' So regarded, it has no inherent power : indeed, in any strict sense, it has no ' power ' at all : it has a ' function ' to discharge, and a ' service ' to render, on behalf of the community, and it is confined to that function and that service. ' It commands only because it serves : it owns only because it owes. It creates rights not as the lordly disperser of gifts, but as the agent of society for the creation of rights. The servant is not greater than his master ' (p. 480). The very language, and the very form of antithesis, have their parallels in the *Vindiciae*. ' Imperare ergo nihil aliud est, quam consulere : Imperii finis unicus populi utilitas . . . Regia vero dignitas non est proprie honos, sed onus ; non immunitas, sed munus ; non vacatio, sed vocatio ; non licentia, sed publica servitus ' (pp. 108–9).[1] Again, ' num regia dignitas possessio est, an potius functio ? Si functio, quid cum proprietate commune habet ? ' (p. 138). And again,

---

[1] The passage is an excellent example of the punning antithesis to which the author of the *Vindiciae* is prone.

'regis nomen non . . . proprietatem, non usufructum, sed functionem et procurationem sonat ' (p. 152). Professor M'Iver speaks of ' State,' and the author of the *Vindiciae* speaks of ' Rex ' ; but the difference does not go deep.

Professor Krabbe contends for the sovereignty of impersonal law as opposed to that of any person or body of persons, ' The modern idea of the State recognizes as sovereign Might the impersonal Power of Right ' (p. 2). And again, ' instead of personal Power we have now impersonal Might : instead of *sic volo, sic jubeo*, we have a spiritual sovereignty. In this conception the modern idea of the State reaches its zenith ' (p. 37). But the conception of the impersonal sovereignty of law is a very old idea. True, it must be vindicated afresh in each age ; but its vindication began a long time ago. Aristotle said, in a famous passage which affected all subsequent thought, that ' the rule of law is preferable to that of a person, and, on the same ground, even if it be better for persons to govern, they should be made guardians and servants of the law ' (*Politics*, iii. 16, §§ 3-4). He also said, in another famous passage (Ibid., iii. 11, §§ 1-2), that 'the generality ought to be sovereign' (ὅτι . . . δεῖ κύριον εἶναι μαλλον τὸ πλῆθος), and he grounded his argument on the idea that the meeting of the generality produced as it were a collective person with a collective capacity of judgment. These two sayings were put together in the thought of the Middle Ages, with the result that the people were regarded as the author of law by the power of their collective reason, and the law thus formed was regarded as the final sovereign. Dicta from Roman Law, enshrining the idea of the power of the popular *comitia* to make laws, and the idea that the *princeps* was bound by the laws, added a new corroboration to this way of thinking.

The author of the *Vindiciae* inherits and enforces these ideas. Steeped as he was in law—knowing the civil law, the canon law, the feudal law : the *Sachsenspiegel*, the *Liber Feudorum*, the ' Spanish Code '—he vindicates strenuously, in one of his best passages (pp. 114-116), the sovereignty of law. The ' dooms ' of kings (*arbitria regum*) were found various and contradictory ; laws, 'speaking to all in one and the same voice,' were discovered by the wiser men and the other magistrates ; and kings were assigned the ' function ' of acting as ' guardians, servants, and keepers ' of these laws. From the quasi-historical beginning he rises to a more general argument, in which the basis of law is carried deeper than the invention of ' the wiser men and the other magistrates,' and its sovereignty is more amply and broadly founded. *Sic volo, sic jubeo, sit pro ratione voluntas* is a saying utterly alien from true monarchy and the nature of the normal state. *Ratio*, and not *voluntas*, is the true guide of men. Now *lex est ratio sive mens, ab omni perturbatione vacua* (a translation of Aristotle's ἄνευ ὀρέξεως νοῦς ὁ νόμος ἐστίν) ;[1] and therefore, as pure reason, it is the true guide. Again, starting from what Aristotle had said about the collective capacity of the generality, and extending his saying to the sphere of the making of law, we may say that *lex est mens, vel potius mentium congregata multitudo* ; or we may say more simply, and with more obvious reference to the saying of Aristotle, *lex est multorum prudentum in unum collecta ratio et sapientia*. On this it follows that law is not only reason, but the common reason ; and on that it follows that it is sovereign not merely in virtue of being *ratio*, but also in virtue of being the expression of what we may call *communis ratio*. Thus the sovereignty of law is connected with the sovereignty of the community ; or rather (for we must not talk of the sovereignty of persons or bodies of persons *as such*), it is connected with the sovereignty of the ' common mind ' of the community and its ' common sense ' of right and law. This is the conclusion at which Professor Krabbe also arrives. He too connects the ' impersonal might ' and ' spiritual sovereignty ' of law with the community, and with the presence of representative institutions which permit the community to express a ' common mind.' ' Only where the formation of Law rests exclusively in the hands of a popular representative body can the pure sovereignty of Law appear externally ; for a popular representative body derives its significance from what it represents, which is the sense of Law inherent in the nation ' (op. cit., p. 36).

NOTE C

The ' Vindiciae' and the Second ' Treatise of Government'

Parallels in detail between the thought of Locke and that of the author of the *Vindiciae*, even if they can be established,

---

[1] *Politics*, III. xvi. 5.

are of no particular value. The real similarity is general, and a matter of the general trend of the argument in the two writers. Locke was not a scholiast or a glossator: he thought out his problems afresh, in the light of contemporary conditions, and with particular reference to his own country. But there are some analogies between the *Vindiciae* and the Second *Treatise* which perhaps deserve notice.

1. In an important passage, the author of the *Vindiciae* inquires into the origin of the State, and of that government of kings which he assumes to be its essential attribute (pp. 107 sqq.). It must, he argues, have been for some great utility that men who were by nature free spontaneously chose *imperium alienum*, and renounced *suae quasi naturae legi ut alienam ferrent.* That utility was twofold. Kings arose to protect individuals from one another by doing justice, and to protect all from external violence by using force to repel force. The Bible and the classical writers of antiquity both illustrate the double function: from both we may see that all kings have been always *judices et duces belli.*

To Locke, too (§ 88), 'the commonwealth comes by a power' vested with two functions—the function of punishing transgressions committed among the members of the society, and the function of punishing injuries done to any of its members by external force. Locke, too, uses the Bible in illustration, more expecially of the second function ; and some of the passages which he cites (e.g. 1 Sam. viii. 20) are the same as those which are cited in the *Vindiciae.*

2. The author of the *Vindiciae* argues that justice is imperfect as long as the decisions given *alia aliis loquuntur* : that it only becomes satisfactory when there are laws *quae cum omnibus una eademque voce loquuntur* (p. 114) ; and that such laws must proceed from ' a congregated multitude of minds ' (p. 116). Locke similarly argues that justice needs ' an established, settled, known law, received and allowed by common consent,' to serve as ' the common measure ' (§ 124), and to remove variety and partiality.

3. The emphasis of Locke is laid upon property. The ' great and chief end ' of commonwealth and governments is the preservation of property (§ 124). To the author of the *Vindiciae* also the purpose of the State is to settle *meum illud et tuum,* and

to pronounce *de rerum dominio* (p. 109). Indeed, he protracts a long legal argument to prove that kings are not the creators or owners or disposers of property, but the agents for securing *ut sua cuique diviti aeque ac pauperi constarent* (p. 134).

4. The author of the *Vindiciae* is full of the language of *curatio*, the *tutor*, *pupilli*. Government, he is always insisting, is a trusteeship. Locke in the same way harps on the ideas of 'trust,' 'fiduciary power,' action 'against the trust reposed,' action 'contrary to the trust.' To Locke, indeed, the trusteeship is vested in the legislature : to the author of the *Vindiciae* it is vested in the nobility and officials as well as (and apparently even more than) in the Estates General. For both, however, the conception of trusteeship, while it is intended to benefit the people, reduces the people into a sort of tutelage. Just as the *pupillus*, though he is really *dominus*, cannot bring an action without the agency of the tutor, says the author of the *Vindiciae*, so the people cannot act without the agency of the magistrates or representatives to whom it has transferred its authority and power (pp. 210–12). Locke, it is true, is less drastic, and allows the people to act for themselves—even imagining, in one passage, a 'perfect democracy' in which the people act directly as principals without the intervention of any agents ; but even Locke seems to think that normally the people have appointed a legislature to act as a permanent trustee, so that they have given up their political power to the legislature, and cannot resume it—unless for some breach of trust which is in its nature exceptional.

5. It is in his final chapters, on 'usurpation,' 'tyranny,' and 'dissolution of governments,' that Locke approaches nearest to the particular theme of the *Vindiciae*. It is here that he quotes Barclay's attempt to confute the *Vindiciae*, and seeks to show that Barclay has himself, after all, left a right of *vindicatio contra tyrannos*.

Note.—Since this essay was written, the writer has had occasion to go further into the question of the authorship of the *Vindiciae*. The reader is referred, for his conclusions, to the *Cambridge Historical Journal*, 1930.

PURITANISM [1]

T HE name Puritan seems to have taken its origin, early in the reign of Elizabeth and by the year 1570, as a nickname given by their enemies to a body of would-be ' purifiers ' of the ceremonies, the government and the doctrine of the incipient Church of England. They were puritans, ' because they think themselves to be *mundiores ceteris* ' : they were puritans, because the word might convey the suggestion and affix the imputation of the ancient heresy of the Cathars, a term of Greek origin exactly analogous to the Latin term of Puritan. But what was hurled by the enemy as an insult was caught up by the faithful and turned into an honour ; and it was not long before the Puritans could pride themselves on professing ' the pure or stainless religion.' It is the same alchemy which transmuted the nickname of Whig into the cherished appellation of a great party.

In its strict sense the term denotes those members of the Church of England who, while remaining in the Church, would have transformed its ceremonies into the plain ritual of Calvinism, its government into the Presbyterian system, its doctrine into the Calvinistic doctrine of election and reprobation. In that sense the Puritans were a Low Church party, walking to the left of the *via media Anglicana*, and anxious not only to follow Calvinistic opinion and practice themselves, but also to make such opinion and practice the general rule of the Church. But it is difficult to confine any term to a strict and limited sense ; and the term Puritan gradually came to receive a double

[1] A Paper contributed to the *Listener* in November 1929.

extension. On the one hand it could be applied to Presbyterians pure and simple, whether they sought to remain inside, or were recognized outside, the Church of England. In such an application the term no longer connoted, as one of its necessary attributes, any membership of that Church. On the other hand, the term could be applied, though this was a far greater extension, to the ' Separatists' who definitely sought to go and to remain outside the Church of England, and to organize themselves in local congregations (such as those of the Congregationalists) or in general sects (like that of the Baptists), on a basis of ' independency.' It has been much debated, particularly by American scholars, whether the term Puritan can properly be applied at all to the Separatists. They did not seek to purify the Church ; they simply stood outside, and how can they be called Puritans ? There is logic in the contention ; but the fact remains that, in England at any rate, the term received a wide extension, and included the Congregationalists and the Baptists as well as the Low Church party and the Presbyterians proper.

NONE the less, it is important to remember that until the year 1662—the year of the revised Prayer Book and the passing of the Caroline Act of Uniformity—the year in which, after a century of struggle in the Church of England, there was a definite parting of the ways—Puritanism was a body of opinion within the Church as well as a body of opinion without. It was not only a matter of the sects who had seceded : it was also a matter of the left wing which had remained. In the century with which we are mainly concerned—the century from the beginning of the reign of Elizabeth to the beginning of that of Charles II —the members of that left wing (and indeed of the whole general body of Puritanism) were never very numerous. During the period of the Civil War—the period which S. R. Gardiner called by the name of the Puritan Revolution—the numbers of the Puritans were swollen partly by the zeal and passion of the times, and partly by the force of fashion which always augments a triumphant party. If, however, we seek to make some enumeration of the body of the Puritans either at the beginning of the seventeenth century, or towards the close, we shall find that their numerical strength was surprisingly small. Scholars have calculated that in the first decade of the century about 3 per cent. of the clergy, and from 2 to 6 per cent. of the laity, were Puritan. When William III attempted a religious census, just after the Revolution of 1688, the statistics showed just over 100,000 male Nonconformists to nearly two and a half millions of male Conformists—that is to say, about 4 per cent. of the one to 96 per cent. of the other.

Puritanism was thus no more than a leaven. Why was it so vital a leaven ? The ultimate cause is the strength of its religious zeal and its moral ardour. But there were contributory causes which deserve notice. It is sometimes said that the Puritan clergy were more learned than the rest. This is perhaps dubious. Professor Usher records the fact that in a list of 281 Puritan clergymen, only 105 had University degrees. But Puritan theology, none the less, had a hold on the Universities in the early part of the seventeenth century, and particularly on the University of Cambridge. The Church of England had no body of theology which could vie with the *Institutes* of Calvin. Puritanism, again, seems to have been strong among the new landed gentry which had arisen in the century of the Reformation, and even in a tolerably large circle of the nobility. It was also strong in the towns, where Puritan ' lecturers ' were paid to preach sermons, often in the afternoon, outside the regular circle of matins and evensong. It is a curious fact that when a Puritan clergyman held a living he had often a salary higher than that of the general run of the clergy. The contributions of the faithful were paid in augmentation ; and when the average salary was £10, or less, a Puritan vicar with a Puritan congregation might receive about £50.

Considerations such as those help to explain the paradox

of Puritanism, the paradox of a strength entirely disproportionate to its numbers. That strength was reflected in the House of Commons. From the new landed gentry and the towns there came to Westminster an abundance of Puritan Members ; and it was commonly said at the time that three parts of the first House of Commons which met in the reign of James I (1604) was Puritan. This character of the House accounts in its measures for the rise of a Parliamentary Opposition, which, beginning on the grounds of objection to the religious settlement, passed to the ground of defence of the Constitution, and culminated in the Civil War.

The geographical distribution of Puritanism was another source of its strength. It was chiefly concentrated in the centres of population and wealth—in London and the Eastern Counties. The Eastern Counties in the seventeenth century were the Lancashire and Yorkshire of their time. They were the homes of the most intensive agriculture ; they were the homes of the woollen industry. The Puritanism of the Eastern Counties made them the core of the Parliamentary cause and the New Model Army. It also made them largely the source of that movement of Puritan colonization which helped to populate New England and to make the American Republic. The place-names of Massachusetts—Boston and Cambridge, Lynn and Ipswich—still recall Eastern England.

BUT to understand Puritanism we must turn to its fundamentals—fundamentals of religious zeal and moral ardour. Predestination is an iron creed ; and it made, or tempered, souls of an iron zeal. God is an inscrutable will, always acting, as it were, by specific decision in every issue. He is will rather than law—specific decision rather than general rule. By His will some are chosen to be of the elect, and called to salvation ; and others, by what Calvin called an ' irreprehensible but incomprehensible judgment,' are condemned to reprobation. But it is not for the elect, in any mood of fatalism, simply to acquiesce in the operation of inscrutable will and fore-ordinance. Who shall be certain of his election ? No man : and therefore it behoves each man, in the solitude of his soul, to scrutinize himself and to struggle until he attains some inkling of the Divine purpose. And even if a man have conviction of his election, that is no end, and it gives no acquittal from struggle. If I am elected and called, I must remember my election and calling, and do according thereto. I am not called into bondage, still less into indolence : I am called into the liberty of the elect and the strenuous activity of the chosen. There is an athleticism, an asceticism, in the Puritan, as of one running for a great prize which is set before him. This is the rock of Puritan faith ; and by its side the formalism of Puritanism—its objection to the cross in baptism, the ring in marriage, the surplice—are a very little thing. Not but what the little thing sometimes became a large beam in the eye of the Puritan ; not but what, again, his formalism in objecting to forms tended to make him a precisian, with a great power of irritation and even, when he had his way, of destruction. Stained glass windows and stone sculptures were forms anathema to his formalism ; and yet that formalism stiffened itself in its own prim forms of rigid expression. None the less, when we have made all allowances for the rigour of its outward case, we must always come back to the real vitality of the inner spirit of Puritanism.

That spirit was a spirit of struggle. The symbol of the Puritan is the figure of Samson Agonistes in the temple of the Philistines. There was a struggle to be waged in the inward man—a struggle for deliverance from the body of death and for assurance of salvation : there was a struggle to be waged with the outward world—a struggle against its cozening forms and all its subtle deceits. The Puritan was at war both with himself and the world ; and the warfare was hard and long. This conception of warfare gave a negative quality to Puritanism : the Puritan must say ' No ' and again ' No,' to himself, to the Church, to the State, to society at large. It also gave a certain dualism

to the general cast of thought : it made the world a place
of unresolved contradictions, and opposed a great and
defiant Devil to the merciful God of Grace. But there
was a positive behind the negative ; and there was a unity
behind the dualism. We must seek the positive core : we
must discover the unity of Puritan life.

THE positive core of Puritanism was a deep sense of
individual personality, and a resolute practice of individual and personal will. ' Will,' it has been said by Mr.
Tawney, ' is the essence of Puritanism.' It may seem a
paradox that a creed which emphasized the absolute will and
predestined purpose of God should make each of its votaries
also the centre of a firm and resolute will of his own. But
the Puritan never interpreted God's predestination as his
own subjection : he made himself not the slave of divine
will, but its image and microcosm. If the will of God
ranged the world, and made specific decision on every issue,
man's will must act with a similar range. It followed that
life confronted the Puritan day by day, and hour by hour,
with issues of anxious decision : it followed that his will
was kept taut and braced by the exercise of daily and
hourly practice. We may call this, if we will, individualism ; and in that sense the Puritan was an individualist.
Primarily, indeed, he was the individualist only of the
religious life ; but then the religious life was all life, and
the religious principle controlled every issue ; and the
individualist of the religious life thus became the individualist of the whole of life. In this way solitude—the
solitude of a fiery burning soul—became an essential attribute of Puritanism. Now there is a sense in which solitude
is one of the greatest of the virtues. It may almost be
said that the art of living is the discovery of a balance
between the gregarious habit which carries us into society,
and the solitary habit which throws us back on ourselves
—between the peace of social companionship and social
conformity, and the effort of individual life and individual
decision. The balance tilts easily towards the gregarious

side ;   and the Puritan who threw all his weight on the other side did much to redress the balance, not only for himself, but in the whole general working of our national life ; not only in the century of his greatness, but also in succeeding centuries. These are simple and mundane matters in which we may trace the effects of his influence. He helped to make citizenship an individual responsibility, a matter in which each must exercise his thought and practise his will.   He helped to make commerce and industry find their own feet and go their own way, escaping an old system of paternal protection.   He helped to make colonization a spontaneous movement ; and when the colonists had settled in lonely lands beyond the seas, he helped to give that temper of self-reliance which could face and conquer solitude.   Yet the solitary habit is only one part of the balance, and the Puritan was perhaps too apt to behave as if it were almost the whole.   Any social system must rest on the virtues of sympathy as well as the virtues of solitude.   Our English system was long defective in the virtues of sympathy ; and the solitary quality of the Puritan life was a contributory cause of that defect.

IF the positive core of Puritanism was insistence on individual will, and a cultivation of that solitude in which individual will is tempered and hardened, there was also a unity in Puritan life ; and there were ways in which it sought to transcend the tendency towards dualism which was implicit in its nature.   We have spoken of Puritan asceticism ; but the asceticism of the Puritan was never of the sort which renounces the world. We have spoken of the solitary habit of Puritanism ; but its solitude was never that of a fugitive and cloistered virtue.   Puritanism was saved from such consequences by its doctrine of election, which readily passed into a doctrine of ' calling ' in the ordinary sense of that term. Not only had the Puritan been called to grace : he had also been called to a vocation.   It was his duty to be about its business : in that way he could show forth fruits, and by these fruits he could furnish a visible testimony of what was in him. The world was not a place to be denied : it was a place to be conquered and shaped. The way of conquest and shaping was work—faithful work in an earthly calling or vocation, by which a man might give evidence of the reality of his heavenly calling. Work became a part of the Puritan creed ; and work was the mother of production. The effort and the struggle of the Puritan were thus translated into a shaping of the material world, a conquest of its resources, a victory over its obstacles ; and the unceasing working of God thus found its parallel in the unceasing working of man. This, again, was good stuff for the national fibre ; but this again had the defects of its qualities. Two of these defects have long remained with us. One is a tendency to let work engulf life to the exclusion of thought and reflection. The Puritan cultivated solitude ; but he lost the fruits of solitude when he made his solitude into an office in which he ceaselessly pursued his calling. Another is a readiness to glide into the conviction that the garnered fruits of a secular calling are somehow the evidence of divine election and moral worth, and that property has thus a sort of sanctity. It is only too easy to glide in turn from that conviction into a feeling that an absence of property is an absence of testimony, and an absence of testimony is an absence of worth. And on that basis even a glaring system of social inequality may be condoned, and not only condoned but justified.

WHAT has been said may bring into relief some features of Puritan ethics—the resolute practice of will ; the stoical cultivation of solitude ; the conception of the duty, and even the sanctity, of work duly done in a calling. A system with these features cannot but be informed by a deep moral zeal : but there was an uncomfortableness even in the zeal. The Puritan could not rely on the accumulated moral experience and tradition of his generation. He looked at it and saw that it was evil ; and in any case he was bound, by his faith, to bring the fresh initiative of his will to face each issue. Not only so, but the issues which he had to face were innumerable. Every issue was a moral issue ; and since morality was religion, and to do good was to do the will of God, every fresh step meant an anxious searching of the unsearchable dispose of God. There was a noble anxiety in such a morality ; but it had its dangers. For one thing, it stretched conscience on a constant rack ; and the man who was thus strained might fall into a morbidity of introspection. For another thing, it involved a steady tension of moral effort ; and the man who felt himself keyed to such a pitch might fall into a satisfaction with his own standard which was also a contempt of the standard of the ordinary man. It was a sort of self-complacency which contemporaries criticized in the Puritans. (' Dost thou think, because thou art virtuous, there shall be no more cakes and ale ? Yes, by Saint Anne ; and ginger shall be hot i' the mouth too.') Saddest of all, perhaps, in the Puritan scheme was the absence of any free space of life. If every issue was a moral issue, nothing was in-different, and everything was a matter of moral regimen. If, again, every moral issue was also a religious issue, and every religious issue involved reference to the will of God and to the Bible which revealed His will, it followed that the Bible became the obligatory canon of the whole of life. It was a canon you were bound to follow, and, if you could, to enforce. A Bible despotism was thus a logical outcome of Puritanism ; and in Massachusetts that despotism was for a time realized. The Puritan clergy and the Puritan elect who held the magistracies dispensed with laws on the ground that the Bible was sufficient ; but they made their interpretation of the Bible a rule not only of legal action, but also of moral behaviour. It is another of the paradoxes of Puritanism, but a paradox inherent in its nature, that its philosophy of the resolute practice of individual will could be made to issue in a stringent form of theocracy.

IF we turn from the moral world to the intellectual, we find similar contradictions in the attitude of the Puritan. One of the most fundamental of his theological tenets was that of the inscrutable Divine will acting by specific decision —a tenet parallel to that of the human will acting, in its own small and yet solemn sphere, by a similar rigour of particular will. It was not a tenet favourable to that idea of uniform law on which all growth of human knowledge is ultimately based. John Winthrop of Boston could regard it as a special providence when a spider was discovered in the porridge before it was eaten. It was another remarkable providence when, in a whole library, a mouse confined its ravages to a copy of the Book of Common Prayer. Apart from this way of thinking, theological preoccupation inevitably diverted attention from other and more secular studies. The libraries of New England, till the later half of the eighteenth century, were theological libraries. On the other hand, education, in the whole of its range, from the primary school to the University, owes much to Puritan impulse. The Puritan life, after all, demanded a man who could read and think ; and were it only for the purpose of reading the Bible or training a ministry, schools and colleges were necessary. It was a Puritan Parliament which, in 1649, voted a sum of £20,000 per annum, partly for the two old Universities of England, but mainly for the maintenance of schoolmasters and ministers. Massachusetts had only struggled through some seven years of existence when it founded Harvard College in 1636. But the greatest monument of the Puritan zeal for education is the village school of New England. Wherever a Puritan congregation settled, there was also founded a school. Yet Massachusetts, the home of the village school, was also the home of a strict censorship of the press. Puritanism would teach men to read. But where it had its way, it was resolved to show that it knew—knew only too well—what it was good for them to read.

We may turn from Puritanism in theology, and in the moral and intellectual sphere, to Puritanism in politics. But we must take politics in a wide sense, and interpret

it to include both Church and State and the relations between the two. Here we must make a distinction between
Puritanism triumphant—the Puritanism of New England—
and Puritanism militant, militant as the creed of a minority,
the Puritanism which was that of old England except for
its brief period of triumph in the years of our Civil War.
In the one we may see Puritanism carried to its logical
outcome and expressed in its logical essence ; in the other
we may see it struggling with circumstances and battling
under adverse conditions. But a bruised herb may best
express its own inward scent and savour ; and perhaps
we may come to the conclusion that it was struggling
Puritanism which best evolved the genius of its true inner
self.

Among the settlements in New England it was
the Puritan Colony of Massachusetts which most clearly,
and indeed almost solely, showed the qualities and the
defects of triumphant Puritanism. Rhode Island, under
the influence of Roger Williams, was a home of liberty
and toleration of religious differences : Connecticut, guided
by Thomas Hooker, practised a democracy which demanded
no religious qualification for its franchise. Massachusetts
was of a more granite quality. Here the State was a
Church, and the Church was a State ; citizenship was
confined to those who showed churchmanship of the Puritan
type, and churchmanship of that type gave to citizenship
its character, its policy, and its methods. The system, it
is true, did not permanently last. By the end of the
seventeenth century it was radically changed. A democratic movement within brought the members of the community who were not of the elect into some share of control
of the common life. The more liberal tradition of her
neighbours in Rhode Island and Connecticut penetrated
into Massachusetts. The influence of the English government, when in the later part of the seventeenth century it
began to recover the reins, was exerted in the cause of
civic liberty and religious toleration. But while it lasted,
the Puritan policy of Massachusetts was a logical *reductio*

ad extremum of Puritan ideas, and it is instructive to study the main features of that policy.

In the first place there was as rigorous an identification of State and Church, of Citizenship and Churchmanship, as ever Elizabeth or Clarendon attempted. ' No man shall be admitted to the freedom of this body politic, but such as are members of some of the churches within the limits of the same.' As we shall see, the only churches tolerated were those of the Puritan way ; and here was thus a State Church, as much as in contemporary England, to whose members the privileges of citizenship were confined. A law of 1635, parallel to the Elizabethan Act of Uniformity, made attendance at church compulsory under pain of fine and imprisonment. A law of 1638 went further. It enunciated the principle, reminiscent of mediaeval belief and practice, that excommunication from the Church must ultimately entail entire exclusion from civil society and civil existence. It provided that an excommunicated person must seek restoration within six months under pain of ' fine, imprisonment, banishment *or further*.' No wonder that Puritan friends in England warned Massachusetts not ' to fall into that evil abroad which you laboured to avoid at home, to bind all men to the same tenets and practice ' ; no wonder, again, that even the Puritans of England ceased to emigrate to Massachusetts, lest they should lose the liberty they prized. Triumphant Puritanism was at least as rigorous as triumphant Anglicanism.

On this drastic unification of life—the life political and the life religious—there followed other features. One was the absence of democratic principle and practice. We naturally, and justly, associate the English Puritans of the seventeenth century with the rise of English democratic ideas. But the English Puritans advocated these ideas in the winter of their discontent ; and the Puritans of Massachusetts were in a summer and heyday of victory. They believed in the rule of the elect ; and the elect were a small minority. The Puritan village church, though it was based on the democratic idea of a ' church covenant,'

was a dominion of the elect; and the Puritan Commonwealth of Massachusetts was of the same type. ' Democracy,' said John Winthrop, ' is accounted the meanest and
worst of all forms of government.' In actual practice the
government of Massachusetts was something of an aristocratic theocracy, a combination of the leading Puritan
laymen with the Puritan ministers. Alike in theory and in
practice the idea of the free commonwealth, moved to
common ends by the common will of all its members, was
absent. It could hardly be otherwise so long as the zeal
of righteousness was dominant, and righteousness was conceived as the jewel of the elect. Nor was toleration more
welcome, or more present, than democracy. Indeed, on
strict Puritan principles it would have been a vice rather
than a virtue. No new churches could be organized without
the consent of the magistrates and of a majority of the
elders of existing churches; and this stereotyped a single
type of church of the Puritan way. When the Quakers
sought entry into Massachusetts, soon after the middle of
the seventeenth century, a law was passed against them
inflicting banishment on pain of death. Four who defied
the law were put to death; many more were whipped or
imprisoned.

More curious, and perhaps more dangerous, than the
absence of democracy or toleration was the absence, in early
Massachusetts, of any real system of law. We have learned
to believe that law is the guarantee of liberty; we have
learned to believe that it gives that security, that sense of
acting under known rule in a sure expectation of regular
and fore-known consequences, which is the necessary
condition of an ordered life. But to the early Puritans of
Massachusetts the State was an organ not of the mere
justice of law, but of the abounding righteousness of grace
and election. ' Whatever sentence the magistrate gives,
the judgment is the Lord's.' It was accordingly voted,
in 1639, ' that the word of God shall be the only rule to
be attended to in ordering the affairs of government.' In
practice the Massachusetts assembly passed occasional

laws ; but even the laws were vague. A law which enacted
that a man spending his time idly or unprofitably should
undergo such penalty as the court thought meet to inflict
was a law which left the magistrate a large latitude. When
he was instructed by the assembly that, in the absence of
such law, he should determine cases as near the law of God
as he could, the latitude was still larger. So long as this
system continued, a godly arbitrariness brooded over men's
lives ; and a magistrate uninstructed by law, and acting
in the strength of moral zeal and religious fervour, became
an inscrutable will capable of irreprehensible but incomprehensible judgments. But this was the inexperience of a
new society ; and it is only fair to add that by 1648 Massachusetts was already beginning to realize the necessity of a
certain and known law.

FROM the triumphant Puritanism of America, which
only enjoyed its triumph for some decades of the
seventeenth century, we may now turn to the militant
Puritanism of England, the Puritanism of a minority
struggling against odds, and necessarily adopting its
tenets to the exigencies of struggle and the conditions
of its environment. The same strength showed itself
on either field ; but it showed itself to more enduring
consequences on the field in which Puritanism was a
minority, engaged in struggle and facing defeat. It is an
old characteristic of the English, that goes back to *Beowulf*
and the days of the Heptarchy, to love dearly that 'fetter-
ing up of the heart ' (as it is called in an old Anglo-Saxon
poem) and that ' fight against odds ' which the conditions
of the seventeenth century imposed on minorities. Puritanism, with its insistence on the resolute exercise of a will
trained by spiritual discipline, added a new moral zest
to an old native instinct. Fighting for faith, against all
powers and principalities, it left a large legacy, even when
it seemed defeated, to the English Commonwealth. What
were the elements of that legacy ?

French writers have sometimes compared the Puritan

Revolution of the seventeenth century, in its abiding results, to the French Revolution of 1789. There are some respects in which the comparison may be said to hold good : there are others in which, as we shall see, it cannot be justified. One thing we may say of both revolutions : they disengaged clearly the notion of the non-clerical State, which stood on its own account, as a human society, working under a human law on the simple ground of justice and equality. We have seen that this was not in the necessary logic of Puritanism, and that in early Massachusetts a very different notion was followed. But we must allow that it was in its conditional logic ; and we may say that when Puritanism had to face the condition, and accept the limitation, implied in its being the faith of a minority, it adopted freely the principle of the non-clerical State. Clericalism, indeed, never exercised the power in England which it exercised in France. But if it was never *the* enemy, as Gambetta declared it to be for France even at the end of the nineteenth century, there were times when it seemed one of the enemies, and one of the gravest of enemies. Bishops had a control of education, through their power of licensing teachers. Their church courts had a large cognizance even over the life of the laity. Laud attempted to carry the Church still more into the State. The Court of High Commission was not an inquisition, but it assumed large powers ; and the general alliance of monarchy and episcopacy might well seem to menace a clerical régime. Perhaps the lay genius of the English lawyers—always a powerful factor in English life—would of itself have defeated any such tendency. But it was Puritanism which made sure the defeat : it was Puritanism which brought the zeal not of a profession, but of a faith, to curb the enemy. It is true that relics of the old system long lingered. Not till 1871 were the old universities of England fully opened to every citizen, irrespective of religious profession ; and even now their nationalization may be said to be incomplete. None the less, we may say that after 1660 there was no danger of a clerical State in

England. Parliament, indeed, might long require conformity to a particular Church, and long exclude Nonconformists from its own body. But it was the lay parliament of the nation which made the requirement and imposed the exclusion ; and the rigour of such a parliament would alter with the alterations of the public opinion on which it rested.

If Puritanism may thus be said to have contributed to the conception of the non-clerical State, it also contributed to the conception of the limited State. Here the Puritan Revolution differed from the French. The French Revolution installed, early in its course, an unlimited State armed with indefinite power by a community which had banished or suppressed minorities. The Puritan Revolution, even in the period of its brief triumph, adopted, under the influence of its ' Independent ' wing, the notion of ' fundamentals ' which Parliament itself could not touch or vary. A defeated minority after 1660, the Puritans clung all the more intensely to the notion of the limited State ; and they passed to the idea that they were bound to resist if the State overstepped its limits. That idea became embedded in the Whig Party, which, as it included the Puritans in its ranks, included also something of their spirit in its principles. Blackstone was a Conservative Whig, who could speak of unlimited sovereignty ; but even Blackstone embalmed a right of resistance in his *Commentaries*. Nor was it only a matter of a theoretical right. The Nonconformists of the eighteenth century were engaged in actual resistance. They had their children taught as they wished in spite of the law : they stood fast in their faith against the State, and the State, at first *de facto*, in the way of quiet ignoring of things perhaps better left unnoticed, and then *de jure*, in the way of express consent, recognized the ground on which they stood. Gradually the idea of the limited State became almost a fashion. It spread from the world of religion to the world of economics. Was not *laissez faire* best ? Would it not be wiser for the State not only to allow men to think their own thoughts and conduct their own worship, but also to manage their own business and regulate their own trade ? In this way the Puritan tradition passed, as it were, from the chapel to the counting-house : Puritanism, we may say, became allied with political economy ; and the faith of free trade was added to the faith of free religion. It was an alliance which had its dangers. Freedom in the world of religion—essentially a non-competing world, even if churches disagree—is different from freedom in the competitive world of economics. Economic freedom, if it is to mean an economic freedom for all, is a freedom which does not come naturally, but has to be made. It is here that we have to unlearn some elements of the old Puritan tradition. But even as we unlearn them, we may recognize that they had their day, and their justification in their day.

Puritanism was favourable to the principle of the limited State : was it also favourable to the principle, and the practice, of the democratic State ? We have seen that it could reject democracy as a ' mean ' form of government— a breach, as one of its adherents said, of the Fifth Commandment. And yet, wherever it established itself, whether in England or in America, Puritanism carried within itself, whatever might be its opinions of outward and political democracy, the principle of an inner and spiritual democracy. We have to remember that however Calvinistic their theology, the Puritans only rarely practised the full form of Calvinistic organization, with its organized hierarchy of *classes* and synods. Cartwright might attempt such an organization about 1580 : it might be generally attempted, though only for a few years, after the Solemn League and Covenant of 1643 ; but the essential unit of the Puritan scheme was the individual congregation. The members of the congregation were united by a ' church covenant ' ; and though the numbers of those within the covenant were often restricted by a requirement of effective-conversion, and of public profession thereof, the idea of the covenant was essentially democratic. It could easily be transferred to the political sphere ; and it was so transferred by the Pilgrim Fathers of the *Mayflower*, when in 1620 they made the compact whereby they agreed ' solemnly and mutually, in the presence of God and one of another, [to] covenant and combine ourselves together into a civil body politic . . . and by virtue hereof to enact constitute and frame such just and equal laws ordinances acts constitutions and offices, from time to time, as shall be thought most meet and convenient for the general good.' Here is the fundamental democratic idea of the people combining to form a commonwealth and to give it a constitution. Not only in the original framing but also in the actual working of the Puritan congregation democratic ideas were apparent. The congregation chose and ordained its pastors and elders : the mainspring of its life was in itself : authority proceeded from it, and authority was responsible to it. Though Massachusetts might object to democracy, and object logically, Thomas Hooker of Connecticut was also in the logic of Puritanism when he maintained that the people chose its magistrates, and ' they who have the power to appoint officers and magistrates, it is in their power also to set bounds and limitations.'

IN New England as well as in Old England Puritanism was thus a force which helped to lay the foundations of a free Commonwealth, freely based on the common purposes and consent of its members. And it also served, as we have already had occasion to notice, in the laying of the foundations of the British Commonwealth. It was from the Eastern counties of England, in which Puritanism was strong, that the tide of emigration set strongest towards America ; and it was the resolute will and the capacity for solitude inherent in the Puritan temper that made the American settlements successful and permanent. Not that Puritanism was the sole motive for emigration, or that Puritans were the sole emigrants. On the contrary, the land-hunger of the Eastern counties was a potent cause of the English colonization of the second quarter of the seventeenth century, and among the colonists there were a large number who emigrated for the simple purpose of acquiring the free land, owned in freehold, which the New World offered. It has been remarked that even among the 102 passengers on the *Mayflower*, only one-third were certainly Puritans ; and it has been calculated that, of some 65,000 persons who had emigrated to North America and the West Indies by 1640, only 16,000 had settled in the Puritan colonies, and of these 16,000 only about one-quarter were regular church-members of Puritan congregations. But Puritanism was the spear-head of the colonial movement, if it was not also the shaft ; and when we reflect on the great part played by the Puritan colonies of New England in the development of North America, both in the period down to 1776 and in the great period of ' Western movement ' up to and across the Rockies during the nineteenth century, we must conclude that here again the effects of Puritanism were out of all proportion to its numbers. The village church and the village school of the Puritan type have crossed the whole American continent. When we think of Puritanism, we must not think of it only in terms of England, but also in terms of the greater part of the United States of America. We must think not only of Oxford and Cambridge, of English towns, of our English Eastern counties, but also of Harvard and Yale, of American cities, of Ohio and Iowa and the great region of the American Middle West. On our side of the Atlantic, and in our European environment, Puritanism was a factor which stood by the side of, and ultimately had to be mixed with, many other factors — the culture of a neighbouring continent : the German and Swiss evangelical tradition : the Latin and Catholic tradition : and, behind all, an ancient and rooted English conservatism. In North America, even if Puritanism was not entirely isolated (we must not forget the Southern Colonies), it grew in a freer ground and a far less mixed environment. It is in the history and character of North America that its genius accordingly displayed some of its most native and inherent qualities.

THE social and economic aspects of Puritanism have
been no less powerful and profound than the political.
Critics have sometimes animadverted on the chilling influence
which the Puritan spirit exerted on family life. Samuel
Butler, dwelling bitterly in *The Way of All Flesh* on the un-
satisfactory relations between parents and children at the
beginning of the nineteenth century, finds the cause in
Puritanism. 'The fathers and sons are for the most part
friends in Shakespeare,' he writes, ' nor does the evil appear
to have reached its full abomination till a long course of
Puritanism had familiarized men's minds with Jewish
ideals as those which we should endeavour to reproduce in
our everyday life.' Doubtless Puritanism did something
to turn the family from a home of loving service to a home
of sombre duty. But Puritanism is a familiar cause, which
is apt to be alleged in explanation of all sorts of effects,
from the rigour of parents to the disrepair of church fabrics.
It was not always, or indeed generally, inimical to family
life (which it invigorated far more than it corrupted) ;
nor was it, again, always — though perhaps it was more
generally — inimical to art and the gracious pleasures of
life. If we think, for example, of music, we must confess
that there was more music in England in the time of Elizabeth than there was in the time of William III. But we
need not blame an intervening Puritanism for the decline.
There was music to be heard in good Puritan houses in the
seventeenth century ; and if there was but little to be
heard anywhere in the eighteenth (at any rate, in comparison
with Tudor times), the blame is general and national.
We may blame Puritanism ; but we may blame no less the
English Church, which spent itself less than in earlier days

> ' To let the pealing organ blow
> To the full-voiced quire below
> In service high and anthems clear,'

and we may blame the English squires and nobles, who,
if they could rebuild their houses and have them decorated
by Italian workmen, forgot other and less visible arts.

The economic affinities and the economic consequences of Puritanism are a theme which has been much discussed of late, and nowhere more justly or sympathetically than in Mr. R. H. Tawney's *Religion and the Rise of Capitalism*. Early Puritanism, as he has remarked, tended towards a belief that the Bible—the rule of all life—should regulate all economic dealings and activities. That economics was in any sense a domain exempt from the operation of that rule was an idea which Puritanism, in its very genius, could not but reject ; and the seventeenth-century Puritans, no less than the Mediaeval Church, were opposed to the sin of usury and to anything that departed from ' justice ' in the fixing of prices or wages. Such a way of thinking made for a moral and religious regulation of the sphere of economic life. But there were elements in Puritanism which drew it gradually in a different direction. In the first place there was, as we have seen, an individualism in the Puritan life which might readily extend itself from the sphere of religion to that of economics, and might claim ' liberty ' in both. Freedom of worship might lead by analogy, even if the analogy were mistaken, to the idea of freedom of trade. In the second place, as we have also seen, there was an insistence in Puritanism upon ' calling,' and upon steady work in the pursuit of a calling. This readily led to an emphasis on production ; and that might lead to a view of production as something which was moral as well as economic—something which, because it was moral, at once possessed moral worth and might justly claim the autonomy which belongs to the moral sphere. In this way, once more, *laissez faire*—and a *laissez faire* almost sanctified by the ground on which it was based—could be deduced from the Puritan system of thought. In this sense, too, we may say that the Puritan cause, in its essence an Antigone protesting against the mere edicts of the State in the name of the higher and eternal law of God, became also a business figure protesting against ' State-interference ' in the name of the sanctity of property. Finally, and in the last place, we have to remember that the Puritans belonged to the middle classes of our towns. They had the great qualities of a middle class ; and they accentuated those qualities by the stern edge of their self-discipline. They saved and accumulated resources : they gathered capital ; and, denied by the laws of the State any fullness of outlet in political life, they turned to the life economic. Foreign observers have thus been drawn to ascribe to Puritanism the origin of the capitalistic system in England. We cannot deny that it was a contributory cause. It had something to do with the rise of what the Germans call ' Manchesterdom,' and with the growth of the economic habits of Victorianism. It had something to do with the gulf between employer and employed—between those called to production and possession, and those who were called to neither. But if Puritanism, in its later phase, was a contributory cause to such developments, this is not the whole of the matter. Puritanism had an earlier phase in which it enthroned religion as the sovereign of economics. Even in its later phase, it was only one among many forces encouraging the growth of capitalism ; and the capitalism which it encouraged was older, in its origins, than the Puritanism which encouraged it. Above all, it was from the ranks of Puritanism, and from village chapels in which they had learned to think and to speak, that there came many of the leaders of the working-class movement of the nineteenth century. Thus Puritanism helped to supply the antidote to what it had contributed—but only contributed —to produce ; and its ultimate spirit of free individuality expressed itself not only in capitalism, but also in the criticism of capitalism—not only in the idea of freedom of trade, but also in the idea (the idea we are now struggling in England to realize) of freedom of labour.

V

CHRISTIANITY AND NATIONALITY [1]

CHRISTIANITY arose, and grew to power, in a Mediterranean world—Latin in its western half, Greek in its eastern, but everywhere penetrated by ideas of Greek origin—which was generally conceived in contemporary thought as a single unit or society. That conception was not primarily or essentially a political conception, even though, in the days of the growth of Christianity, a single political structure of Empire embraced and contained the Mediterranean world. It was rather a philosophical, or, we may even say, a theological conception. It had been originally elaborated by the Stoics ; but in the form in which it was current towards the beginning of the Christian era, it was the construction of Posidonius of Apamea, an eclectic philosopher, combining elements of Platonism with the tenets of the Stoics, whose lectures in the University of Rhodes were attended by Cicero, and whose teaching appears in passages of the sixth book of Vergil's *Aeneid*. On this conception the world was regarded as a single city of God. God was Reason ; Reason was a subtle substance, a fiery pervasive aether ; and this aether, in the form of ' a pure influence flowing from the glory of the Almighty,' as it is written in the Book of Wisdom, or, as the Greek philosophers said, in the form of a material spirit or πνεῦμα, was always ' passing and going through all things by reason of pureness.' A world so penetrated by Reason was a world congenial to man, in the breath of whose being Reason also resided as ' a fragment

1 The Burge Memorial Lecture for the year 1927.

of the Divine ' ; and God was thus knit to man, and man united to God, in a common and intimate city. The ending of human life was the way to a still closer unity. The soul of man sought at death to rejoin the upper aether, which was at once its magnet and its own true nature : angels and ministers might aid it in its ascent ; and even in death man might ' feel at home,' as Dr. Bevan has said, in a universe which was knowable, comfortable, harmonious, and compact.

The philosophical or theological conception of a single city of God, even if it was something distinct from the political order under which it was evolved, neverthless found a natural corollary in that order, which could not but appear to be a reflection, as in a glass, of the ideal laid up in the heavens. Zeno, the founder of Stoicism, who had already taught that mankind should form a single city, had before his eyes the actual pattern of the empire of Alexander. Posidonius lived before the days of the Roman Empire, but he lived in a world whose peoples the Romans already governed by their authority, and on which they had imposed the habit of their peace. The definite foundation of the Empire, and the deification of the Emperors, brought political facts still closer to philosophical and theological conceptions. When the Emperor was worshipped as a manifest god and saviour by all his subjects, the society of the Empire became a quasi-religious society, cemented by a common allegiance which was also a common cult. The city of God penetrated by a subtle Reason was something different from the political society of an empire penetrated by the *numen* of Caesar ; but if there was difference, there was also congruity. The philosopher could count, after all, on an actual political scheme which was one and undivided, like his own ideal scheme of the Universe. The two corroborated one another ; unity answered to unity ; and the harmony which the philosopher sought might seem to be happily established in the correspondence between the πόλις Διός and the *imperium Romanum*.

OUR Lord had spoken, again and again, of a kingdom of Heaven. His teaching, which grew and expanded in the Hellenistic East, among Greek ideas, came readily under the influence of current conceptions of a single and universal society. That influence is already apparent in St. Paul, who held that the Christan Church was a single organic unity—' the fulness of him that filleth all in all '—fitly joined together and compacted by that which every joint supplied, and transcending, in virtue of its unity, all earlier distinctions, whether of Jew and Gentile, or of Greek and barbarian, or of bond and free. But if Christianity could thus make its peace with current philosophic conceptions of the city of God, substituting the penetration of the personal spirit of God for that of an impersonal and material $\pi\nu\epsilon\hat{\upsilon}\mu\alpha$, it was vastly more difficult for it to come to terms with the actual political order of an empire resting on emperor-worship. As it grew and consolidated its organization, it found itself confronted by the gravest of possible problems. Should the Christian society be purely religious, and should it subtract its members accordingly, in a complete isolation, from a quasi-religious society which cast its incense on the altar of an anti-Christ ? Could a Christian ever appear in the imperial courts, or serve in the imperial army, or acknowledge imperial citizenship in any way or by any act ? Were all these things external, and even diabolical, and was the genius of Christianity a genius of protest, of dissent, of nonconformity ? Or was it possible for the Christian Church, as it had absorbed and transmuted the philosophic conceptions of pagan antiquity, to absorb and transmute its political structure ? Could the Church became a world-society, coextensive with the world-empire ? Could it give the Empire the new aspect of a Christian society and the new cement of a Christian allegiance ; and could it get for itself, in the act of giving, an establishment of its life in the concrete form of an organized and recognized ecclesiastical system ?

The die was cast in favour of the latter choice.

Christianity became both a city of God in conception and an organized universal society in action. The Empire became Christian ; Christianity became imperial. There were deep and cogent reasons for the union between the Church and the Empire. On the one hand, the Church tended strongly to universality ; and the Empire lay ready to hand as a universal scheme in which that tendency might find satisfaction. On the other hand, the Empire, sustained by no common force of public opinion, and resting on no common basis of general will, could only maintain its unity by some common scheme of religious belief ; and as emperor-worship became less of a belief and more of a form, a common Christianity became more and more the one scheme of belief by which unity could be maintained. In this way, and for these reasons, Christianity became, during the fourth and the following centuries of our era, not only Christian, but also Catholic—an organized universal structure, acting from the first through the deliberative organ of its general Councils, and gradually developing for itself the executive organ of a central Papacy. It was a city of God or kingdom of Heaven not merely in idea, or as a conception, like the πόλις Διός of Marcus Aurelius, or the *civitas Dei* of St. Augustine (which was an ideal society of the elect), but as an actual and organized substance. It belonged to the stuff of the visible world of institutions ; and if, as such, it was subject to imperfections and blemishes by which an ideal society cannot be touched, it was yet a living and moving reality, engaged in the process of history and affecting the course of its movement.

The Roman Empire vanished in the West : the Catholic society remained. The one Christian commonwealth of all mankind, conceived indeed partly as an Empire— the surviving image of ancient Rome—but conceived mainly and generally as a Church, is the essential society of that long period of human history which we call by the name of the Middle Ages. It was a fact, and not merely an idea : and yet it was also an idea, and not altogether a fact. Universality was less universal in the world of reality than it was to the vision of thinkers ; and the catholic society, even while it was concrete, faded on its circumference into an ideal haze. The Byzantine Empire and the Greek Church went their own way ; the tribal societies of Franks and Lombards and Saxons were contained, but hardly incorporated, in the body of Catholic Christianity ; and while, in the earlier centuries of the Middle Ages, the assumed fact of a universal society had no actual fact of some other form of society to challenge its vogue—no nation, and still less any national State—it never squared exactly with the facts of contemporary life. Neither a pure idea nor an absolute fact, the universal society was a half-way house between the theological idea of a single city of God and the institutional fact of a regular and operative organization of all mankind. The tribal societies of the Teutons had less of the nature of self-conscious societies : perhaps, indeed, we can hardly say that they had any consciousness whatsoever of their own nature ; but they had their roots in reality, and their kings and assemblies were the potential nuclei of new forms of organization and new conceptions of society.

THE new organization and conception of society which we call by the name of the nation has been gradually built, at different times in different countries, here earlier and there later, during the millennium of human history since the year 1000 A.D. It germinated within the Christian commonwealth : it sprang from the ashes of the tribal society. If we examine its origin, we shall find that at some geographical centre, such as London or Paris, a political authority or State arises (the Plantagenets in London, the Capetians in Paris), which gradually gathers a territory around that centre, gives to the inhabitants of that territory a common allegiance, common memories, and a common tradition—a tradition of uniform law and government, uniform speech, a single literature, a common history—and thus establishes the necessary conditions of a national society and national consciousness. A nation is not a physical fact or racial group. Racially all nations are composite and heterogeneous : they are composed of different stocks and breeds ; and it is not in virtue of any physical factor of common blood that the unity and identity of a nation may be vindicated. Nor, again, is a nation a political structure, or scheme of law and order, as the old Roman Empire had been. It may be that in part ; but it must always be something more than that before it can be dignified by the name of nation. Neither a physical fact of common blood, nor a political structure of common law and order, a nation is essentially a spiritual society. It is what it is in virtue of a common mental substance resident in the minds of all its members—common memories of the past, common ideas in the present, common hopes for the future, and, above all, a common and general will issuing from the common substance of memories, ideas, and hopes.

When Christianity meets the nation, and has to make its peace with national societies and national traditions, it is meeting something new, and something different in kind from the Empire with which it had come to terms a thousand years before. The old political world-society of antiquity had possessed a universality which answered to the aspiring and universal genius of the early Church. Nor was this all. The very defects of the old Empire had been the opportunities and the satisfaction of the Church. The Empire, if it had a common law, had no common language or body of common literature : it had no common tradition or community of public opinion : it was destitute of the essential qualities of a spiritual society. It was a cadre, but it had no *esprit de corps* : it was a channel, but it needed to be filled with living waters. The Church could pour its spiritual tradition, its enthusiasm, its passion for unity and universality, into a mould which lay waiting for the influx. The nation was made of different stuff. In its essence it was a negation of universality : it was a particularist society, confined to a given territory and peculiar to a given body of persons. In its essence, again, it was a spiritual society. So far as it was true to itself, and so far as it attained to itself, it was based on the spiritual factors of a common tradition, a public opinion, and a general will, and it drew its inspiration from the spiritual legacy of the past. When Christianity, in the power of its long centuries and the spirit of its great tradition, met the nation, it met something which, if it differed in being particularist in its scope and secular, or mainly secular, in its aims, was none the less, on other and essential grounds, *in eodem genere* with itself.

The problem early arose of the relations between the nascent nation, represented by its monarch or ' State ' (in the original sense of the word in which it is used to denote the person or persons of ' state ' and eminence who are vested with powers of government), and the world-society of the Christian commonwealth, represented by its clergy and above all by its pope. In the early days of the growth of nations it is the monarch who serves as the magnet of national loyalty and the symbol of national feeling ; and nationalism, which in our own days is so closely associated with the cause of democracy that it may almost appear to be the same thing, appeared for many centuries (and not least in the century of the Reformation) under the form and guise of monarchism. National monarchs readily fell into conflict with the clergy of their territory who sought to vindicate independence of royal authority and to plead the overriding claims of their membership and office in the Catholic religious society ; and since the clergy could find comfort and support from the Papacy, such conflicts issued in struggles between kings and popes—struggles such as those which mark the reign of Henry II of England at the end of the twelfth or that of Philippe le Bel of France at the beginning of the fourteenth century. There is a sense in which the Reformation itself, if it be regarded in its political aspect, may be viewed as the last, or, if not the last, at any rate the greatest of those struggles. But Henry VIII, when in the name of nationalism he broke the bonds of Rome and made a national Church, raised deeper issues than had ever been called in question in the previous struggles of kings and popes.

The old struggles between kings and popes had been struggles not so much between rival societies as between rival authorities ; and they had turned on specific questions of jurisdiction, or taxation, or the control of preferments. The deeper question which began to emerge in the age of the Reformation was that of the general relation of Christian society, conceived as a single kingdom of God under the single law of Christ, to the society of the nation, regarded as the realm of a secular yet spiritual tradition covering a particular territory and peculiar to its people. Even before the Reformation the old Catholic society had long been subject to a process of fission. The orthodox Church of the East, so closely associated with the Byzantine State that it might seem one of its aspects, was divided by a gulf from the West ; and within the orthodox Church itself, as it spread among Bulgars and Serbs and Russians, new sub-divisions emerged, which corresponded, in some measure, to societies which contained the germs of a national life. Even in the West it was possible, in the height of the Middle Ages, to speak of an *ecclesia Anglicana* and an *ecclesia Gallicana* ; and as the Middle Ages drew to their close we may find a peculiar position vindicated for the Church in France by the Pragmatic Sanction of Bourges in 1438, or again peculiar rights, such as that of communion in both kinds, accorded to the Bohemian laity by the Compactata of 1433. But the Reformation, as it pursued its course from the Diet of Worms in 1521 to the Treaty of Westphalia in 1648, brought clearly into the light a principle of organization which, whatever its harbingers, marked none the less a new phase in the history of Christianity. Where reformed churches were established—in Scotland, in England, in Geneva, in Holland, in the principalities of North Germany, in Scandinavia—we may see the nation taking for its province the profession of its own form of Christianity, and establishing a national form of religious organization. The spiritual tradition of the new and secular nation is fused with the spiritual tradition of the old and Christian society ; and the result at its best is twofold. On the one hand, the national society may be raised to a higher power by the consecration of its life through its own peculiar form of religion. The nation becomes also a Church ; and it may be something greater in virtue of being both. On the other hand, the religious society may be increased in its content and range by the incorporation of a national tradition and intimacy in the substance of its own life. The Church becomes also a nation ; and it, too, may conceivably be something greater in virtue of being both.

IN no country, perhaps, was the identification of the Church and the nation more clearly apprehended than it was in England. The nation and the Church were held to be one society : membership of the one involved membership of the other : the good citizen was necessarily also the good churchman. Yet even in England the identification was rather the vision of Hooker and Laud than the actual and established fact of daily life. The ideal of the national Church has been challenged among us during the last three centuries from two different sides. In the first place—in order of time, and perhaps also in order of importance—there was the challenge of Nonconformity. To the Nonconformist the radical principle of the Reformation was not a national Church, which would only be a new body of death in place of the old, but liberty of conscience. Liberty of conscience meant the right of all men to associate freely in voluntary societies according to the inclinations of their belief ; and the voluntary religious society, as wide or as narrow as the number of its free adherents might determine, was accordingly vindicated as the proper organization of Christian life. In the second place, there was the challenge offered to the national Church by the old universalism and the Catholic tradition—a challenge which sprang to new life in the Oxford Movement, and lives to-day among those who are still inspired by its principles.

To the convinced Catholic, if we may use that word in a broad and general sense, the Reformation left intact the continuity and the universality of the Catholic tradition ; and to him the proper organization of Christian life is the historic and universal Church of Christ, transcending the nation, as it transcends the sect or confession, and uniting the whole round world in a single society.

Fundamentally as the two challenges differ, and widely as Catholicism diverges from Nonconformity, they are yet allied in their attitude to the principle of nationality and the conception of a national Church. The one would assert the principle of the free Church within the free nation : the other would vindicate the august and sovereign nature of a single Church which lies outside, and yet embraces, the nations ; but both would refuse to accept the identification of religious and national society. Both, too, may be said to have shown in the past, and to show in the present, an international trend. The Nonconformist bodies of one country maintain their connexions with cognate bodies in others ; and the Nonconformist influence in our national politics has been generally directed towards the support of liberal ideas of foreign policy—the encouragement of struggling national causes ; the advocacy of the free course of trade across national barriers ; opposition to wars of aggression ; sympathy with the restriction of armaments and the general cause of peace. Driven into opposition to a national State which sought to enforce religious conformity, Nonconformists have also been led to support international policies which similarly sought to curb its aggressive tendencies. The international activities of Catholicism have been less conspicuous, but the adherents of the Catholic tradition have also sought to maintain contact, and even to achieve reunion, with cognate religious bodies in other countries ; and the genius of universalism which informs their creed has made them alive to the general movement of European opinion and tender towards the general cause of European comity. The members of a national Church may have narrower sympathies. Wrapped in the intimate life of their own country, they may be inclined to support all its public policies : they may corroborate national pride and encourage national isolation. Christianity, it may be said, should be a brake upon the nation. It should check by its universality the self-centred particularism into which a nation may readily fall : it should meet with its own gospel of peace the combative passions which are so easily roused by national sentiments. Balance is a law of life ; and it may be urged that a balance is better obtained if Church and nation are organizations of a different order, rather complementary to than identical with one another.

THE question of the relation of Christianity to nationality is, however, even more fundamental than the questions which are raised by the existence of national Churches. What we have to ask ourselves, in the last resort, is whether the nation itself—the principle of nationality and the passion of nationalism—can really be fitted into the Christian conception of the order of the world and the purpose of history. A devout Christian may well say to himself, in the secret of his soul, that the essence of Christianity is peace, the inclusion of all mankind in a single faith, and the union of all humanity in a single body under Christ its Head. Why, he may ask himself, should national differences persist, and why should the world be divided among different national traditions, with all their inevitable divergencies and antipathies ? Can such an order of the world be divine, and can a process of history which has achieved such a result be justified ? These are questions that have to be faced. In any attempt to reach an answer we may begin by reflecting that the unity of human society is indeed a precious thing, but that no unity has any real virtue unless it has some content, some substance of common feeling, some depth of spiritual tradition. A society is only a real society in virtue of such content, such substance, such tradition. Now the essence of the nation is the substance of its tradition. It is a real society of the mind,

with a common mental content resident in the minds of all
its members—a content which has been built by the generations, and is at once a large inheritance from the past and a
generous bequest to the future. When we think of such a
society, we cannot call it merely secular, or altogether
earthly. We are rather driven to the generous faith of
Mazzini, to whom the nation was a divine society. Man, he
believed, was united to God by a communion which issued
in duty to Him ; but he was also, and in consequence,
united to his fellow-men (because they also were united
in communion with God) by associations, especially the
associations of the family and the nation, which were units
divinely appointed for the discharge of man's duty to
God. The association of the nation was thus consecrated :
its essence was mission : its purpose was the discharge of
the duty divinely laid upon it both by the riches of its
own internal development and by the aid which it gave to
other nations in the development of their life. No nation,
Mazzini held, could live for itself alone : each owed a duty
to others, to the general system of Europe, and to humanity
at large.

Nations, like men, must be judged by their fruits ; and
it is not possible to applaud all the fruits of national activity,
either in Mazzini's own country or elsewhere. But it is
equally impossible to regard nations and nationality as an
aberration of the process of history. It has always been
one of the tenets of Christianity—a tenet which it inherited
from Hebraism ; a tenet by which it was, from the first,
distinguished from contemporary Greek philosophy with
its doctrine of the repetition of cycles—that God has a
purpose ; that each event in history is unique ; but that
all are links in the progressive chain of the unfolding of
that purpose. The units and associations through which
the divine purpose has operated in history are various.
There have been city-states ; there have been would-be
world-empires ; there have been tribal societies, large and
small ; there have been, and there still are, nations. Of
all these forms it can hardly be denied that the nation has

the greatest power for good, whatever the harm it has also done or may yet do. If we look at its origin, we shall recognize how deeply religious elements were implicit in its very beginnings. The nation is a product of Western Europe : it sprang to life among the tribal societies which had entered the western half of the Roman Empire after it had become Christian ; and it was cradled in Christianity. It is a just remark of Dean Church that if Christianity came to the peoples of the Mediterranean when they were already formed, it came to the peoples of Western and North-Western Europe when they were still in the process of being made. The religious factor was from the first a great element in the spiritual tradition of the Western nations, and the influence of the Church played a large part both in securing their unity (the unity of Anglo-Saxon England, for example, was in no small measure the work of the Church) and in determining their moral ideas and the very substance of their law. We may not follow Mazzini in regarding the nation as a divinely appointed society, but we have none the less to confess that religion has entered into its making and become part of the substance of its inherited tradition. Even the secular nation which repudiates any recognition of Christianity is penetrated by a past which is itself penetrated by Christian tradition.

Nor are the fruits of the nation, in its modern operation, alien from the habit of the Christian temper or the spirit of Christian principle. If there is one doctrine which is firmly rooted and embedded in Christianity, it is that of the infinite value of human personality, which makes men capable of sonship of God and inheritance of the kingdom of Heaven. If there is any test of human progress along a line of purpose through the course of history, it is the test of progressive recognition, in human societies, of what we may call the worth of persons. Now the work of the nations has enriched and dignified human personality. From the days of the French Revolution the nations have more and more organized themselves as

States, and national States have more and more arranged their lives on the basis of democratic government. Nationality and democracy have gone hand in hand, not merely as parallel or simultaneous causes, but in virtue of an inner connexion, by which a system of self-government naturally arises as soon as States become coextensive with the national societies in terms of which men readily think and feel, and in the area of which they readily form the public opinion and general will that are the basis of self-government. National States issuing in systems of democratic self-government have enhanced the worth of persons by the gift of the suffrage, and by eliciting and enlisting, for the purposes of national discussion, the interest and the opinion of all their adult members. Where a national system of education has been added, and the nation has determined to awaken the intelligence and to form the character of its children, another and very great force has been brought into play for the enrichment of personality and the increase of worth of persons. Perhaps we are apt to judge the value of nationality too much by the nature of international relations, and too little by the quality of the internal national life which it inspires. Yet men may be fairly judged no less by what they are at home than by what they are in society ; and nations too may be weighed as much by what they do to improve the life and the worth of their own members as by what they do externally in their relations to one another.

All in all, we may say of the nation that it is a creation of the human spirit—feeling its way to an ideal of righteousness, here in one manner, and there in another—which has helped to liberate men by its methods of free self-government and to educate them by its system of free education ; which has incorporated in the substance of its tradition religious elements, and has given expression in its literature to ideals and aspirations made musical and intimate by the appeal of a national language. None of these are small things ; and national literature in particular—at once the expression of national life, and an impression upon it ; at once the gift of a nation to itself, and a national contribution to common human culture—may be counted heavily to the credit of the nation from which it proceeds. In all these things there is at least a potential nobility which deserves recognition. And if we believe, as a convinced Christian will readily believe, that there is a plan and the unfolding of a purpose in the movement of human history, we shall say that a development so long in its continuance, and so comprehensive in its range, as the development of nations has been, must be recognized and even, if possible, enhanced by Christian countenance and comfort. If the nation can be regarded as part of the purpose and plan of the world, it is for Christian faith to wrap itself round the nation, and for Christian doctrine to enfold the nation in its scope.

CHRISTIANITY did not begin as a Church. Our Lord was a teacher of men. Transcending all other teachers, He was yet like all great teachers in this, that He sought to produce a ' conversion of the soul ' which would result in a new ' way of life ' among His disciples. Teaching and discipleship were the words which He used ; but as more and more souls were converted by His teaching, and the new way of life was trodden by more and more disciples, the Christian school became little by little a great Christian Church. Yet the essence of all teaching remains the teaching itself ; and whatever the organization in which it has issued, the essence of Christianity is still the teaching and spirit of its Founder. Organization is a human mould ; but the human mould does not make the divine spirit which runs into its form any the less divine ; and different moulds may contain the same spirit at different periods of time. The original mould of Christianity was the mould of the universal society, which the philosophers and the statesmen of antiquity had combined to proclaim or to establish. But it was the mould of a particular time and a particular season in human affairs ; and the fertility of that process of human history, which is no mere series of chance events or of cyclical repetitions, was not exhausted by the production of that mould. The nation is the new mould of our modern times —a mould originally produced, by particular influences of the historical process, in Western Europe, but a mould which is establishing itself, by the contagion of example and the force of suggestion, in the East as well as the West and the New World as well as the Old. The spirit of Christianity has in each age to make its terms and arrange its accommodation with the developments of the historical process. It did so in the last centuries of ancient history, and formed a universal organization of its life to match the universal society of those centuries. It may do so equally in the later centuries of modern history, forming national organizations to match new national societies. We may readily admit that it is easier for a new Church, seeking a form and a shape of order, to run into some existing mould, than it is for an ancient Church, which has found its form and shape, to change them to suit some change in the contemporary moulds of human life. Christianity has centuries behind it ; and it carries the weight and the casing of the centuries. But whether it assumes a national form, or remains super-national, or runs on non-national lines of voluntary organization, it is everywhere confronted by the great and looming figures of national societies, and it has to adjust its teaching and its activities to their existence and their aspirations.

I have already said that the nation is a deeper and richer society, in virtue of its spiritual tradition, than were its precursors ; and I have already suggested that churches and nations are both the gainers by mutual contact and co-operation. A Church which draws into itself the spirit of a national tradition may increase its appeal to its members ; and the common fund of Christianity may be all the richer, and all the more living, for a larger variety of settings and interpretations. In the same way the nation which draws into itself continuously, and not merely in its first beginnings, the inspiration of a religious faith and a religious purpose will increase its own vitality. A nation is most active, and most truly national, when it is possessed by a religious conviction—not, I hasten to add, the conviction of those moments of aberration in which a nation regards itself as God's own chosen instrument for working out His intentions, but the conviction of a resolute and permanent faith which makes a nation firm in the pursuit of a cause, such as (to take but one example) the cause of the abolition of the slave trade and slavery as things contrary to Christian principle. Our own nation has suffered from its moments of aberration, in which it has dreamed sad dreams of an English God and God's Englishman ; but in its more sober and permanent disposition it has been inspired by a not ignoble notion of national duty to aid the oppressed—the persecuted Vaudois, the suffering slave, the oppressed nationality—and it has been most characteristically national when it has most felt such inspiration. And indeed it follows, if a nation be in its nature a spiritual society, that it will be most itself when it is most stirred by spiritual motives and purposes.

I am far from believing in the pure divinity of the nation, or from subscribing to any doctrine of the divine right of nationality to an absolute self-determination. Nations are human societies, created in time, with the imperfections of the temporal ; and they are subject to the eternal religious principles which exist not in to-day or yesterday, but for ever. They live and move in the ambit of the Christian spirit, and the actions which their leaders take in their name must be judged by the degree of their conformity with that spirit. But if they are human societies, it does not follow that nations are also secular—at least in that sense of the word in which it is used as the antithesis and the negation of the religious. We offend against the essence of the nation if we emphasize its secularity, or regard it as merely an earthly unit for earthly purposes. Its tradition began its life at the breast of Christianity ; and its development in time, through the centuries of our millennium, has not been a development utterly away from its nursing mother. There is something of a plan in its growth : there is something of progress in its achievements. We are prone to make distinctions in our thinking, and to harden them by the terms which we use for their designation. But life and the heaving movement of history are sometimes less distinct than our thought, and much less distinct than our terms ; and the distinction between the secular and the religious—the nation and the Church— is perhaps less profound than we are apt to think. France, it is true, has tended to follow, since the Revolution of 1789, the lines of a secularist nationalism ; but in England our national tradition has been opposed to the idea of a merely secular society for secular purposes standing over against a separate religious society for religious purposes. Our practice has been in the main that of the single society, which if it is national is also religious, making public profession of Christianity in its solemn acts, and recognizing religious instruction as part of its scheme of ˙education. It is a practice which has its sanctions. Our national Church was perhaps something of an accident in its beginnings, but it is neither fortuitous nor erroneous in its continuance. The form of Christianity which seeks to penetrate and to elevate the nation, making itself coextensive with the national society, and seeking to infuse its own essence into the national tradition, is a form which may carry furthest, and infuse deepest, the teaching which is the essence of Christianity.

I MAY seem to have dwelt long on nationalism in an address which in its nature should be devoted to internationalism. I can only plead that, if we are to have a healthy and effective internationalism, those who are labouring to promote the union of nations must first of all understand the nature of the units to be united, and understand them no less—and indeed even more—in their strength than in their weakness. There is a form of facile internationalism which lays such stress on the first part of the word that it tends to forget the second.

A League of Nations means nations as well as a League, and if there were not nations the League would be a bond uniting a number of zeros. Nationality is not in its nature an enemy of internationalism—though it may be in its excesses. We may even say that the more nationality there is—the more each nation has developed and deepened and enriched its tradition—the more there is likely to be a League of Nations. A developed and deep and rich national tradition makes a nation less discontented, because it can rejoice more in its own abundance ; and it may make it more ready to give, because it has more to give. It is here, perhaps, that the work of Christianity lies, in the development and deepening and enrichment of the national traditions of the different nations. A national Church has its way made easy for such work ; but any form of organization based upon Christian faith can operate, in its measure, on the nation within which it is active. The great international function of Christianity lies in the deeper spiritualizing, within each nation, of that national tradition which is already, in itself, a spiritual thing. Links of junction and leagues of union matter, and matter profoundly ; but the intimate concern of Christianity lies perhaps even more in the penetration by its spirit of the bodies to be linked and the nations to be leagued than in emphasis on the machinery of junction or union. The kingdom of Heaven is within you ; and it is within each nation that the foundations of the ideal world of fair dealing and justice and goodwill and peace have to be laid. And this is the accommodation or adjustment which Christianity can everywhere make to the supreme fact in the social structure of our modern world—the existence and aspirations of nations.

It has been the gist of this lecture that Christianity and nationality are not enemies, and indeed are so far from being enemies that the union of their two traditions, whether in the form of a national Church or in some other way of interaction and interpenetration, may be conceived as a natural stage of the historical process of human life.

The more that Christianity acts upon each nation in its own internal life, the more it elevates all nations to a height at which they can dwell together as equal spiritual societies —the more, again, it unites them by giving a common content to their various traditions. A nation is no ignoble thing. If men can be led by its appeal, as we know that they can be, to lift themselves out of themselves into a concern for its general well-being, they can escape by their devotion to it from the narrow and individual selfishness which so readily besets us all ; and if in turn the whole nation can ' lift itself out of itself,' with the aid of the Churches, into a conception of national mission—an ideal of national ' station ' in the general society of mankind, and of the national duties appurtenant to that station—it can also escape, through that conception and that ideal, from the broader and corporate selfishness which is the defect of nationalism. It is the mission of the Churches within a nation to co-operate for common action upon its life towards that end ; and it is equally the mission of the associated Churches within each nation to aid the associated Churches of other nations, wherever and whenever they can, in promoting the cause which is common to all—the deeper steeping of all the nations in the spirit of a common Christian teaching and tradition. The work of Christianity, in its relation to nationality, is that Christianity should penetrate more and more the spirit of each nation, and that, upon that basis, a common Christian effort should play its part in ensuring that common understanding among the nations which is at once the root and the fruit of any abiding friendship.

VI

THE DISCREDITED STATE [1]

I T is perhaps not an untrue saying, that the State has
generally been discredited in England. Indeed, foreign
lawyers have been known to say that the State has never
existed in England. Notions of *imperium* and *majestas*
have not flourished in these islands, except in the Byzantine
days of Henry VIII. Austin, who, one is told, was not
particularly skilled in English law, and could blunder
shockingly in Roman law, may have theorized about
majestas ; but his own difficulties in fitting his theory of
sovereignty into the framework of English politics seem
to show that it is fairly remote from the *genius loci*. A
sovereign and majestic State, a single and undivided *imperium*, lifted above the conflicts of society, neutral,
mediatory, impartial, such as Hegel conceived and such as
German theorists still postulate—this we have not known.
Our State is on its executive side a bundle of officials,
individually responsible for their acts, and only united by
a mysterious Crown which is responsible for nothing and
serves chiefly as a bracket to unite an indefinite series of
integers. Our State on its legislative side, as Hegel told
us a hundred years ago, is no pure State, emancipated
from society : it is trammelled in the bonds of *bürgerliche*

[1] A Paper delivered before a Philosophical Society in the University
of Oxford in May 1914. I should express myself differently in some
respects to-day. The experience of the last sixteen years has altered any
theory I may have had when I wrote the paper. But I have reprinted
it here as it was originally delivered, partly because I thought it might
have some historical interest, and partly because the last two paragraphs
indicate that I was aware, when I wrote, of the ' relativity ' of the views
which I was then expressing.

Gesellschaft; and our legislature, composed of members of this society, 'sacrifices objective freedom or rational right to mere formal freedom and particular private interests' (*Philosophie des Geistes*, § 544).

With a bracket-enclosed bundle of officials, and a socially trammelled legislature, we cannot have a State, a German will say; or if we have a State, it can only be discredited. History cannot elucidate, but it may at any rate illustrate, this discredit. Let us take three illustrations. The feudal baronage of the days of Magna Carta were good syndicalists —and indeed the best syndicalists throughout history have been the upper classes. For organized labour like theirs they felt that the State had no message. They asserted a right of striking against the State : they claimed a class-privilege of legalized rebellion whenever the class-privileges which they had defined in Magna Carta suffered infringement. Their syndicalism had a good mediaeval philosophy at its back. They could appeal to contract and natural law. The king ruled on contractual terms ; if he transgressed the terms which he had promised in his coronation oath to observe, they were quit of their *fides* and might betake themselves to *diffidatio*. Moreover, natural law rules the world, including States and kings ; and if class-privileges are included under that elastic head, class-privilege rules, or overrules, the world of States and kings. In other words, the feudal barons were not unacquainted with the eminent dominion of natural rights.

A second illustration follows logically, if not chronologically: 1688 is no far cry from 1215. Locke speaks of property instead of class-privilege ; and since we all *may* have property, he seems more universally kind. Be that as it may, he inaugurated a long period of our history. The right of property, not only in things but in persons— not only for use, but also for power—has raised its head against the State for these last two centuries. Once more contract, always inimical to the State, has served as a philosophy ; and in the name of freedom of contract a great organ of freedom has had its long winter of discredit.

But two may play with the same doctrine. The natural rights of labour may be urged as well as the natural rights of property. They are being urged to-day. This revenge of labour on property has its ironies. The worst of the natural right of property was its want of logic. While it claimed immunity from the State, it could only exist by the protection of the State. Its motto was, You must keep your hands off me ; but you must stand in front of me. Labour has learned its lesson from property ; and with an almost equal want of logic, perhaps the more pardonable because it has good precedent, it claims immunity from the State for its trade unions in the same breath that it demands recognition by the State of their rights.

A third illustration touches different ground. Men may claim not a mere natural right to privilege, or property, or labour, but a right divine to worship free. Robert Browne, of Corpus Christi College, Cambridge, had little use for the Elizabethan State. Henry Barrow, of Clare, was of the same way of thinking. Congregationalism, which ranks these two Cambridge men among its founders, simply turned its back on the State. Calvinism, in one sense more drastic, in another sense more complacent, recognized the State, but made it the organ of a spiritual consistory, and enlisted its secular arm for enforcing the final judgments of an ecclesiastical tribunal. It is Congregationalism, however, and not Calvinism, which has influenced English political thought most deeply. The first and most striking agent of that influence was Sir Harry Vane, Milton's contemporary. Vane, taught by his experience of religious intolerance in America, had early come by the principle of ' soul-liberty,' which Roger Williams, father of toleration, had made the basis of his community at Providence in 1636. Soul-liberty, Vane urged, was exempt from and higher than the State. ' Magistracy,' he wrote, ' is not to intrude itself into the office and proper concerns of Christ's inward government and rule in the conscience ; but it is to content itself with the outward man, and to intermeddle with the concerns thereof in reference to the

converse which man ought to have with man.' The
doctrine may seem to us trite and conservative; it was
new-minted and radical to an age which thought in terms
of the one society, the church-state, whose membership was
compulsory, and whose rules, alike the ecclesiastic and the
politic, were equally binding on all its members. Milton
celebrates Vane as a new Cortez who has seen a new Pacific:

> 'To know
> Both spiritual power and civil, what each means,
> What severs each, thou hast learned, which few have done.'

Believing that the individual can never forfeit to the State
his soul-liberty, Vane equally believed that the community
can never alienate its own inherent if limited sovereignty.
The responsibility of each individual for the saving alive
of his own soul, the responsibility of each community for
the determining of its own life, these are the two divine
burdens of humanity. No wonder that Vane's philosophy
had a deep influence on T. H. Green, who had a notable
sympathy for English Nonconformists. Vane said on the
scaffold, 'The people of England have long been asleep.
I doubt they will be hungry when they awake.' 'If the
people of England should yet awake and be hungry,' Green
writes, 'they will find their food in the ideas which, with
much blindness and weakness, he vainly offered them,
cleared and ripened by a philosophy of which he did not
dream.'

English Nonconformity has been the main influence in
the discrediting of the English State, just because it has
been the noblest. Antigone has confronted Creon these
250 years with the declaration that his mortal decrees were
not so strong as to outspeed the unwritten and unfailing
law of God. The pity is that our English Antigone has
had Midas for her ally. For the Nonconformist defiance
of the State has been confirmed and corroborated by the
defiance of the economic man, with his appeal to the unwritten and unfailing law of free contract and free competition. Our two distinctively English products in the

sphere of the mind—and we may take these to be Nonconformity and political economy—have been shrewd enemies
of the State. It is curious to notice that he who wrote
The Man versus the State was reared in Nonconformist
circles and nourished on political economy. It was for a
paper called the *Nonconformist* that Herbert Spencer wrote
his first essay on politics—*The proper sphere of Government* :
it was in the agitation against the Corn Laws that he first
took any active part in politics. And the whole assumption
of the validity of natural rights which Spencer so largely
drew from these two influences is an assumption that still
lies at the back of ordinary English thought and prejudice.
Few Englishmen might know what you meant if you spoke
to them of natural rights ; but most Englishmen believe
in natural rights. Professor Halévy, a close observer of
things English, noted, in a recent letter to the writer, that
' the old eighteenth-century idea, exploded as it is, of the
abstract rights of the individual is quietly gaining ground
in the world of actual English politics.'

THE measure of the ground gained is the number of the
new ' isms ' that are current. Their number sometimes
surprises, and men feel that they live in new and unstable
days. The quiet Victorian peace of the last half of the
nineteenth century has perhaps lulled us into forgetfulness.
But there were many ' isms ' abroad in the tumultuous
years between 1789 and 1848 ; and there were ideas spreading even in the years of Victorian peace which are now sown
broadcast. Two of these—Tractarianism and Marxianism
—suggest some reflections. They have in some sense taken
the place of the old Nonconformity and the old economics in
resistance to the State. Curiously enough Nonconformity
is now if anything conformist. It is Elizabethan : it will
accept a State definition of religion for the purposes of teaching in elementary schools. The real Nonconformist of these
days is the high Anglican. Ever since 1833 he has felt the
claim and urged the rights of the Church of his conception
against the State and its menace. He has felt that his

Church is a substantive body independent of the State, with its own origin in divine foundation, its own continuity in virtue of apostolical descent, its own rights in virtue of its origin and continuity. Newman wrote to his fellow-clergy in the first Tract for the Times : ' A notion has gone abroad that [the people] can take away your power. They think they have given and can take it away. . . . Enlighten them in this matter. Exalt our holy fathers the bishops, as the representatives of the Apostles . . . and magnify your office as being ordained by them to take part in their ministry.' Here the protest is not the protest of Roger Williams for individual soul-liberty : it is a protest for group-liberty. And Marxianism, a philosophy which probably owes much to English inspiration, and certainly owes something to the inspiration of Thomas Hodgskin, indicates a similar change. The economic defiance of the State is no longer the individualist claim of the economic man for *laissez faire* : it is the cry of class consciousness, the collective voice of Labour. Interpreted and expanded by Sorel, Marxianism urges the need for the liberty of the proletariate consciousness and culture from the contamination of the bourgeois State, just as Catholicism demands the freedom of religious consciousness and the religious idea of life from the coercion of the secular State. Nonconformist soul-liberty and economic individualism have both surrendered the defiance of the State to new challengers. The challengers are now groups, challenging in the name of groups ; but the challenge is still there.

The English State is thus accustomed to discredit. And to tell the truth it has never sought to take great credit to itself. It has not magnified its own office, or exalted its own dignity. It has left its officers to be responsible for their official doings to the ordinary courts and by the ordinary rules of the common law. Habeas Corpus enables the judges to review any act of the executive which has resulted in the imprisonment of a subject. No official can swell with pride as the embodiment of the State, or boast that the clothes he wears distinguish him from his civic brethren. Our forefathers at the end of the seventeenth century would not even allow the State, in the shape of the Crown, to contract our National Debt. The National Debt is owed, and the interest on the National Debt is paid, by ' the Publick.' While law has not been tender to the State, it has been tender enough, intentionally or no, to all manner of groups. Here we touch on that peculiarly English thing, the Trust. The State replied to Nonconformist defiance, at any rate in the eighteenth century, by turning the other cheek. For one thing it passed annual Acts of Indemnity to secure those Nonconformists who had violated its laws by taking office without the due subscription ; for another, it permitted the conception of trust to shelter Nonconformity in possession of its chapels and funds. The trust, as Professor Maitland has shown, preserved religious liberty. And the trust has also served trades unions. It has permitted them to accumulate and to hold the funds without which their activities would have been impossible. It may indeed be urged that the trust has sheltered group-life more fully than any legal recognition of the ' real personality ' of groups could have done. Hidden behind their trustees, groups have thriven and grown unnoticed. The recognition of their real personality would have meant their coming more fully under the public eye ; and the public eye might have refused to wink at the doings of bodies which it could see, while it never even blinked at the activities of groups which were hidden by the screen of trust.

Nor have groups merely flourished in our country under the shelter of trusts. They have flourished anyhow and anywhere. England is a place where they seem always to have been budding and maturing. In this clubable country groups and associations are always arising freely and acting as freely. We have thrown off in an easy and light-hearted way groups like the East India Company, which, as we may read in our statute book, can have financial transactions with the English ' Publick ' as an independent entity, so that in 1786 the Public stands indebted to the

Company in a sum of more than four millions. In the same easy way this English State has thrown off groups like colonies, which manage to combine independence with allegiance ; and within her own borders she has thrown up those associations called parties, which are well within the State, and yet so far from being altogether under the State, that they have a habit of taking the State in tow and 'running' it after their own devices. Nonconformist bodies, trade unions, great semi-sovereign companies, self-governing colonies, political parties—they have all budded freely, matured easily, and gone very much their own way.

IT is curious that, while English thought and practice have never been particularly favourable to the claims of the State, two Englishmen, Hobbes and Austin, should have been preachers of a doctrine of *majestas* which recognizes and, one may almost say, consecrates those claims. The doctrine has a long history, and its history proves that it is not of English origin. As stated by Austin it runs as follows : ' Every positive law, or every law simply and strictly so called, is set by a sovereign person, or a sovereign body of persons, to a member or members of the independent political society wherein that person or body is sovereign or supreme.' In other words, all laws are the fiat of a sovereign ; all sovereigns are persons or bodies of persons of a determinate character ; each independent political society has one and only one such person or body of persons ; and every such person or body of persons has indeterminate or unlimited power. This is a theory of an admirable simplicity ; but it is not the theory of Bentham, who recognizes the possibility of a limited sovereignty [1] ; it

---

[1] Cf. the *Fragment on Government*, chapter iv. §§ 34–6. ' What difficulty there should be in conceiving a state of things to subsist in which the supreme authority is thus limited [by an instrument of convention, setting assignable bounds to its power], what greater difficulty in conceiving it with this limitation, than without any, I cannot see.' Bentham, writing in 1776, thus anticipated, more than ten years in advance, the principle of the United States Constitution. (I owe this reference to the kindness of Sir F. Pollock.)

fails to square with the facts of English political life and structure ; and it is, one may suspect, French in its immediate and perhaps papal in its ultimate origin. In the eighth chapter of his first book, the French legist, Bodin, defines *majestas* as *summa in cives ac subditos legibusque soluta potestas*. This majesty is the *differentia* of a State : ' a state transcends a corporation by the fact that it embraces a multitude of citizens and towns within the protection of the majesty of its power.' For support of the transcendence and omnipotence of this majesty Bodin appeals, and very naturally appeals, to the supremest of all sovereigns, the papal chair. Innocent IV, he writes, ' who understood best of all men the rights of sovereignty, and who had put under his feet the authority of almost all emperors and Christian princes, said that supreme power belongs to him who can take away from ordinary law.' It is indeed the high papal view of the *plenitudo potestatis* which really inspires Bodin, as Bodin inspires Austin. As the Papacy is the *fons et origo* of the government of the august commonwealth of Christian men, so the sovereign is the ἀρχή—the ἀρχή in both senses of the word—of the public conduct of the members of each independent political society.

A modern clerical writer—inspired by the teaching of Acton, who fought papal infallibility, and stimulated by the writings of Gierke, who champions the real personality of those corporations relegated by Innocent IV to the category of *fictae personae*—has set his lance against this high and dry doctrine of sovereignty. Dr. Figgis, representing those tendencies of advanced Anglicanism which have been mentioned before, has written more than one philippic against the Innocentine and Austinian notions of sovereignty. If one looks at the ecclesiastical community in itself, he contends, the Innocentine notion is fatal to the true federal character of the Catholic Church ; if one looks at the ecclesiastical community as engaged in the life of a State, he argues, the Austinian notion is destructive of the rights of that community, because it is fatal to the true federal character of the State, and because it is only on the

basis of the recognition of its federal character that the rights
of its component communities can be preserved. Advocating
a federalistic view alike of the Catholic Church and of the
State, Dr. Figgis ingeminates the phrase 'inherent rights
of associations.' He returns, in a word, to the old idea of
natural rights, but he resuscitates that ghost by giving it
blood to drink—the red blood of real corporate personality.
It is in the name of real group-persons that Dr. Figgis can
renounce the doctrine of an ' omnicompetent State ' con-
fronting and controlling a ' sum of atomistic individuals ' ;
it is in this sign that he will victoriously instal the doctrine
of a partially competent State of a federal character, embrac-
ing in a kind of co-partnership—and not, as Bodin says,
in the transcendent majesty of power—real groups which
have also their competence in their sphere.

II

THE problem of resistance is in actual life always a problem of groups. Theorists may set limits to the State
in the name of the individual ; practical resistance is
always a matter of group-consciousness. What is a group ?
Has it a personality beyond the persons of its members,
and a will beyond their wills ? Maitland, following and
interpreting Gierke, has answered that ' the fellowship is a
real person, with . . . a will of its own.' Professor Geldart,
in an inaugural lecture on legal personality, cautiously
writes that ' there seems to be at least a *prima facie* case
for holding that our legal theory ought to admit the reality
of a personality in permanent associated bodies, or at least
of something so like personality that we may provisionally
call it by that name for want of a better.' The problem is
perhaps the simplest and most terrible of all problems. It
is the problem of universals : the problem of identity and
difference. It is as easy for a mind without the philosophic
compass to drift into the *res praeter res*, and to see all as
identity, as it is to run up against the *nomen de rebus*, and to
see all as difference. Perhaps neither fits the facts ; perhaps

the Identical, in this matter of groups, is neither a real person nor a nominalist fiction. Let us call it an idea, and see into what dim port we drift with that pilot. William of Wykeham had an idea, somewhere about 1378 ; to-day there is a group, or fellowship, of St. Mary College of Winchester in Oxford, and this Paper has been written in a room that belongs to this idea, and its writer is somehow, being Fellow of Wykeham's college, related to this same idea. What has happened is that this idea has entered into a continuous succession of persons. They have retained their personality, but they have coloured their personality with the idea : a new personality has not arisen, but a new organizing idea has served as a scheme of composition for existing personalities. We have it on Aristotelian authority that the State is the same as long as its scheme of composition is the same. Its identity resides not in any single transcendent personality but in a single organizing idea permeating simultaneously and permanently a number of personalities. As for the State, so for all fellowships ; there may be oneness without any transcendent one. We may alter our organizing idea ; we may turn a tragic chorus into a comic chorus. We do not kill a personality that existed before, or create a personality that did not exist before : we alter our organizing idea.

Law has to bring these permanent and organizing ideas, which unite persons together in lasting schemes, under some rubric or title—trust, contract, *persona ficta* or real person. The rubrics of law are not reality ; they are cases in which to put reality ; but the cases may fit reality well or badly, and since reality has a way of growing, they may help or hinder its growth. Apparently the cases called trust, contract, and *persona ficta* all hinder growth, and cramp the living texture of reality within the limits of a rigid trust-deed, or a hard bond of contract, or a limiting charter of incorporation such as must go to the creation of a *persona ficta*. Much may be said for the rubric of real personality as a rubric of the lawyers and for the lawyers ; and much might be said in this connexion on a fascinating problem—how far legal categories are created by the demands of social growth, and how far legal categories create or rather determine social growth itself. But to the plain man the simple necessity is the necessity of preserving the organizing idea fresh and growing, freshly apprehended as a motive by each mind in the organization, and freely growing with the growth of mind, as a wider outlook discovers fresh implications and fresh relations of the idea. Ideas have their pathology ; and they suffer from two main diseases. They may become mere bundles of blue paper swathed in red tape : we may have trust-deeds in lieu of ideas ; and the religious idea itself, which is the true and only unity of any Church, may pass from an idea to a creed, and from a creed to an empty formulary. Again, they may become office chairs and organizing secretaries. This is the tragedy that is always enacted when an institution becomes mere officialdom, or a Church mere sacerdotalism. Great is the magic of office chairs, and the hard-driven word organization too often covers an ample paucity of ideas. But we need not escape blue paper and office chairs by flying to real personalities which are perhaps, in any other sense than that of legal categories, the ghosts of imagination. Ideas are, and are not fictions : they have hands and feet ; but they are not persons, any more than they are fictions.

We may eliminate personality and will—transcendent personality and transcendent will—from associations ; we may be content to speak of associations as schemes in which real and individual persons and wills are related to one another by means of a common and organizing idea. We may conceive the State as such a scheme based on the political idea of law and order ; we may conceive it as containing, or at any rate co-existing with, a rich variety of schemes based on a rich variety of ideas. We are all members of the one scheme and partakers of the one idea ; most of us are also members of many other schemes, and partakers of many other ideas. The ideas are in relation to one another ; perhaps they are in competition with one another. If it is so, it is a competition of ideas, not of real collective personalities. To apprehend this point of view is already a certain gain. We are rid of the idea of an internecine struggle between the real personality of the State and the real personality of other groups. We cease to feel murder in the air. Real ideas cannot be killed : they can only die by the suicide of their own excess, or the slow internal decay of their own life. Again, when we talk of real persons, we attach to them an intrinsic value as such, because we feel that all personality has value. At that rate we should see value in the Mafia [1] or Camorra. If one talks rather of ideas, one can keep something more of critical poise. One can argue with ideas : one can show that they are partial or erroneous ; one can deflate a bubble idea with a prick of logic.

BUT the problem remains to be faced—if not to be solved, for it is perhaps theoretically insoluble—whether there is any graded hierarchy of associating ideas, and whether we can ascribe sovereignty to one associating idea. A passion for the *reductio ad unum*, such as inspired the *De Monarchia* of Dante, may urge us to seek a dominant One ; and finding that One in the associating idea of the political community, we may speak of the sovereignty of public opinion. We may urge that there must be a single source of adjustment to determine the relations of associating ideas one with another, to criticize each scheme of association on its merits, to abolish associating ideas that are dead, to reinvigorate associating ideas that are dormant. Whether empirically or theoretically considered, the matter is by no means easy. Empirically we may see that other associating ideas than that of the political community have claimed,

---

[1] It is curious to note that the word Mafia is applied both to the organizing (or disorganizing) idea, and to the society which it unites. Dr. Murray defines Mafia as ' the spirit of hostility to the law and its ministers prevailing among a large portion of the population (of Sicily) . . . also the body of those who share in this anti-legal spirit.' It would seem that the Sicilians are good enough philosophers to give the name of the organizing idea to the society which it constitutes.

and—what is more important—have received a final and absolute allegiance. This is most conspicuously true of the religious idea, which political theory has a way of neglecting. The final allegiance of the thorough Romanist lies with Rome, and not with Westminster. The allegiance of Sir Harry Vane, ' in the office and proper concerns of Christ's inward government and rule in the conscience,' lay not with the magistracy, nor even with the sacerdocy, but with the indwelling Christ. The mediaeval world knew no unitary political sovereignty. Mediaeval thinkers might indeed conceive of a final and ultimate law of nature, whether as an ' indicative law ' and the dictate of reason as to what is right, or as an imperative rule and the will of God ; but just because they ascribed sovereignty to this law of nature, insomuch that all laws and all executive acts contrary thereto were *ipso facto* null and void, they could not and did not ascribe any sovereignty to a political superior. It was possible for the associating idea of the feudal privilege of a class to erect itself into an ultimate value, and to claim and exercise the right of legal rebellion against the authority of the State. The conception of an ultimate State Sovereignty entered England with the Reformation. Its zenith is the year 1539, when Parliament ascribed to Henry VIII's proclamations the force of law, and by the Act of the Six Articles took the very ark of the religious idea itself into the sphere of its regulation. But State Sovereignty was shattered by Nonconformity and shot-ridden by the Great Rebellion. And if to-day some may see a new Henry VIII in the guise of a sovereign public opinion, the syndicalist will none the less claim exemption from the bourgeois State for his idea of class, the nationalist will claim immunity from the denationalized State for his idea of the nation, and the right hand of the churchman will lose its cunning if he forgets Jerusalem. Even a quiet and cautious scholar like the President of Harvard will tell us in his last book that public opinion, which is in effect the opinion of the majority, is only dominant within the sphere of those things in which the minority will voluntarily consent to the decision of the majority, and that outside this sphere there lies an area of issues which a prudent State will never raise, because it is impotent to decide.

Public opinion, the associating idea of the political community, would be uniquely sovereign if it were absolutely homogeneous. That it never is ; and that, some of us may hope, it never will be. Any community is a field of competing ideas ; and with the growth of mind we can only expect a richer competition. It may be urged that heterogeneity of opinion is a symptom of an imperfect community, which has never thought itself together. It may also be urged that the opposite is true. The pullulation of new organizing and associating ideas is not a sign of poverty of the mind. The formation of new idea-centres, and the organization of men round those centres, is not likely to cease. One may rejoice as well as grieve to see Ulstermen and Irishmen, labour-men and churchmen, swarming after new guiding ideas to new hives. The apiarist is troubled : he wants all his bees in his own private orchard. But there is something to be said for the bees Their guiding idea may be imperfect. It may contain a narrow and imperfect synthesis of data ; and the nationalist idea, for instance, may on occasion lead men to seek a life that is narrow and poor in comparison with the wider and richer life of a great culture-state. But ideas have also to be measured by their effects on persons — in a word, if a very loose word, by their subjective value. An idea may be one-sided, but it may enlist the whole personality in its defence as nothing else could. If it does, it has after all its value as a vital and energizing factor for the individual. One defends democracy not as a form of government but as a mode of spiritual expression—an eliciting and enlisting force, which draws from us energies of thought and of will which we should never otherwise expend. The same defence may also cover this sphere. And there is another thing to be said. Admitting for the moment that the State idea is the broader and wider synthesis, it may, just because of its breadth, be an imperfect synthesis, which only achieves success by neglecting factors for which it should find room. It may be a forced and bare universal, purchased at the cost of many of its individuals. The very attempt of factors which conceive themselves neglected to push themselves forward as absolute wholes on their own account may serve as an incentive to a truer synthesis. If bare unitary sovereignty is, as it seems to be, such a forced and bare universal, we should only rejoice in its practical criticism by the logic of fact.

III

ON what lines men may achieve, if ever they can achieve, a single associating universal, it is difficult to see. Churches, at any rate, seem likely always to be recalcitrant elements. As things now are, the high Hegelian unification seems at least premature. When Hegel tells me that ' the being of the State (on its objective side) is the in-and-for-itself universal,' and that yet ' the State, as self-knowing and self-acting, is pure subjectivity and *one* individual ' ; when I hear that I, ' seeking to be a centre for myself, am brought by the State back into the life of the universal substance ' —I throw up my hands. When I take things as I find them, I cannot see that universality, sovereignty, call it what you will, is the unique property of any one association. Other times, other fashions ; and again *tot sententiae, quot societates*. At different times different societies may claim a final allegiance ; and at one and the same time two or more societies may tug at the same heart-strings with equally imperative demands. No associating idea seems to engulf the whole man ; and any man may have to face that solemn conflict of duties, which his membership of two different societies, his divided allegiance to two divergent ideas, may at any moment awake. There is no set solution of the dilemma. One is thrown back on the ' leaden canon ' of Lesbian builders—' for the canon of the indeterminate is itself also indeterminate.' Either way one seems bound to lose. Whether one unsheathes the sword for the idea of the political society—the idea which requires as its bare minimum the observance of law and order—or for the idea of the other and rival society of religion, or nation, or class, the thumb is turned down against the gladiator. Either the pains and penalties that attend outraged law and order, or the ostracism or excommunication which attends desertion of the other group.

The prospect seems desolating. And most of us are not Childe Rolands, nor do we come to the dark tower. From anxiety and suspense, from the condition of unstable equilibrium, we deliver ourselves into the obvious and primrose path towards the greener valleys of law and order. *Quod principi placuit legis habet vigorem.* No associating idea, we may comfort ourselves, can have absolute validity or inherent right save one. Men who live together in a community must have an ultimate source of adjustment of their relations. That ultimate adjusting force, itself unadjusted, gives all rights except its own ; and all rights are therefore derivative, none are inherent. You may talk—and here you hit most shrewdly—of the inherent rights of Churches ; but what of Mormonism ? You may talk of the inherent rights of proletariate consciousness ; do you also admit the inherent rights of capitalistic consciousness ? You may talk of the inherent rights of nationality : what of Albania ? After all, the Idea of the State is the idea *par excellence*—all-embracing, all-subsuming, all-adjusting. Other ideas are partial ; other ideas need criticism and adjustment. One may praise famous associations such as did bear rule in their kingdoms ; but the tyranny of the association over its own members may be greater than any coercion exercised by the State over associations ; and the State may and will be an organ of the freedom of persons, which is the only freedom, if it curtails the freedom of associations, which is only a paper freedom.

Yet some may still set a lance against the State, however daunted. The State is the organ of freedom : it is also a vehicle of force. Its sphere is automatism ; it does external acts to produce external results. Other associations need consent the more as they use force the less ; they must act more in the spiritual sphere, and seek to supply motive ideas in order to produce spiritual reactions. Again, the State may be broader ; but is it many-sided, or one-sided ? It rests fundamentally on the idea of law and order in the external converse of man with man ; and the cultural ideas which it has superadded, turning itself from a plain grocer's shop into a Whiteley's emporium, have not altered its foundations. And therefore it is perhaps after all no final source of adjustment. It may be that there is no other source of adjustment among the associating ideas of a many-sided community except omniscience, which we admittedly do not possess. It may be that the State-idea is but *primus inter pares*—as ultimate as, but hardly more ultimate in the last resort than, other ideas which can quicken the pulse and fire the heart. Our universal may thus turn out to be a federal sort of thing. The State may be an educator of citizens : the Church may also be an educator of church-men, with a ' right of entry ' as such. The State may have its Westminster Parliament : the nation may also have its Dublin Parliament. The State may be an area of political action : the trade union may also be a field of political action. It hardly meets the point to urge that the Church will not have its right of entry, or Dublin its parliament, or trade unions a political levy, until the State has issued its permissive law. The State is not prior to law ; and Gierke will tell us that ' law is the result not of a common will that a thing shall be, but of a common conviction that it is.' Browning can write

> Justinian's Pandects only make precise
> What simply sparkled in men's eyes before,
> Twitched in their brow or quivered on their lip,
> Waited the speech they called but would not come.'

In a word, law, as has already been said, makes cases to hold reality, though it may affect reality very vitally by the kind of case it makes.

The Austinian notion of sovereignty is such a case.

The reality it seeks to contain is the associating and organizing idea of law and order. The difficulty is that reality is wider than the case, for there are other ideas, in practice equally ultimate with this idea ; . and reality is therefore cramped by its case. In foreign affairs, it is true, there is a point in emphasizing the independence or ultimacy of a determinate political authority : only upon such terms can it negotiate with any finality. Indeed, changing the venue of our metaphor, we may say that sovereignty is a lotion for external application. But it ought to be labelled ' Poison—not to be taken internally.' Internally, it leads to a false view of law, which it degrades into the mere will of the sovereign. ' The human mind,' Professor Wallace wrote in one of his lectures, ' must be disabused of the delusion that it makes laws.' Sovereignty fosters the delusion. Internally, again, it leads to a false unification and simplification of the rich complexity of the fact. It substitutes unitarianism for federalism, a corner in lieu of competition.

This may seem anarchism. Really it is polyarchism. And as for the problem of polyarchism—the problem of unstable equilibrium—why, after all, *solvitur ambulando*, it is likely to be settled by the needs of mere ordered life. This is the ultimate necessity ; but it is not an absolute or invariable necessity. It varies with times and seasons. The sixteenth century was a time and season for *salus populi lex suprema*. Within, there was need of taming fully a still half-tamed nobility, of laying securely the red spectre of social unrest : without, nations were assuming ' the state and posture of gladiators ' in their dealings one with another. Machiavelli could preach the State ultimate, the State undivided : he could warn his new prince that he would ' often be forced, in order to maintain his state, to go to work against faith, against charity, against humanity, against religion.' Years of ordered life have permitted the germination of other ideas than the indispensable minimum idea of law and order ; they have brought us polyarchism for monarchism. If the indispensable basis of law and order has been well and truly laid in sound hard concrete, it is all for the good. If that basis is not secure, if the building of our common life shows cracks and signs of subsidences, if the enemy without should see a gaping opportunity for his battering-ram, the cry of ' Back to law and order ' will be great, and will prevail. Perhaps the hour is not yet. But if it should strike, there is no fear for the State, or for the idea of law and order. There is rather fear for other societies, other ideas. The idea of law and order, when it is roused, is one of the cruellest things in history. Think of the suppression of the Parisian Commune in 1871.

THE discredit of the State is a sign that it has done its work well, and is doing its work well. When the judge gets white gloves at assize after assize, we can afford to think of putting up the shutters of the jails. The State will come into credit again, with a rush, at the double, as soon as it is seen to be doing its work badly. In the use of my private income I like to support charity and all manner of good causes. If it comes to a pinch, I have to say to myself, as somebody said to Talleyrand, ' It is necessary to live.' In our social life we are swarming hither and thither after associating ideas not only of law and order, but of religion, nation, class. If it comes to a pinch, we shall forget that we are anything but citizens. Through our mouths the State, which is nothing but ourselves organized in an ordered life, will then say to itself, ' It is necessary to live.' And there is no Talleyrand to say to the State, ' I do not see the necessity for it.'

VII

THE STUDY OF POLITICAL SCIENCE [1]

I

A PRELIMINARY modesty becomes a new professor ; and a deprecatory preface to his inaugural discourse is not only a decency, but also a debt, when the new professor is sitting uneasily in a new chair to expound a subject which, he well knows, many of his hearers will regard as certainly nebulous, probably dubious, and possibly disputatious. Happy is the Cambridge man, with history bred in his very bones, who returns to Cambridge, after years of devotion and service, to declare the ascertained mysteries of the muse Clio ; [2] but unhappy, thrice unhappy, is the Oxford man, who comes to Cambridge for the first time, dripping from seven years of immersion in the bewildering complications of the University of London, to profess an uncertain subject about which he has already forgotten more than he ever knew. To come to Cambridge—the home of exact knowledge, where men walk on the razor's edge of acute analysis—and to come, with such an equipment, for the exposition of such a subject, is a bold and desperate thing. I can only promise, as I do with a genuine sincerity, to attempt to ascertain the nature of my subject : to seek to discover the facts, if such there be, which form its basis ; and to try to analyse, as best I can, their significance and implications. And I may perhaps be allowed to

[1] An Inaugural Lecture delivered in the University of Cambridge in 1928.

[2] Professor G. M. Trevelyan, who had only the term before delivered his Inaugural Lecture as Regius Professor of Modern History.

take some measure of comfort from the reflection that such experience of affairs as I have had in London during the last seven years may give to my lectures that tang of reality which my subject especially needs. No philosophy of human life can live by books alone ; and political philosophy, no less than other forms, must study the busy hum of affairs in the cave before it can move into the upper light of contemplation.

You will not expect me, after what I have said in my preface, to begin the body of my discourse by any precise definition of my subject. It is a subject which has come to be known in this place by the name of Political Science. I am not altogether happy about the term ' Science.' It has been vindicated so largely, and almost exclusively, for the exact and experimental study of natural phenomena, that its application to politics may convey suggestions, and excite anticipations, which cannot be justified. If I am to use the designation of Political Science, I shall use it, as Aristotle used πολιτικὴ ἐπιστήμη, to signify a method, or form of inquiry, concerned with the moral phenomena of human behaviour in political societies. I should prefer to call such a method or form of inquiry by the name of Political Theory, because I should hope, by the use of that name, to avoid the appearance of any excessive claim to exactitude, and I should be indicating more precisely the nature of the inquiry, as simply a ' speculation ' (θεωρία) about a group of facts in the field of political action, a speculation intended to result in a general scheme which connects the facts systematically with one another and thus gives an explanation of their significance. If that name be adopted, a respectable and honourable antiquity may readily be vindicated for the subject I have to profess. It was studied by Aristotle : it was expounded by St Thomas Aquinas : it was discussed by the venerable Paley, a light of this University, in his *Principles of Moral and Political Philosophy* ; and it has been treated continuously, during the last seventy years, by a succession of distinguished men in both of the older Universities.

IN the cultivation of political theory as a subject of University study Oxford has perhaps been more systematic, if less many-sided, than Cambridge. The Oxford school of Literae Humaniores, the glory of my old University, has produced what itself may almost be called a school of thinkers (for Oxford naturally runs to ' schools ' and ' movements ' of thought) in T. H. Green and F. H. Bradley and Bernard Bosanquet. Nurtured on a double inspiration, the ancient oracles of Greek philosophy and the modern mysteries of German idealism—blending Plato with Hegel, and Aristotle with Kant—these Oxford thinkers have advanced to the creation of original philosophies on the principles of political obligation, the duties of social station, and the general theory of the State. Their influence on generations of Oxford men has been profound ; some who have sat at the feet of their political wisdom have in after days been called to handle the political destinies of their country ; and they have shown that they had not forgotten the lessons which they once learned.

Cambridge, always more individualistic, has never produced a single dominant mode or prevalent body of opinion in the field of political theory. But Cambridge has none the less been the nursing-mother of a rich and various speculation. Now it has fostered a philosopher, and now an historian—now a lawyer, and now a churchman—who has turned to the study of politics and made, from his own particular angle, some new and vigorous contribution to its development. There is the honoured name of Henry Sidgwick, a philosopher who took both politics and economics for his province, and who, steeped in the teaching of John Stuart Mill, expounded with a rigorous integrity, and a scrupulous analysis, the purely English tradition which makes the utility of individuals the canon of all institutions and the criterion of every policy. There is Sir John Seeley, Regius Professor of Modern History, one of the earliest discoverers of the existence of the British Empire, a scholar of masculine vigour and a robust realism, who regarded political science as the fruit on the branches of history, and, drawing his principles of politics from a study of the modern working of the English constitution, turned the attention of Cambridge scholars towards that study of political institutions which has continued to be endemic. There is Lord Acton, Seeley's successor, *clarum et venerabile nomen*, a profound and pregnant thinker on all European affairs ' as well civil as ecclesiastical,' who cherished a delicate and fastidious love of liberty, believing that the independence of the Church in the State had been, and should continue to be, its bulwark, and dreading those nationalist enthusiasms which seek to make a national State into a destructive tyrant ' crushing all natural rights and all established liberties for the purpose of vindicating itself.' No influence has been more profound in this place than that of Acton ; and I would commemorate among those who felt and propagated that influence the name of Neville Figgis, whom I was proud to call a friend ; who adorned with incisive wit and industrious scholarship all the themes of political theory which he touched ; who loved and prophesied the cause of liberty, both political and religious (I shall never forget his taking me round the garden of the house of the community in which he lived at Mirfield, and suddenly exclaiming, ' Barker, I really believe I'm a syndicalist ') ; and who, if he had lived, would have been an occupant as proud as he would have been worthy of the chair to which, in his stead, I am called. I cannot but glow as I think of his memory. Admiration and affection were his due ; and he had his due from many. And there is another name which comes last, but is very far from being the least—a name which also kindles a glow in the minds of those who have heard his voice and fed on his thought—the name of one who was worthy, in his field, to be counted by the side of Acton, and who, along with Acton, filled the mind and determined the thought of Figgis —the name of Maitland. I can cite no greater name. I can only record the measure of the debt which I owe to the man who wrote, in his own inimitable style, the opening chapters of the *History of English Law*, the introduction to *Political Theories of the*

Middle Age, and the essays which deal with or touch on the problems of politics in the three volumes of his *Collected Papers*. How massive was the monument which he erected ; how stately and delicate was the style of its architecture ; and how far-reaching has been the influence which his teaching, and in particular his teaching about the character of associations and the nature of their personality, has exerted.

I cannot but reflect, as I think of the writings of these Cambridge scholars, how many of them were vowed to the cause of liberty. If Oxford, with its strong corporate sense, about the origin of which I have often wondered, has professed the cause of the body politic, Cambridge, once the apostle of Protestantism and always the apostle of freedom, has followed the banner of individual autonomy. It is the banner which claims my allegiance ; and I am proud and comforted to think of the great men who formed the tradition which I shall follow. The chair of Political Science is a new chair ; but behind it stretches a line of solemn and majestic shadows. There is Sidgwick, with his scrupulous regard for the canon of individual liberty : there is Acton, for whom history was above all the history of freedom : there is Maitland, whose dissertation for his fellowship at Trinity was ' a historical sketch of liberty and equality as ideals of English political philosophy,' and whose theory of associations has nerved both defenders of the liberties of Trade Unions and champions of the rights of churches in the modern State. Thinking of these things, and seeing behind me these great figures, I may say of my efforts, as with infinitely less reason Ranke said of his in his inaugural lecture, *Non attingunt metam, sed meta posita est*.

II

AMONG the precursors whose names I have mentioned there were at least four—Seeley and Acton, Figgis and Maitland—who had devoted themselves to the study of history ; and Sidgwick himself, philosopher as he was, had studied the development of European polity. There is an obvious affinity between history and political theory ; and it may well be a way to the better understanding of the nature of political theory if I turn to consider how far it proceeds on the ground of history, and how far it takes wing and transcends the bounds of historical study. Herodotus, the most garrulous and lovable of story-tellers, could not tell the story of the Persian wars without passing into political reflections ; and in his third book he makes a number of Persian grandees, after compassing the death of the false Smerdis, proceed straight from assassination to a calm discussion of the inherent merits, and the inevitable defects, of monarchy, aristocracy, and democracy. The austere Thucydides mingles a pithy and astringent philosophy with his severe narrative of the Peloponnesian war ; and alike in the Melian Dialogue, the funeral speech of Pericles, and the passage on sedition in his third book, he gravely attempts *rerum cognoscere causas*. As the historians of Greece became philosophers, so the philosophers became, if not historians, at any rate students of history. Plato himself, idealist as he was, and however cavalier he might generally be in his treatment of history, attempts a review of the lessons of the past, in the third book of the *Laws*, before he proceeds to build an ideal State. The *Politics* of Aristotle is built on the solid foundations of Greek experience ; and its political theory was compacted and corroborated from a study of 158 constitutions, of which we possess an example in the treatise on the Constitution of Athens. The practice of the Greeks may seem to confirm the theory which Seeley expressed in a well-known jingle, ' History without Political Science has no fruit : Political Science without History has no root.' And if this be so, history will be but philosophy—political philosophy— teaching by examples ; and political philosophy in turn will be simply history precipitated in a patterned shape of generalities.

But I take leave to doubt whether Professor Trevelyan should be termed a root, and, still more, whether I deserve the appellation of fruit.   History and political theory march together for all the length of their frontiers ; but they are separate and independent studies.   Let us assume, for the purpose of argument, the truth of Croce's proposition that ' every true history is contemporary history '—that it is a history of the present regarded as containing the past, or, if you will, of the past regarded as constituting the present. Let us further assume the truth of another saying of Croce, that ' dead history revives, and past history again becomes present, as the development of life demands them,' or, in other words, that in a given present some element of a distant past, acquiring a new vitality from a new congruity with the life of that present, may become once more a creative force, as the Greek past did at the Renaissance. On these assumptions we may proceed to admit that there is much political theory which has been bred partly from the stimulus of present experience, but partly also from the study and stimulus of some congruous past which has become alive and present from its congruity with present experience.   The political theory of Rousseau, for example, was born of Rousseau's experience of the Republic of Geneva and of his study of the parallel city-states of the Greek past in the biographies of Plutarch and the dialogues of Plato.   The political theory of the Whigs in the seventeenth century sprang equally from a mixture of contemporary political experience and the study of precedents and analogies in a congruous past—particularly, perhaps, the reign of Richard II, which was affected by the Whigs for its records of constitutional opposition and its example of a king's deposition.   But while we may readily admit the debt of such political theory to the study of history, we must equally admit the possibility of a great and influential theory of politics which has no definite basis in history.   It may be the method of a political thinker to assume as his axiom certain views about the nature of the human mind and the end of human life, and to deduce a systematic theory from those views.   This was the method of Spinoza ; it was the method of Plato when he wrote the

Republic ; and it is fundamentally the method of Aristotle, who—however historical, and even empirical, he may appear—was none the less purely philosophical in his explanation of the existence, his conception of the purposes, and his derivation of the institutions, of the true or normal State. In this way, and in this sense, history and political theory may be independent, if conterminous, powers. You may have a political theory which is a good theory without being rooted in historical study, just as you may have history which is fine history without issuing in any fruit of political science. For to relate what actually occurred, *wie es eigentlich gewesen ist*, is a task worthy of the greatest historian ; and he who tells some noble and stirring story in noble and stirring prose may mix true art with genuine history and carry every vote.

NOT only is political theory a study which is, or may be, independent of the study of history. We may go further, and say that it is a study which loses its true nature, and puts its neck unnecessarily under the yoke of happening and the routine of historic sequence, if it occupies itself largely with problems of history. It is concerned with questions of being rather than with those of becoming : it has to discuss what the State is *semper et ubique*, rather than what it was at this time or in that place, or how it developed from one form into another. It is true that John Stuart Mill once wrote that the fundamental problem of all social speculation was ' to find the laws according to which any state of society produces the state which succeeds it.' He was following Comte and the Positivist theory of successive stages in a superseding process of development, by which, for example, the industrial regime ejects the military as ' positive ' thought ousts ' metaphysical.' But to anatomize the history of society and thought into separate sections divided by deep abysses—as if it were a desert of Arizona traversed and split by great cañons—is to forget the continuous eternities both of society and of thought. There are questions of political theory which are the same

yesterday, to-day, and for ever. Why does the State
exist ? What are the purposes for which it exists ? What
are the best and most congruous means for their realization ?
These are its fundamental problems ; and it is thus concerned less with historic processes (however generally and
even abstractly they may be conceived) than with the
fundamental realities—essence, purpose, and value—which
transcend the category of time. We must admit, indeed,
that the state exists in time, and may vary in form, if not
in substance, from age to age. We must equally admit
that political speculation has often dressed itself in historical
language, and that the theory of the Social Contract, for
instance, has sometimes been expressed in terms which
suggest an historical account of the actual genesis of the
State. But even the theory of the Social Contract is, at
bottom, a philosophical theory rather than an historical
narrative. It is an attempt to explain, not the chronological antecedents, but the logical presuppositions, of the
State—to show, not how it came to be, but on what assumptions we can explain its being. Hobbes himself, after an
account of the state of nature which imposes the necessity
of a social contract, remarks ' It may peradventure be
thought that there never was such a time . . . and I
believe it was never generally so . . . howsoever it may
be perceived what manner of life *there would be,* where there
were no common power to fear.' In a word, the whole
theory is a matter of an hypothesis, or assumption, on
which the existence of the State and its government can
be explained ; and it does not profess or claim historical
validity. There is a profound remark of Hobbes which
may serve as the conclusion of the whole matter. Philosophy ' excludes history as well natural as political, though
most useful—nay necessary—to philosophy ; because such
knowledge is but experience, and not ratiocination.'

' Most useful—nay, necessary.' Nurtured as I have
been in history, I should be the last to decry its utility, and,
indeed, its necessity, for the purposes of my subject. Any
true philosophy must be one which has been immersed in

experience—and yet has escaped the peril of submersion in its wide and brimming flood. A philosophy of politics must especially be immersed in a double experience—that of the past and that of the present. It must be based, in the first place, on a knowledge of what Sidgwick called ' the development of European polity '—a knowledge of Greek democracy, of Roman imperialism, of mediaeval institutions both feudal and ecclesiastical, and of the mingled parliamentarianism and nationalism of modern Europe. It must be founded, in the second place, on a real acquaintance, deeper than can be derived from the study of books alone, with the forms—and not only the forms, but also the spirit and working—of contemporary institutions. The parallel chair in the sister University bears a double designation : it is a chair of political theory and institutions. In this University too the study of political institutions has been cultivated, for many years past, by a number of lecturers ; and one of the papers set in the first part of the Historical Tripos is primarily concerned with ' a comparative survey of Political Institutions and their development, with some reference to the history of Political Theory.' Such study, and such survey, has a natural and obvious fascination. Who is there who cannot read with delight the memorable works of Bryce on *The American Commonwealth* and *Modern Democracies*, or President Lowell's lucid treatises on *Governments and Parties in Continental Europe* and *The Government of England* ? From this point of view I can well understand why the University, even if it has not specifically used the word institutions in the designation of the new chair, has included in the Professor's terms of appointment a generous clause which permits his absence, during one term in every three, in order that he may study abroad the actual working of institutions or the actual development of theory. I have thought how I could best take advantage of this permission, and while I may take some liberty to myself, I am inclined to think that I shall not fly away much, or for long, from the cage in which I am more than content to sit and sing. There are some far flights (I can think of three) which I desire to undertake during my tenure of the chair ; but I believe that I may occasionally desire to spend the academic year in the company of my colleagues. For one thing, my own bias leans towards the side of theory, and it is probably best for me to run with the bias. Other professors will contribute, in time to come, what I have failed to give ; and the subject of the chair is vast enough to permit some measure of selection and specialization. Meanwhile I am happy to think that a number of University lecturers in the field of history are lecturing, and will continue to lecture, on political institutions. I will help whenever I can, and wherever I have fresh knowledge to contribute ; and though it may not be given to me to survey mankind in China and Peru, I will remember that Capetown and Delhi and Washington are not inaccessible, that vacations are sometimes long, and that continental journeys are often short. For the rest, I will cultivate my garden in Cambridge, and I will comfort myself with the austere reflection that though absence might endear me more, presence may make for greater continuity of study and instruction. The uninterrupted movement of a University's life, as I have had some occasion to observe, does not pause for the absence of any Professor ; nor does the business of any other body or society in which he may be interested. And I feel it the duty of a Professor of Political Science to interest himself, as far as he may, in the life and affairs of the community in which he lives. It is difficult, I confess, for a professor to practise what he professes ; but χαλεπὰ τὰ καλά—all good things are difficult.

I SEEM to have diverged from history into an auto-biography of the future ; and I must return from green fields into the dusty road. I have spoken of history and political theory as separate things : let me put them together and treat of the history of political theory—or, as it is often called, the history of political ideas. It is a fascinating subject, just as the history of philosophy is a fascinating subject. And just as, I imagine, you must know something of the history of philosophy to be a good philosopher, so you must certainly know a good deal of the history of political ideas to be a tolerable political theorist. In thought, as well as in action, the roots of the present lie deep in the past ; and Hegel had his foundations in Plato, as Bosanquet, in his turn, had his foundations in both. The more the development of political ideas is studied, the richer will be the development of political theory—provided, I hasten to add, that it is studied as a means and not as an end, and provided again that it is studied in its breadth as well as its depth. Let me explain these two provisos. The first is simple. To study and to understand previous theories about a subject does not absolve a teacher from the duty of himself understanding the subject itself. It is possible, but not perhaps very useful, to know all political theories without attaining a theory ; and there may be more wisdom in less knowledge, if it is brought to a point and used as a tool of original thought. The danger of some subjects of speculation—I would cite in evidence literary criticism as well as political theory—is that they may be choked, as it were, by the history of their own past. The second proviso which I have made raises larger considerations. When I speak of considering breadth as well as depth, I mean that besides political theory there is what I would call political thought, which is as broad and wide as the general community from which it proceeds, and which, in any study of political ideas, must be considered no less than political theory, however deeply such theory may delve. Political theory is the speculation of individual minds, self-conscious and analytic ; political thought is the thought of a whole society, often but dimly conscious of itself, and yet pervading and shaping political life and growth. The complex of political ideas which we may call by the name of political thought is implicit in, and has to be gathered from, its own actual and historical results—the development of Athenian democracy, the growth of the English constitution, the general unfolding of national

ideas and aspirations in modern Europe. It is embedded
in institutions, from which it must be disengaged ; and it
may even be, as it were, interred in the political vocabulary
of a language, from which it may have to be exhumed, as
Professor Myres has shown in a recent work on *The Political
Ideas of the Greeks*, by a patient study of etymologies and
the nuances of meaning attached to political terms. Whatever the sources from which it may be discovered, it is a
matter of profound moment ; and no history of political
ideas can be complete which does not reckon with *Staats-
gedanke* as well as with *Staatslehre*.

I HAVE spoken long of history in its relation to political
theory. If I speak but briefly of a study cognate to history—the study of law—my brevity must be regarded less as
the measure of my respect than as the index of my ignorance. But I hasten to say how readily I admit that political
theory can never afford to neglect the study of legal ideas,
and how gratefully I recognize the debt which my subject
owes to a succession of great legal thinkers. Legal ideas
have formed, or contributed to form, the institutions of the
state ; and they are still the bony substance, or supporting
vertebrae, of its subtly compacted organs. The family is a
legal rather than a natural institution—an institution which
was thought into existence by the primitive lawyers who
made its rules, rather than brought to birth by innate
instincts [1] : property, too, is a conception of the lawyers ;
and the State itself, in one of its aspects, is a legal framework which lawyers have largely built and whose anatomy
they have discussed in treatises on *Staatsrecht*. In England,
indeed, with its unwritten constitution and its conception
of the general sovereignty of a single law, there has never
been any separate *Staatsrecht* ; and the study of constitutional law has been part and parcel of the general study
of common law. But perhaps for that reason, and because
there has been no separate compartment of study, but only
a disengaging of broad constitutional principles from the

[1] Eduard Meyer, *Geschichte des Altertums*, I. i. (3rd edition) p. 17.

body of our law, the thought of the lawyers has exercised all the more influence on political ideas and speculation. Blackstone is justly famous ; the name of one of his successors in the Vinerian Chair—that of Dicey—deserves to be had in lasting remembrance ; and I have already celebrated the name of a great occupant of the Downing Chair of the Laws of England in this University, Maitland, who not only showed that the history of English Law was an essential part of the history of English politics and political ideas, but made his exposition, by his style and his genius, a part of English literature. In the more general field of Jurisprudence Cambridge produced Maine, if Maine adorned Oxford ; and Maine, pursuing an historical method of inquiry, made the general history of law at once illustrate and check political theories, whether of the patriarchal origin of society or of the formation of the State by a Social Contract. Nor, outside England, and not to mention other English names, such as that of Austin, can I forget the work on my subject done by the lawyers of the Continent— Bodin, Grotius and Montesquieu, Gierke and Jellinek, Duguit and Esmein. The debt is profound ; and I cannot, even at the risk of egotism, forbear to mention what I owe to the teachers of law in my own old University with whom I have had discussions, or, I had perhaps better say, from whom I have had expositions. I will only add that I hope to be allowed to renew the indebtedness here. Political theory and its teachers must consort not only with history and historians, but also with law and the lawyers.

III

BEFORE I turn from history and the cognate study of law to consider philosophy, I desire to say some few words about psychology, which is, as it were, a half-way house on the road I am travelling. If in the days of Seeley, and in the general tradition of Cambridge, the study of politics has been mainly connected with the study of history ; if again in the days of T. H. Green and his successors, and in the general tradition of Oxford, it has been connected with the study of philosophy—in the world outside it has come more and more to connect itself with the growing study of psychology. Political theory would sometimes seem to be turning itself before our eyes into social psychology. Theorists of an older type are censured for basing their theory on a very imperfect observation of the human mind and the tendencies of human conduct, and the new science of mental and moral behaviour is promising to supply the defect. There is some justice in the censure, and some actual delivery accompanies the promise ; nor can I be blind, even if in this matter my eyes are a little held, to the new substance and new inspiration brought into social studies by writers such as Tarde, MacDougall, and Graham Wallas. But I cannot but say to myself—it may be from hardness of heart and an obstinate clinging to the gospel I once received—that psychology is a fashion (I have seen, in my lifetime, more than one fashion of thought) : that fashions change ; and that the quiet hodden grey of philosophy endures.

In its modern form psychology runs into the mould of natural science. Like physics, it decomposes its subject-matter into atoms and electrons which it calls by the name of instincts. Like biology, it works from the primitive to the present ; it explains the present in terms of evolution from the past ; and it may be led to refer the behaviour of civilized man to the instincts developed in man's rude beginnings. Decomposing the mind into instincts, it may miss the unity secured to the mind by a pervading and freely moving reason which ' passeth and goeth through all things by reason of her pureness,' and makes the mind move freely as a whole towards its chosen purposes. Referring the present to the past, and explaining social behaviour to-day by primary and primitive instincts, it may forget any standard of value, and blend the high with the low in a common continuous substance. The dignity of man may suffer, and he may become not a little lower than the angels, if the study of his mind is treated as the study of so much mechanism. On the other hand there can be no doubt that the study of psychology in its various forms—and there are very various and divergent forms of the study—has added new substance to political theory. If the study of political institutions and legal principles brings us face to face with what Hegel would call Mind Objective—mind concrete and deposited in a solid and stable fabric—the study of psychology presents us with mind subjective, the subtle spinning of mental processes which forms the living stuff of Society and the State, the play of emotions, sentiments, instincts, and habits, which lies behind and peeps through political and legal systems. Nor does social psychology only add to knowledge : it may also claim to be a practical and applied science. I have been told that its aim is entirely practical ; that it might be described as a sort of social therapeutics ; that just as the doctor studies physical processes with a view to stimulating or inhibiting or modifying those processes, so the social psychologist studies psychical processes with a view to similar control. In a word, he wishes to know how normal man behaves in the presence of a given stimulus in order that he may discover how far you can change his behaviour by changing the stimulus. Perhaps there may be a remedy for the evils of states if psychologists are kings, or kings have the spirit and power of psychology ; and a statesman who has studied psychology may be the better aware both of the difficulties which he has to face in men's instincts and modes of behaviour, and of the methods by which he may overcome those difficulties. But there is a certain danger in that form of applied psychology, not unknown to statesmen, which leads to spell-binding and *réclame* ; and there is also a tendency even in pure students of the subject to let their view of human nature suffer from their observations of the working of the human mind. The political theorists who used psychology even before it existed—and one may perhaps speak in such terms of Machiavelli and Hobbes and Bentham—were apt to think that mankind was a little breed. Greater knowledge has bred greater respect ; but even now the observation of mass-behaviour may lead the psychological student of ' human nature in politics ' to feel —half in sadness, and more than half in kindness—how little real wisdom goes to the government of the world.

THE affinities of psychology, when it is regarded or studied as a branch of natural science, are affinities with biology. If it be true that psychology has added new content to political theory—and of that, whatever else may be said, there cannot be any doubt—it is also true that biology has laid it under a debt. It is not only a matter of the theory of evolution, which has influenced all thought in every field, and has turned political theory to the study of social development ; nor is it a matter merely of the idea of adaptation to environment, which has led some political thinkers to regard a people's political ideas and institutions as a way of life adjusted to suit regional features and needs. The service which biology can render to political theory goes farther than these things. What has happened in the past is that biologists have elaborated their own theories in their own field, and that students in other fields have borrowed these theories and applied them to their subject without adequate consideration of their relevance or validity in the study of that subject. Ideas of struggle for life and survival of the fittest, which have their value in the domain for which they were elaborated, have thus been, as it were, lifted and transported to the alien domain of human society. It is the natural fate of new and seminal theories that, by being applied too generally —as if they were panaceas or universal ' open sesames '— they should again and again be misapplied ; but neither Darwin nor Einstein can be blamed for the indiscriminate zeal of those votaries of novelty who find the secret of the universe in each new discovery. I need not, however, linger over what has happened in the past. What has now begun to happen in the field of biology, and what is likely to go farther, holds far more promise. Instead of sustaining a sort of theft, biologists are beginning to lend. They have turned their attention to ‘the biological foundations of society,’ if I may quote the title of a work by an old colleague of mine, the late Professor Dendy : they have taken into their province (to quote again, and this time from the title of a lecture by a great Cambridge biologist, Dr. Bateson) the study of the relation between ‘biological fact and the structure of society.’ The growth of Eugenics—a subject of profound importance for political theory—is an example of the contribution which biology may make when it turns to the study of biological fact in its connexion with social structure ; and that is perhaps only one example of what we may justly expect. Biology has perhaps greater contributions to make to the study of human welfare than any other science. And in this place, celebrated by the names of great biologists, it is fitting for a Professor of Political Science to acknowledge existing debt, to anticipate further obligation, and to promise neither to neglect biological fact in his own inquiries nor to be slow in grasping any chance of co-operation with students of biology in the general field of social investigation.

IV

I COME in conclusion, and I come with a genuine feeling of modest stillness and humility, to the great subject of which I conceive the subject of this chair to be a province, a border-province, if you will, but none the less a province. That subject is philosophy, and especially moral philosophy. As I see it, political theory is primarily concerned with the purpose, or purposes, which man proposes to himself as a moral being, living in association with other moral beings, who at once desires and is forced to pursue his purpose or purposes in the medium of a common life. It is a study of ends, and of the modes of realization of those ends ; and since ends have supreme value, and determine the value of other things which serve as their means, it is a study of value or values. Here it may be said to touch the sister science or theory which is called economics. Economics is also concerned with values ; and if originally it concerned itself only with money value, it has been led inevitably to the study of social value and the measurement of the difference between the one and the other. ' This consideration,' Marshall has remarked, ' will be found to underlie nearly all the most serious modern economic studies.' Economics and politics thus run up together into philosophy ; and moral philosophy (or moral science) is the basis, or apex, common to both. For such philosophy is a study of ultimate value ; and that is a necessary criterion for those who pursue the study of social value, whether in the field of political life and institutions, or in that of economic life and production.

It is here, and in this conception of political theory as moral philosophy applied to the life of the whole community, that Plato and Aristotle still remain masters. Plato combined ethics and politics in a single dialogue which he entitled, ' polity, or concerning righteousness '— the dialogue which we call the *Republic*. Aristotle wrote separate treatises on *Ethics* and *Politics* ; but the one is related to the other, and both are concerned with the study of the human good, which is ' the same for the individual and the state,' though it ' appears a greater and more perfect thing to have and to hold ' when it is exhibited in the life of a good community. In the *Elements of Politics* and the *Principles of Political Obligation* the method of Henry Sidgwick and T. H. Green is fundamentally similar. Whatever the difference of their views, both of these thinkers postulated a conception of the human good, and both of them attempted to determine, on the basis and by the criterion of that conception, the system of relations which ought to be established in a political community. In its essentials the problem of political theory is a constant. It has to determine the end, or ultimate value, which governs and determines the life of political society : it has to discover the appropriate and congruous means by which that end may be realized, that ultimate value actually enjoyed. But in one age one aspect of the final good may be emphasized, and in another another ; and the means of realization also vary, not only with variations in the aspect of the final good selected for emphasis, but also with the variations of the medium—by which I mean the congeries of contemporary institutions, customs, conditions, and problems—in which realization has to be achieved. That is why political theory is always new as well as always old, and why it is constantly changing even while it remains the same.

IS there any aspect of social well-being which particularly needs emphasis to-day, and is there any means for its attainment which offers particular promise and demands particular study ? If I can answer these questions, I shall have given some clue to the prepossessions with which I start and the lines which I hope to follow. I will say at once that there is one aspect of social well-being which lies heavily on my mind at the present time. I assume that the general end of society is the development in each member of a full personality, which on the one hand issues in the individual doing or enjoying of things worth doing or enjoying, and on the other hand flows in the channels of harmonious co-operation with other and like personalities. The human good, in the form in which it is pursued in the state, is the energy of individual moral wills acting for their own appropriate objects in a regular system of organized co-operation. On the one hand individual energy, on the other social co-operation ; on the one hand free initiative, on the other organization. The pendulum swings slowly from this side to that in the development of humanity ; and now it may seem to pause here, and now there. Yet freedom remains a precious thing ; and an individual moral will, even when it has to act in harmony with other and similar wills, must essentially be free if it is to be moral— for free action only is moral. The cause of liberty was proclaimed by Mill, as it was proclaimed by Milton : it seemed a cause which was accepted : it is a cause which is being threatened. Its enemies wear no ignoble faces. There is the puritanism of administrative zeal, concerned for the setting in order of a thickly populated and sadly complicated society, full of contacts and conflicts of interest which seem to cry for adjustment. There will always be men who would fain leave the world a tidier place than they found it ; and we cannot readily blame them for a misguided zeal. There is, again, the passion of social enthusiasm, aflame for a creed and consumed by desire for grasping quickly the sorry scheme of things and remoulding it instantly new. Such passion will not readily stay to gain consent, and it may move to its end like a rushing impatient wind, taking ultimate acceptance for granted, and ready to impose a dictatorship until it comes. Liberty is thus threatened alike from the right and the left—at once by the sober administrator and by the ardent reformer. And meanwhile the methods by which men once thought that liberty could be made secure have themselves fallen into discredit. It is not so long ago since democracy was a word of power, and men were ready to suffer for the cause of free parliaments and a free suffrage. To-day the word and the cause are under suspicion ; and there is a feeling abroad that the people, too vast to be moved except in moments of passion, when movement may become a tyrannical frenzy, are a managed multitude which the controllers of the machine can manipulate at their will. We have to face a reaction against the old faith in liberty and popular government ; we have to admit that the political hopes in which men once dressed themselves were sanguine. But the faith and the hopes abide. There is no better way for the management of men than the way of self-management ; and in the long run it is the only possible way. It is true that the burden of self-government is heavy. It makes great demands on the intelligence and the interest of every citizen. But the demands which it makes are its justification. A form of government which elicits and enlists the mental and moral energy of a whole civic body for its working is a good form of government. Yet the justification will only be theoretical unless the energy is really present. And it will only be really present if electorates can develop an instructed and interested public opinion, which is neither tyrannical in its occasional pressure nor apathetic in its general laxity. The formation of such a public opinion is the crux of our politics.

IF liberty is the aspect of social well-being which needs emphasis to-day, and if liberty demands a living body of public opinion for its realization, is there any means for attaining such a body of opinion which offers particular promise and demands particular study ? There is an answer which is painfully obvious, but which, in the hope that the obvious may also be true, I shall none the less venture to give. That answer is ' education.' It is an old saying that we must educate our masters. It is an older saying, repeated again and again in the *Politics* of Aristotle, that the citizen must be educated in the spirit of the constitution under which he lives. That saying, with a new application, and, it may be, with a new depth of interpretation, is one which may well be repeated to-day. The theory of education is essentially a part of political theory. It is not so much a matter of psychology, with which it has been generally connected in the Universities and Training Colleges where it is taught (though I admit that the study of psychology has a value for the theory of education, as it has for political theory in general) : it is rather a matter of social theory—of grasping and comprehending the purposes, the character, and the needs of Society and the State, and of discovering the methods by which the young can best be trained to achieve these purposes, to maintain and even improve that character, and to satisfy those needs. To Plato the State was essentially an educational society, and its activity was first and foremost a training of its members to understand, and understanding to fulfil, the duties of their station in the community. I believe that we shall come to take the same view. A national system of education is a comparatively new thing with us ; and we only see in part the services it can render, and the significance it may assume, in the scheme of our national life. That it may give us the instructed and interested public opinion which we need for the safety of democracy is only one of the expectations we may perhaps legitimately form. It may also help to form, and even to strengthen, civic char-acter, banishing some of those shadows—the shadow of a restless instability ; the shadow of a gregarious and imitative habit—which have been cast upon it by the urbanization of our life. It may train men not only to do their work in the world, but also to use the time of their leisure—that time which is the growing-time of the spirit ; that time in which the spirit of man, casting aside its shackles, can expand and exult in the free play of its faculties, released, and at the same time realized, in the delight of music and literature, the joy of thought and discussion. For to bring the matter to a clear and simple point, I cannot but believe that it may well be part of the function of the state, and a part which ought to be emphasized in political theory, that it should promote from its own funds, and encourage by its own institutions, not only education in the narrower sense in which we habitually use the word, but also (if I may use a word soiled by some dubious use) that broader and more general culture which includes, among many other things, the hearing of good music and the seeing of good plays.

BUT this is too exciting a theme for the end of a lecture ; and I must fall into a quiet final cadence. I know enthusiasts who would call the theory of education the core and centre of social theory ; and I am almost persuaded to be such an enthusiast myself. I do not wish, in devoting myself to political theory, to relinquish the interest which I have more and more come to feel in the matter of educa-tion. I believe, on the contrary, that in virtue of that very devotion I am likely, and indeed bound, to feel an even greater interest. Any scheme, therefore, that may be launched in this University, either for its fuller par-ticipation in the training of teachers, or for its sharing, in other ways, in the preparation of social workers (and are we not all such ?) in other fields—any plan intended to secure, in the noble words of the Bidding Prayer, ' that there may never be wanting a succession of persons duly qualified for the service of God in Church and in State '— must necessarily command the fullest measure of my attention. Not that I come with any scheme which I wish to press. μὴ γένοιτο. I only come with a desire to learn and a wish to help.

VIII

HISTORY AND PHILOSOPHY[1]

PLATO spoke of an ancient difference between philosophy and poetry. We may perhaps speak of a certain modern difference between philosophy and history—or at any rate between teachers of history and teachers of philosophy. Every teacher is apt to magnify his own subject, and naturally prone to magnify it most at the expense of the nearest and most closely related of other subjects. When teachers of different subjects are brought closely together—as they are in Oxford common rooms and Cambridge combination rooms—they are driven to take stock of one another ; and the philosopher may rally the historian with a nimble dialectic, while the historian, who has more of the *esprit positif*, will pursue his Parthian foe in the heavy armour of 'facts.' ' You philosophers,' he will say, ' love to theorize about provinces, such as the State, into which you have not travelled and of which you have made no survey. The real stuff is not in you. You are detached from affairs : you say you are spectators of all time and existence, but when it comes to the point, you retire from the dust and heat under the shelter of a wall. It is we historians—students of things that have actually been done or are actually being done— who have an instinct for affairs and a sense of reality : it is we who can bring the lessons of the past to guide the making of the future.' The philosopher, with his ironic modesty, may admit the impeachment ; but he will shoot some rankling arrow. ' Yes,' he will say, ' you historians

[1] Based on an Address delivered before the Historical Association in London, January 1922.

are great travellers and surveyors. You accumulate much knowledge (or rather memory—for knowledge is a deep thing) of events and institutions ; but I wonder whether you ever attempt to think together all this memory, or to find its significance and plan. It may be that you do ; in fact, I believe that I have noticed an occasional attempt here and there. But I doubt if these attempts have carried you very far. For you assume, whenever you make these attempts, that historical process is the explanation of existence, and that the sequence of events preceding any given thing is the explanation of that thing. Does that assumption really help you to think things together, or to find any significance or plan ? ·

If I may make a personal confession, I would admit that these sayings of the philosopher long left me with an uncomfortable feeling. I remembered (as a teacher of history I hope I may be forgiven for ' remembering ' rather than thinking) the dictum of Hobbes, that philosophy ' excludes history as well natural as political, though most useful (nay, necessary) to philosophy : because such knowledge is but experience, and not ratiocination.' I said to myself that any knowledge I had was ' but experience ' ; I admitted to myself that history only dealt with ' How ' and not with ' Why '—that it only explained how things came to be, and did not and could not explain why they were or should be. I realized (or thought that I did) that to know how private property came to exist is not to know why it should exist, any more than to know that common property once existed in the dawn of time—if indeed it did—is to know that it ought to exist in these latter days. History does not explain values, on which alone a *raison d'être* can be grounded ; and this is because values are not due to the growth (or, as I would rather say, remembering that history is the record of human will and action, to the *making*) which constitutes the historical process. Nothing possesses value because it has grown, or was made long ago, or has been made by a long process : everything possesses such value as it possesses, in that field of institutions with which history deals, because it serves, and to the extent to which it serves, a moral purpose. We are always cheating ourselves into the conviction that continuity of duration or antiquity of origin is itself a value ; but we must always criticize continuities and antiquities by a criterion which is beyond time. In a word, the historian, with all his historical values, must come before the bar of philosophy. And there—to take one instance—all the many nationalisms which feed on the historic method, with their memories of Cuchulain and Stephen Dushan and other heroes and glories, will be asked to change their language ; and the question will be, not ' What have you been ? ' but ' What can you do for the moral betterment of humanity ? '

While I was in this frame of mind, I came across, and I read, a work by Benedetto Croce on history.[1] The thesis of this work, if I understand it rightly, is that there is really no difference between history and philosophy. History *is* philosophy, and philosophy *is* history. If we are to adopt such a thesis, and to make such an identification, it would seem that we must change the connotation of one or both of the terms which are thus identified. It may be that we must assign a new sense to the term ' philosophy ' ; but at any rate it appears necessary that we should give a new meaning to the term ' history.' If the terms are identical, an investigation of either should lead to an understanding of the other. A philosopher would naturally start with philosophy. Those who have been trained in history may be forgiven for starting with history.

WHAT then, is history, and with what does it deal ? It is natural to answer that it is a method of inquiry which deals with what has happened, exactly as it happened, or, as Ranke said, ' *wie es eigentlich gewesen ist.*' In other words, which appear to be words of an obvious truth, it deals with the past. But does it really deal with the past ? That is exactly the question.

[1] *The Theory and History of Historiography.* Eng. Trans., Harrap, 1921.

We have to remember, first of all, that much of the past is irretrievably gone and forgotten, and has left no memorial, as though it had never been. This is partly the result of accident ; but it also springs from the wise economy of the human mind, which has forgotten the unessential. And this may remind us that in our modern civilization, with all its apparatus, we are debarred from forgetting. We have paper, the printing press, libraries, archives : we preserve everything : the wise economy of the mind cannot operate ; and trouble is prepared for our descendants. But of the past that is past we can at any rate say that what survives is a part—the part which accident and economy have conspired to leave—and not the whole.

In the next place we have to notice that when we deal with such of the past as still remains, and still is present with us, we select. We select not only in the obvious sense of choosing this particular period, or this particular country, or this particular aspect (economic, or constitutional, or biographical), but also in the further sense of picking this or that part of the record of our period, or country, or aspect, as the substance of our thought and the staple of our exposition. An historian is like an artist—like the painter of a portrait or a landscape : he selects what has significance and interest. Such significance and interest are present in two cases and under two conditions. They are present, in the first place, when the element selected is a root of the present, which survives in the present and is thus contemporary with it. The institutions of our Teutonic ancestors—their villages and their assemblies—are elements of the past which are roots of our present ; and they have a significance and an interest for us accordingly. But significance and interest may also be present when the element selected is an analogue of the present ; when it is spiritually akin to the present ; when it is an inspiration, and, as it were, a spiritual root of the life of the present. The past of republican Rome was such an analogue to the men of the French Revolution : it was something spiritually akin, from which they drew inspiration ; it was a motive force for the time in which they lived—a force surviving and contemporary. And age by age we may similarly see some period of the past flashing into contemporaneity with the present, as the wheel of time revolves, and becoming, in a spiritual sense, which is none the less deep because it is spiritual, a living part of the real present.

It follows that history is, after all, concerned with the past which is present—present either as a root or an inspiration of the present—and that ' past history, if it really is history, that is to say, if it means something and is not an empty echo, is also contemporary.' This view, that all history is contemporary history, depends ultimately upon a conception of philosophy. According to that conception time is the area of the operation of mind or spirit. In each age the spirit is struggling for self-consciousness. In order to attain self-consciousness it must comprehend those elements in its present life which have come from the past. It is the function of history to aid the attainment of self-consciousness by giving a description and by showing the derivation of those elements. If we think of his work of description, we can only say that the historian is describing the ' present ' and writing ' contemporary ' history. If we think of the elements described, we may say that they existed in the past, or that they are derived from the past ; but we must also say that they are still present, because they are forces still operative in the operation of the spirit.

A T this point we may pause to make an observation. The spirit has its phases, which vary from age to age. Its constitution and operation were one thing in the age of the Renaissance ; another in the age of Enlightenment, of which Voltaire was the prophet ; and still another in the age of Romanticism which followed the French Revolution. On this it follows that the past which was present to the spirit, and was a part of its constitution and operation, in each of these phases, was a past that varied with each phase. The mediaeval past, for example, viewed as a past which was still present, was one thing to the men of the

Renaissance, to whom it was a dark and inimical age of obscurantism, to be overcome at all hazards : it was another thing to the men of the Enlightenment, who pitied its ' Gothic ' absurdity : it was still another thing to the men of the Romantic movement—an enchanting Age of Faith, with its church-bells still ringing through the centuries to call humanity to its devotions. The past thus varies according to the phase of the spirit in which it is present : it is not a fixed datum, but a Protean thing which can change from shape to shape. This is not to say that its facts, events, happenings, institutions ever alter. It would be a pure absurdity to say anything of the kind. It is only to say that the significance and interest of the past alter from age to age. There is a past which is constant ; and there is also a past which changes. Of the two it is the past which changes—which undergoes re-interpretation—which matters most ; for it is this past which is part of the fibre of the present. And here we touch another paradox. Not only does the past change : it also lives and dies. A past age may sometimes be alive, because it is present and part of the life of the present ; and it may at other times be dead, because it has no significance or interest, and is no part of the constitution of the spirit in its present phase. The Greek past, for instance, lived in the age of the Renaissance ; but it was dead—or very nearly dead—in the early Middle Ages. To-day it is alive and vigorous again. ' If the twentieth century searched through the past for its nearest spiritual kin,' writes a Greek scholar, ' it is in the fifth and following centuries before Christ that they would be found. We are to-day in a position, as no other age has been, to understand Ancient Greece, to learn the lessons it teaches, and, in studying the ideals and fortunes of men with whom we have so much in common, to gain a fuller power of understanding and estimating our own.' These words may lead us to a final paradox. What is nearest to us in thought—what must particularly and primarily be comprehended if we would comprehend ourselves and our own age—may be what is very far from us in time. We are naturally apt to believe that, if we would understand the twentieth century, we must first study the nineteenth ; and we push our pupils—or they push us—into the study of what seems emphatically ' modern ' history. But this is perhaps a short-sighted view. It is Pericles, and not Bismarck, who is really modern, because it is he who is our nearest spiritual kin. It is Greece of the fifth century before Christ, and not Prussia in the nineteenth century of the Christian era, which is present in the spirit of this age as its analogue and inspiration. If we would study contemporary history, we must study the history of classical Greece.

BUT it is time to recur to the argument. That argument, at the point at which we paused, and turned as it were down a side lane, had reached the conclusion that the historian describes the ' present,' and writes ' contemporary ' history. We have now to carry this conclusion further. If history describes the present as containing—and indeed as being— all the past that is still present as a root or an inspiration of contemporary life and thought, then we may say that after all history does give an understanding and an explanation of what we are and where we stand. History which is just the record of a past which is past, and an account of the process of that past couched in the form of a sequence of events, is not an explanation, but only a serial or a journal which has no significance or plan. History which is a description of the present as containing in itself the past— history which is an account of the past as still alive in the present—this may be an explanation, and a mother of understanding. On the former conception of history it would follow that it is a temporal sequence, as of a chain with many links, which produces and makes the present. But this is not the fact. It may only be one link of the chain, and that a link which (in time) is far removed and very early, which produces and constitutes the present. The Greek conception and practice of democracy, for instance, may be the link that is present and helps to make the present ; and the other links of the chain of time may be dropped and ignored by the spirit in its present phase, as things which possess no significance or interest for its operation.

But if history be an explanation, and a mother of understanding: if, as the theory of Croce would suggest, 'its ultimate—which is also its present—import is an account of what we now are and where we now stand': if 'its message comes into such an account, distils and sublimates into such a quintessential judgment on the present'—then we may bring the argument to its final conclusion, and we may say that history is philosophy. History makes us spectators of this present time and this contemporary existence, with all the past that they contain: history is the achieved self-consciousness of the spirit in its present phase, viewing itself in all its fulness as containing the past which is part of its present. It was said of old that history is philosophy teaching by examples. If it were that, it would not be philosophy, but a mass of empirical precepts. It is philosophy in the higher sense of a deep and rich understanding of the present—the present seen in all its connexion and contact with its roots and its inspirations in the long far-reaching past. 'When history has been raised to the knowledge of the eternal present,' Croce concludes, 'it reveals itself as one with philosophy, which for its part is never anything else but the thought of the eternal present.'

MANY may demur to this conclusion. There is a history, they will say, which is not philosophy. There is a history which is a story of the past, exactly as it happened; and the human mind, with its boundless and divine curiosity, will always crave to know the story of what has happened just because it happened, and exactly as it happened. There is a touch of nature which makes us all kin: we think nothing human alien from ourselves: the Incas of Peru or the Aztecs of Mexico—they *were*; and just because they were, and because they were men, we shall always desire to know their story, and we shall always turn to history for their story. The wardrobe of a mediaeval king:

the panoply of a mediaeval knight : the structure of the *Great Harry* : the rig of a frigate—these, too, were all in the world once upon a time ; and we desire to know what they were.

Yes, we desire to know ; but we have to avoid the *progressus ad infinitum.* There is no end of the things that were ; and there is no end of the stories which might be told about them. But are such stories history ? And is it not wise to have some definite conception of history—what it is and what purpose it serves ? The danger before historians is that they should become story-tellers of the infinite. ' All things are defined—and limited—by the function they discharge and the potentiality they possess.' It may be wise for the historian to acknowledge that his function is to aid each age to the attainment of self-consciousness, and that his potentiality rests in his ability to describe all the roots and the inspirations of the past which go to constitute the living present. He may be well-advised to become the ally of the philosopher ; and in the issue he may be rewarded—and astonished—by finding that he has become a philosopher himself.

We may make two observations which show the need for an alliance between the historian and the philosopher. In the first place, every history that is a genuine history implies some view of the world. If we call Herodotus the father of history (he is rather the eternal child of history), we shall find in the first book of the father of history, in the story of the fortunes of Croesus, a philosophy concerning the ways of the gods towards men—a philosophy which runs through the whole of his ἱστορίης ἀπόδεξις. And if there is much history nowadays which has no view of the world, and is rather a compilation of facts (which men sometimes call by the name of research), perhaps it is not history. In the second place, every philosophy that is a genuine philosophy implies some knowledge of the present world, and of the factors which have gone to constitute that world ; and the name for that knowledge is history. For the object of the study of the philosopher is spirit, or mind.

And mind is not a timeless or abstract thing : it sits at
the roaring loom, and weaves its living web. Plunged in
time, concrete in history, it is ceaselessly thinking and
making and being in successive presents. In each present
it must attain self-consciousness ; in each present it must
find its philosophy. There is no final philosophy, just as
there is not, and never will be, any final history of any age
or movement—be it the Periclean age or the decline of the
Roman Empire or the Great Rebellion ; and the reason is
in either case the same. And just because there is no final
philosophy, every philosopher should be so far an historian
as to recognize that his philosophy is a philosophy of his
own present, and to ensue accordingly—what he can only
attain if he studies history—a knowledge of that present in
all the fulness of its manifestation.

THIS is the end of the argument, if I have understood
Croce aright, concerning history and philosophy. It
remains to point some morals. One of these concerns the
curricula of the various schools of history which are now
established in most of our universities. If the historian
must also be a philosopher, the historical student must be
trained in philosophy as well as in history. What, then,
are we to say of the curricula in these schools of history ?
We can only say that they are almost exclusively concerned with outlines or surveys of history, partly English,
partly European—outlines or surveys in which the field
of ' ancient ' history (in many ways the history which is
most contemporary) is left uncultivated, and any reference
to the living present is absent ; while, if there be any
philosophy, it has generally two defects—it is treated in
isolation, in a compartment by itself ; and it is only that
one part of philosophy which goes by the name of political
science. Yet moral philosophy is of the first order in a
study which is concerned with the will and actions of men ;
and even the metaphysics of an age may be of primary
importance for the understanding of its life. Who can say
that he knows much of the Middle Ages if Realism and

Nominalism remain to him unfathomed terms of art ?   The study of the history of an age should go hand in hand with the study of its philosophy.   There is much to be said for those Oxford schools which combine the study of the history of the ancient world with that of its philosophy, or, again, the study of modern philosophy with that of the history of the modern world which started with the Industrial Revolution, the Revolution in America and the French Revolution.

There is another moral, which concerns research ; and this must be mentioned with bated breath.   There is a great vogue of historical research in these days.   But it is possible to wonder whether some of this research is not a mistaken imitation of the sort of research that is necessary and valuable in natural science.   Natural science is a great process of discovery of the elements and the facts of the natural world.   In that multitudinous world research is imperative.   To control the natural world, we must know it ;   to know it, we must have at our service a vast mass of induction based on a vast observation.   The world of human action is a different world.   Its facts are not new pieces of matter, or new resolutions of matter into ever tinier and tinier elements.   They are, as it were, fragments of mind—creations of the spirit, and indeed parts of the spirit—which we have to make alive again by thinking them back into life.   Discovery of the fact is important here, as it is in the natural world ; but interpretation and vivification of the fact matter most.   To concentrate simply on the discovery of the fact is to forget the half which is greater than all the rest.   Through such forgetfulness historical research may run to waste.   Whatever may be the needs of natural science, thinking is the thing which we need in the world of human action.   I wish I knew more facts :   I wish I had discovered *any* facts ;   but I wish most of all that I might understand better the facts which I know—and yet do not know, because I do not understand them thoroughly.   We ought all to dig for new facts ;   but if we stop at that, the gain is not very apparent.

All that has happened is much as if we had dug sherds out of a hole in the ground, and piled them in a heap by the side of the hole. It is not clear, if we stop at that point, that the sherds collected in a heap are better than the sherds in the ground. One can only hope that they will be useful to those who come after and can use the material.

I would conclude by saying once more (I only repeat Croce) that the natural world is one thing, and the human world another ; and natural science is one thing, and human history another. Natural science deals with matter, reduced to the nicest and finest subdivisions—all the matter it can find, and all the sub-divisions—an infinity, as it were, of infinitesimals. It employs a busy host of co-operative workers, eagerly watching one another's work : the results attained by an Austrian botanist to-day may affect the conclusions of an English professor of genetics in a few weeks' time. No research need here be wasted : every discovery may tell. It is otherwise with history. History deals with mind and the operation of mind ; and the supreme necessity is that the historian should bring a living mind to the understanding of the operation of man's mind. Co-operation will help ; but the great efforts of the historian have to be made in the loneliness of thought. Thucydides went deeper than perhaps any other historian into the minds of the men whose actions he described. He had researched abundantly for his facts ; but it is his supreme merit, which makes him still the greatest of historians, that he thought his facts through, and thought them down to their foundations in the minds of his contemporaries. And this he did himself, and by himself. And unless this be done, we may say that the writing of history is

> ' Work that obscures . . .
> Making our not-returning time of breath
> Dull with the ritual and records of death,
> That frost of fact by which our wisdom gives
> Correctly stated death to all that lives.'

IX

THE USES OF LEISURE [1]

' The wisdom of a learned man cometh by opportunity of leisure : and he that hath little business shall become wise.

' How can he get wisdom that holdeth the plough, and that glorieth in the goad, that driveth oxen, and is occupied in their labours, and whose talk is of bullocks ?

' He giveth his mind to make furrows ; and is diligent to give the kine fodder.

' So every carpenter and workmaster, that laboureth night and day : and they that cut and grave seals, and are diligent to make great variety, and give themselves to counterfeit imagery, and watch to finish a work :

' The smith also sitting by the anvil, and considering the iron work, the vapour of the fire wasteth his flesh, and he fighteth with the heat of the furnace : the noise of the hammer and the anvil is ever in his ears, and his eyes look still upon the pattern of the thing that he maketh ; he setteth his mind to finish his work and watcheth to polish it perfectly :

' So doth the potter sitting at his work, and turning the wheel about with his feet, who is alway carefully set at his work, and maketh all his work by number ;

' He fashioneth the clay with his arm, and boweth down his strength before his feet, he applieth himself to lead it over, and he is diligent to make clean the furnace :

' All these trust to their hands : and every one is wise in his work.

' Without these cannot a city be inhabited : and they shall not dwell where they will, nor go up and down :

' They shall not be sought for in publick counsel, nor sit high in the congregation : they shall not sit on the judges' seat, nor understand the sentence of judgment : they cannot declare justice and judgment : and they shall not be found where parables are spoken.

' But they will maintain the state of the world, and all their desire is in the work of their craft ' (Ecclus. xxxviii. 24–34).

THESE sentences were written about two hundred years before our era, under the influence of antique ideas, common alike to Hebrew and Greek, concerning knowledge and government and manual work. According

[1] An Address delivered in the Chapel of Trinity College, Cambridge, on the occasion of the Second Annual Conference of the British Institute of Adult Education, in 1923.

to those ideas, knowledge and government belonged to the few who had little business and sufficient leisure ; manual work was incompatible with the acquisition of the one or participation in the other ; and yet it had its advantages, for it gave the worker a technique, so that he was ' wise in his work,' and again it satisfied his longings, so that ' all his desire was in the work of his craft.' I have called these ideas antique ; but you may find them in modern history. In 1541, for instance, a body of Commissioners was proposing to confine a school at Canterbury to the children of the gentry, on the ground that it was ' meet for the ploughman's son to go to the plough, and the artificer's son to apply the trade of his parent's vocation ; and the gentlemen's children are meet to have the knowledge of government and rule in the Commonwealth.' Antique or modern, these ideas are contrary to the Christian spirit, as Archbishop Cranmer roundly told the Commissioners. ' Utterly to exclude the ploughman's son and the poor man's son from the benefits of learning,' he said, ' is as much as to say that Almighty God should not be at liberty to bestow His great gifts of grace upon any person . . . Who giveth His gifts . . . unto all kinds and states of people indifferently.' [1] Challenged by the Christian spirit, the old ideas have also been undermined by the spread of democratic principles, which have vindicated the right of the suffrage and, as a corollary, the right of education, for all the members of the community. Finally, the great change in the nature of manual work which we call the industrial revolution has abolished the advantages which might before be claimed for manual work, and it has thus completed the overthrow of the old ideas. Under the conditions of production by the machine in the factory it cannot be said that the worker, engaged in the repetition of some mechanical process, either becomes ' wise in his work ' or finds that ' all his desire is in the work of his craft.' And just because he cannot get wisdom or the satisfaction of his longings in the course of his work, he too must somehow find leisure and

[1] Strype's *Cranmer*, quoted by A. E. Dobbs, op. cit., pp. 83 *n*. 1, 104 *n*. 3.

release from business, and out of his leisure gain both wisdom and satisfaction.

We may thus vindicate a right of knowledge for all on three grounds—the ground that it is implied in the spirit of Christianity : the ground that it is a necessary corollary to democracy : the ground that it is a necessary corrective to the conditions of our present system of industrial production. The last of these grounds has been emphasized by Mr. Dobbs, in a work on *Education and Social Movements*. He shows how, in the old society before 1760, the manual worker, often engaged partly in farm-work, partly in domestic industry, and partly in the care of the animals which he pastured on the commons, drew a large experience from the variety of his daily life, and might find in that experience an education of faculty and a satisfaction of the longings of the mind. In the society which shaped itself after 1760—the society in which we now live—the old justifications, such as they were, for a life spent solely in doing manual work have dwindled. Such work is not a satisfaction, and it is not an education. Because it is not a satisfaction, but a drudgery, the workers have demanded, and the conscience of the community has agreed with the demand, that there should be a limitation of their hours, and that periods of leisure should be guaranteed to all who work in factories, shops, and places of business. It is now part of the policy of England to guarantee a weekly half-holiday and otherwise to limit the hours of work ; and we have gone beyond the other countries of Europe in this respect. Because, again, manual work has ceased to be an education—at any rate to the extent to which it once was so—the braver and more adventurous spirits among the workers, a chosen band, have been steadily seeking, for the last hundred years, to find a new education for themselves. More than a century ago the first Mechanics' Institute was started by London working men, in November 1823. Nearly thirty years ago the first conference of a national association for the education of workers—the Workers' Educational Association—was held at Oxford, in August 1903. There is a paragraph in one of the novels of one of the greatest of English writers which puts admirably the ideals of the sort of man who has been a leader of this movement. ' He loved his kind. He had a conviction that the want of most men was knowledge of a sort which brings wisdom rather than affluence. He wished to raise the class at the expense of individuals rather than individuals at the expense of the class. What was more, he was ready at once to be the first unit sacrificed.' [1]

Our modern economic society, we have seen, requires leisure and education as its complements and its correctives. They are two things which should go together. Leisure is a time to be devoted — not wholly, for the body has its claims to relaxation, and the mind too needs its gentle indulgences ; not wholly, but at any rate largely — to the purposes of education and the gaining of that knowledge, not to be acquired in the course of work, ' which brings wisdom rather than affluence.' Education, on the other hand, should be a training—not again wholly, but at any rate largely—in the right way of using leisure, which without education may be misspent and frittered away. This vital connexion between leisure and education is a fundamental thing. Unless we grasp it, we are in danger of abusing leisure and misusing education. And in order that we may grasp it, it is necessary that we should have a right conception of the meaning of leisure.

One of the old Greek philosophers made a distinction which may help us here. He thought that we ought not merely to distinguish between work and leisure, but also to distinguish between leisure and recreation. Work, he thought, was something done not for its own sake, but as a means to something else—affluence, let us say, or at any rate subsistence ; recreation was rest from work, which took the form of play, and issued in the recovery of the poise of body and mind, disturbed and unbalanced by work ; but leisure was a noble thing, and indeed the noblest thing in life ; it was employment in some activity (we may almost

[1] Hardy, *Return of the Native*, Book III., c. ii., *ad initium*.

say some form of work) which was desirable for its own sake,[1] such as the hearing of noble music and poetry, intercourse with friends chosen for their worth, or the exercise of the speculative faculty. In this fine sense of the word, we may say that we live for leisure ; that it is the end of our being, which transcends work and far transcends recreation ; that it is the growing time of the human spirit, which in its leisure from necessary toils, and the necessary recreations they entail as their counterpoise, can expand in communion with its own thoughts and with the thoughts of others and with the Grace of God. The sad thing about modern English society is that there is so little leisure in this higher sense. It is not only that we work so hard : it is also that we play so hard. Perhaps the monotony and uniformity of work sends us in reaction to the hazards of games, or the excitement of watching them, or the still greater excitement of betting upon them : perhaps the urban aggregations in which men now live make them unhappy unless they are crowding together to some common game or spectacle. Whatever the reason, poor leisure is far too often out in the cold, while recreation is romping about all the rooms in the house. One need be no kill-joy or Puritan to think or talk in this strain. Life is something more than a series of alternate layers of lean work and fat hearty play. It is meant for the growth and development of the human spirit. And that growth needs its growing time, which is leisure.

If leisure be largely for education, education is also largely for leisure. We too often think and speak of education as something intended to fit us for life's work. Ideally, it should rather be intended to fit us for life's leisure. I do not mean that education should be humane rather than vocational. Education may be humane, and yet directed to work and the better doing of work. I mean something more—that education should mean the filling of our mind with interests and possibilities of high delight, which we can develop for ourselves in all our leisure hours ; that it should be an initiation in the tastes and pursuits which will

[1] Newman's edition of Aristotle's *Politics*, III. p. 422.

crown our leisure with fulfilment ; in a word, that it should be a training and a preparation for the right use of the time of the spirit's freedom. Perhaps education has not hitherto been sufficiently adjusted to this end. Perhaps, if it had been, it would have been directed more to the awakening of a taste for art and music, in order that they might become the permanent possession and the abiding joy of later years. Be that as it may, it is surely true that education is a necessity if men are to gain the faculty of using leisure easily, happily, and fruitfully.

The use of leisure is a difficult thing. The majority of us, when freedom is given into our hands, fly to the excitement of some form of recreation. We must be 'doing' something—preferably something physical : if we are not, we are lost and without resource. We know the routine of work : we know the rules and the routine of different forms of play ; but we do not know how to move freely, originally, and by our own choice in the world that lies above work and play—the world of leisure. This is why holidays sometimes pall, and leave us at a loss : it is why men who have retired from work sometimes fall into melancholy, and find their reason for living gone. Leisure without faculty for its use may even be a mother of mischief ; men may dissipate themselves in frivolities, and worse than frivolities, because they do not know how to concentrate themselves upon better things. A society which guarantees leisure is guaranteeing something which may be useless, and even dangerous, unless it adds, or at any rate encourages its members to add, the one thing which will enable the gift to be used— a continuous process of education.

The world offers to the mind of man many noble joys. There is a joy in knowing the flowers of the field, and calling them by their names. There is a joy in knowing the heavenly bodies which move above us, and in understanding the rhythm and the rules of their motions. There is a joy in knowing the past of our kind, and in unrolling the long record of human history which explains what we are to-day. There is a joy in entering into the vision of the poet and painter, who have seen the ideal beauty which lies hidden from ordinary eyes. There is a joy in wrestling with the thought of great philosophers, who have pondered about the why and wherefore of this mortal world and our mortal existence in it. These are the joys of leisure; and leisure is the growing time of the spirit because it is the time of these joys. But it needs an effort to catch these joys; and you cannot catch them without hooks of apprehension. You must know a little in order to want to know more. Blank ignorance is blank incuriousness, but a little knowledge may be the opportunity and the incentive for more knowledge. The facts presented to mere ignorance are facts which there are no hooks to catch; but when a mind has had some little training, it develops tentacles of apprehension; it is anxious to seize new stuff, to arrange it and co-ordinate it with the old stuff which is already there, and so to make a little systematic world of its own for its own high delectation. The mind which is furnished with these tentacles and hooks of apprehension is a mind which will never be embarrassed or dumbfounded by leisure. It will begin to play at once, in the nobler sense of the word play: the hooks will grip more and more of things seen and unseen into its consciousness; and in the growing time there will be growth. When we say, therefore, that education is a preparation for the enjoyment of leisure, we mean that it is an equipment of the mind with these hooks and tentacles, these curiosities and appetites. And from this point of view we may see that there is a large sphere for the education of the adult, and that education is in no sense only the concern of childhood. The child learns at school; but the child learns at a time when real experience of life has not yet begun. He learns, and is often curious to learn; but what he learns cannot be co-ordinated with, or grappled into, a first-hand experience, because such experience has not yet begun to be gathered. When he goes out into the world, and begins to gather experience, that experience may seem to him the one essential thing, and the schooltime lessons may fade away into the outgrown occupations of a vanished childhood. It is at this age—the age of adolescence, young manhood and young womanhood—that everything turns on the rescue of young minds from being immersed in mere experience. It is now that they need to recover curiosities, and to be furnished with hooks and tentacles of apprehension, by which they can capture a knowledge which can now be co-ordinated with experience. History, for example, is one thing to a child—a record of exciting events which satisfies curiosity : it is another thing to an adult—a record of the moral experience of men and nations which can be compared with and interpreted by the moral experience which the adult has himself gone through. But unless, in adolescent and adult years, the curiosity be reawakened and recovered, the adult mind may remain immersed in its own more immediate experience ; and the high contemplation which lifts it above such experience, and yet explains and interprets that experience, may never be attained. Adolescent and adult education are in this way of primary importance, if man is to rise to that height of his being in which he uses leisure for the purpose of contemplation of the world, in order to explain it, and his own experience of it, and to attain to the justification of faith in its purpose and operation.

TO the Hebrews, as to the Greeks, the end and the height of life was wisdom—' knowledge of the sort which brings wisdom.' The interest of the Hebrew was in the moral order of the world, and his passion was for a God of righteousness, a strength and stay of justice upholding all creation. ' Behold,' it is written in the Book of Job, ' the fear of the Lord, that is wisdom, and to depart from evil is understanding.' To the Greek the problem of understanding was intellectual : he sought to see the world in the guise of eternity, and to be a spectator of all time and all existence. But he knew that wisdom was not to be had except through a rigorous moral self-discipline. ' Wisdom is not to be won, said Plato, ' unless a man make himself a slave to its winning.' The Hebrew and the Greek strains were transmitted together to the Middle Ages ; and the men of the Middle Ages, from St. Augustine to St. Bernard, from St. Bernard to Thomas à Kempis, set their minds upon the life of contemplation, the entry into the divine wisdom, the enjoyment of God. What Job sought, and Plato sought, and the saints of the Middle Ages sought, is still the goal of our seeking. Leisure used in contemplation—leisure prepared and trained for that high vocation—this is the ideal we have to pursue, because this is the way we go to find our souls, and to find our God. Action is a natural ideal to a stock like ours, set in a northern climate, and inured to physical activity ; but contemplation, though it may be more difficult for us than it was for Job among his flocks and herds, or for Plato in the academy, or for St. Bernard in the cloister, is still the appointed way. We have all, indeed, to play our social part—to work for our community or class (I would rather say community than class)—but even to do that properly we have to retire into ourselves whenever we can, and to contemplate the why and the wherefore of what we are doing, and to think of the ends of being and of grace.

But the contemplation which in this age we have to seek is a contemplation in which all the community shares. That is where we must transcend antiquity. Not a lonely and stricken master of flocks and herds, not a philosopher among his disciples, not an abbot among his monks—not these only, but a whole society, is what must somehow come into the light and life of thought. We must dream a dream, and we must dream it until it is not a dream. It is a dream of an England which is not a power that makes war : not an industrial organization that makes wealth ; but an educational society, which makes and diffuses wisdom among all its members. The State which began in war and continued in wealth must one day live for wisdom. It will guarantee leisure, for ' wisdom cometh by opportunity of leisure ' ; but it will also guarantee that training, and that furnishing of the mind with curiosity and capacity for learning, which are necessary for the right employment of leisure. And the wisdom and understanding for which men will be curious and passionate in those days will be the knowledge of the Lord, which comes from contemplation of all His works and ways. For the Lord is a God of Knowledge; and to know Him is our peace. We have each, indeed, an assigned business in this world, and we must each of us be about our business. But the end of our life is not doing: it is knowing—to know, even as we are known. In this age we may pray to be delivered from over-much doing, from the restlessness of action, from the passion of practical energy which is at once the quality and the defect of our nation. The prophets and teachers of Israel pointed to a higher thing. Their prayer was, 'Make me of quick understanding in the fear of the Lord.' 'Give me the spirit of wisdom and understanding, the spirit of knowledge and of the fear of the Lord!' 'O, send her out of thy holy heavens, and from the throne of thy glory, that being present she may labour with me, that I may know what is pleasing unto Thee.' 'O God of my fathers, and Lord of mercy, who hast made all things with thy word . . . give me wisdom, that sitteth by thy throne; and reject me not from among thy children. . . . For wisdom is more moving than any motion: she passeth and goeth through all things by reason of her pureness. For she is the breath of the power of God, and a pure influence flowing from the glory of the Almighty: therefore can no defiled thing fall into her. For she is the brightness of the everlasting light, the un-spotted mirror of the power of God, and the image of his goodness.'

NOTE

I have quoted a number of passages from the Apocrypha in this Address. I cannot refrain from expressing my regret that the Apocrypha should have disappeared from almost all the current copies of our English Bible.

May I add that Burke, in his *Reflections on the Revolution in France* (vol. iv. pp. 53–4, of the edition in the 'World's Classics'), quotes the passage from Ecclesiasticus which is quoted at the beginning of this address? Unlike Cranmer, he accepts the philosophy of the passage. 'The occupation of a hairdresser or of a working tallow-chandler cannot be a matter of honour to any person—to say nothing of a number of other more servile employments. Such descriptions of men ought not to suffer oppression from the State ; but the State suffers oppression if such as they, either individually or collectively, are permitted to rule.' But it is only fair to say that he adds a proviso : ' There is no qualification for government but virtue and wisdom, actual or presumptive. Wherever they are actually found, they have, in whatever state, condition, profession or trade, the passport of heaven to human place and honour.'

ANN ARBOR PAPERBACKS

reissues of works of enduring merit

The University of Michigan Press — Ann Arbor